VICTORY IN OUR SCHOOLS

The day will come when our children are truly first, as demonstrated by our love and caring. The day will come when, after harnessing space, the winds, the tides, and gravitation, we shall harness the energy of love. And on that day, for the second time in the history of the world, we shall have discovered fire.

—TIELHARD DE CHARDIN

VICTORY

IN OUR

SCHOOLS

MAJOR GENERAL

JOHN STANFORD

WITH ROBIN SIMONS

FOREWORD BY
VICE PRESIDENT AL GORE

BANTAM BOOKS
NEW YORK   TORONTO   LONDON   SYDNEY   AUCKLAND

VICTORY IN OUR SCHOOLS
A Bantam Book/August 1999

All rights reserved.

Library of Congress Cataloging-in-Publication Data

Stanford, John, d. 1998.
Victory in our schools / John Stanford with Robin Simons.
p.   cm.
ISBN 0-553-37974-7
1. School improvement programs—United States.   2. Public
schools—United States.   3. Educational change—United States
I. Simons, Robin.   II. Title.
LB2822.82.S83   1999
371.01'0973—dc21   99-18018
                                                CIP

Published simultaneously in the United States and Canada

Bantam Books are published by Bantam Books, a division of Random
House, Inc. Its trademark, consisting of the words "Bantam Books"
and the portrayal of a rooster, is Registered in U.S. Patent and
Trademark Office and in other countries. Marca Registrada. Bantam
Books, 1540 Broadway, New York, New York 10036.

This book is dedicated to teachers,
the real and enduring heroes of our society.

CONTENTS

Foreword by Vice President Al Gore   *vii*

Preface   *xi*

Introduction   *xv*

CHAPTER 1: The Victory Is in the Classroom   1

CHAPTER 2: We Can Achieve the Victory When . . .
We Share a Common Vision and a Plan for Getting There   11

CHAPTER 3: We Can Achieve the Victory When . . .
We Turn Our Schools into Achievement Systems   29

CHAPTER 4: We Can Achieve the Victory When . . .
We Hold Our People Accountable   61

CHAPTER 5: We Can Achieve the Victory When . . .
We Make School More Exciting than the Streets   87

CHAPTER 6: We Can Achieve the Victory When . . .
We Empower Our Teachers to Teach   132

CHAPTER 7: We Can Achieve the Victory When . . .
We Run Our Schools Like Businesses   151

CHAPTER 8: We Can Achieve the Victory When . . .
We Make the Media Our Partners   167

CHAPTER 9: We Can Achieve the Victory When . . .
We Stop Being Afraid of Change   181

CHAPTER 10: We Can Achieve the Victory When . . .
We Use Love to Lead Our Children   195

FOREWORD

When John Stanford was in elementary school, his sixth-grade teacher visited his parents with a sobering message: Their child wasn't ready to advance to the next grade. That warning led his mother to become more involved in John's education, talking regularly with his teachers and checking in with him several times a day after school to make sure he was doing his homework. The Superintendent—a hero to the people of Seattle for mobilizing the entire city to help all children achieve—believed his own rise to leadership would not have happened without the "courage and love" reflected in his mother's and teacher's commitment that young John Stanford could and would succeed.

John Stanford's greatest gift to Seattle was to return that courage and love to all of the city's children. He believed deeply that every child can and must learn. He was determined to make every student, parent, teacher, principal, citizen, business, and civic organization act on that belief. He understood the yearning in a community for strong public schools and found ways for everyone to be part of the solution. He was a powerful advocate for getting children the resources needed to reach high standards—including well-trained teachers, high-quality curricula and assessments, and a support system for all students. With limitless spirit and energy, he transformed every resource and every challenge into realizing his powerful vision of improved achievement for all children. Under John's leadership, involvement in education has become an important part of good citizenship in Seattle.

Even during his difficult battle with leukemia last year, John's courage and determination provided strength to the children and adults of Seattle. The thousands of get-well cards flooding into his hospital room reflected the hope and determination he inspired. Children said that if Superintendent Stanford wasn't going to give up, they weren't going to give up either. His death has not diminished Seattle's resolve. Rather, his philosophy to "love 'em and lead 'em" and his commitment to bold actions to improve our public schools continue to motivate the people of Seattle and a great many others across America to lift up all of our children.

Education has always been at the heart of opportunity in this country. But it is especially so today. And that is why it is so crucial that we carry on John Stanford's work and rededicate ourselves to revolutionary improvements in our public schools.

We have arrived at an important turning point in American education, and John Stanford's life and his book provide a beacon of light and hope to illuminate the right path. With the dawn of a new Information Age, knowledge has become our greatest strategic resource and learning has become our greatest strategic skill. Until recently, many Americans could lead productive, satisfying lives without a high-school diploma. Now, for all of our people, the indispensable key to unlocking the American dream is a good education and the ability, motivation, and confidence to learn throughout a lifetime. We simply cannot leave anyone behind.

Young people in school today have just passed the baby boomers to become the largest generation in American history. Yet our nation will thrive in the twenty-first century only if we make sure that their education surpasses the education we received from the generations before us. As student enrollment grows and an aging teaching force retires, will we attract, train, and retain the million new high-quality teachers needed in the next ten years? Will we rebuild our school buildings and make sure that every child can learn in safe, modern classrooms? Will we set high academic standards and provide the intensive support and accountability needed to help our children meet them? Will each of us help our public schools make the dramatic progress needed to prepare our children for the next century?

To these essential challenges and questions, John's book and life give resounding and compelling answers. In his life, he mobilized an entire community around the education of its children. In his book, he portrays a vision that all children will learn if we push them, ourselves, and each other to make that happen. He writes, "It never occurred to me we would not succeed."

His vision and confidence were backed by specific ideas of how to improve an urban public school system and the strengths of a very talented executive. He quotes Proverbs 29:18 "Where there is no vision, the people perish." But he also recognized the importance of clear, concise strategic plans with measurable objectives to drive each school's budget and activities. And he revolutionized the school system by empowering parents to choose the right public school for their child and by empowering teachers and principals to manage their own schools.

John was perhaps best known for his intensive focus on reading as the foundation for all further learning. He sparked a prodigious citywide campaign to help every child learn to read. It is no accident that parents across Seattle are reading to their children, that thousands of reading tutors from businesses and other organizations have flooded into the schools, and that billboards and television ads have sprung up across the city and airwaves encouraging children to read.

He created "exit standards" to ensure that children acquire the skills and knowledge needed to advance to the next grade. Citing the tough love exhibited by his own sixth-grade teacher, he recommended setting clear promotion standards, identifying children at risk of not meeting these standards as early as possible, and providing intensive, high-quality instruction in school and after school to help children reach these standards. His solution was never to assign blame, but rather to lovingly and relentlessly insist that schools and communities help each child succeed.

Inspired by his mother and father, he wanted the children of Seattle to learn about the power of education directly from their parents. Like John, this is how I learned about the importance of education. My dad started out as a schoolteacher, and later, as a school superintendent, worked his way through YMCA law school at night. My mother worked her way through school as a waitress during the Depression and became one of the first women to graduate from Vanderbilt Law School. They inspired me through a strong commitment to their own education, and then reinforced this lesson through consistent involvement in mine. My wife, Tipper, and I have continued this commitment by becoming actively involved in our own children's education and convening annual conferences looking at how to strengthen the capacity of families to help address vital issues like education.

The dedication of this book to teachers as "the real and enduring heroes of society" reflects a deep conviction about the value and role of our nation's teachers. Stanford fought for teachers and principals, providing the support, recognition, training, and authority they need but holding them accountable for results. He recognized that our schools will improve only through the hard work of the caring, talented, and dedicated people who work in our schools every day.

Above all, John Stanford fought for students—demanding performance, finding every possible way to engage a child's interest and talent through academics, music, the arts, sports, whatever it takes to engage a student in learning and productive activity. John often said the job of educators is to find our children's strengths and work with them until they succeed.

He believed deeply that we must boost student achievement for all children and close the academic performance gap between minority and white children. Indeed, one mission of our nation is to demonstrate that people of different racial and ethnic backgrounds, of all faiths and creeds, can not only work and live together, but can enrich and ennoble themselves and others and build our nation's future together. We must provide all of our people with a quality education if we are to achieve this mission and have one cohesive America providing opportunity for all and demanding responsibility from all.

To accomplish these goals, John enlisted parents, teachers, principals, businesses, museums, civic groups, and thousands of volunteers to help children learn. He put every resource in the community to work on behalf of children. He brought "the public back into public education."

His efforts have paid off handsomely in Seattle. Test scores are up, the gap between minority and white students is closing, incidences of violence are down, and the city is mobilized on behalf of children and education. Moreover, John unleashed an enduring tradition of leadership across the school system and community that will surely continue to move Seattle's public schools in the right direction.

He writes in this book and demonstrated in his life that "children need to feel there is someone in their corner who really wants them to succeed." We should all be profoundly grateful that children across Seattle—and now across America—will fare better because John Stanford stood in our children's corner.

John was a hero to the people of Seattle and a true American hero. All of us can learn from his life, and from the vision and ideas expressed in this book. However we judge all of the specific and impressive strategies outlined here, we can pay tribute to John Stanford and his vision by embracing one central lesson: We can and must rededicate ourselves and our communities to strong public schools that help every child realize his or her promise. We cannot afford to ignore—or even linger while we consider—this challenge. In John's spirit, we must all take bold, constructive action to help our children learn and succeed.

—Vice President Al Gore
April 1999

PREFACE

> *"What's he going to do — make the kids stand at attention, do push-ups, and wear uniforms? That stuff might work in the military but it won't work in the schools."*

After two closed interviews, the Seattle School Board asked me to participate in an open-forum interview with parents, teachers, and the general public. The Seattle media had given a lot of coverage to the board's search for a superintendent, and the fact that I came with no background in education but with thirty years in the United States Army and four as a county executive had raised a small tidal wave of curiosity. Not surprisingly, the room was packed.

As the interview began, I could hear the murmurings of the crowd. Some of the most respected principals sat behind the school board president and whispered adamantly in her ear, "Don't hire the general!" Teachers joked about how they would have to address me, and whether they'd have to salute each other, and polish their shoes. Parents worried that I'd promote excessive discipline, squelch creativity, and transform the schools into boot camps.

I knew, of course, the concerns of the parents and teachers. I knew the stereotype they held of the army general: a Pattonesque commander, inflexible and abrasive, more able to order than to listen, willing to sacrifice our city's children for a questionable cause. But I also knew how far from the mark that was. Thirty years of leading in the military had taught me that most leaders are the *antithesis* of those traits. Leading means *inspiring*, not commanding. Leading means loving the people you lead so they will give you their hearts as well as their minds. It means communicating a vision of where you can go *together* and inviting them to join. The community was right: a TV general could not have led the public schools. They didn't know me, but their stereotypes were different from my reality. Now I had two hours to change their minds.

I felt I was going into the interview unarmed but dangerous. Unarmed because I had no K–12 education experience and I was competing for the job against two experienced superintendents with Ph.Ds. How could I answer questions about Bloom's *Taxonomy* or Gardner's multiple intelligences? Some political leaders had already responded to my candidacy by saying "This guy doesn't have a clue about public education," and, in the strictest sense, they were right: I didn't know the specifics of educational practice. But I felt strongly that to be a successful superintendent I didn't need to know those details: There were already 5,000 educators in the district who did! What the district needed was a leader. That's the reason I was "dangerous"—I knew I had the leadership skills to do the job.

Over the next two hours I listened carefully to the audience's concerns. In response I told them confidently that I could lead their schools to success but I could not run the schools alone; I would need their help and I would actively invite their participation. I told them that the academic achievement of every child would be my highest priority, and that I would ask parents, businesses, and community groups to help us to raise the levels of achievement. I told them that, despite the enormous problems the district was facing—aging buildings, declining test scores, a woefully insufficient budget—despite the fact that someone had said, "Why would you want to be a superintendent of schools? Why do you care? It's too late for public education," despite all those things, *we can do it. We can reach and teach all children.*

This is not a clever slogan, nor simply a rallying cry. It *is* the schools' responsibility to teach and reach each child. I know this in my heart because I was one of the "unreachable." I failed sixth grade.

This should not have come as a big surprise to my family or me: for years I'd been fooling around in class, not doing my homework. But when Miss Greenstein came to my house at the end of the year for a "private conversation" with my parents, and when I saw my parents' faces as they showed her to the door, I was devastated. I felt ashamed. My parents had never graduated from grade school. They each worked two jobs (my father as a truck driver and train engineer, my mother as a cook) to keep our family together and, more than anything, they wanted better for their children. My two older sisters were diligent; they were the scholars my parents wanted. Now I felt like I was breaking their hearts.

But my mother wasn't about to let her expectations for her only son die. She purchased a set of *World Book Encyclopedias* for me. The next school year, and every year after, from wherever she was working, she called me every afternoon—usually two or three times—to make sure I was doing my homework. It was hard for her to check the quality of my school-work since she couldn't do the work herself, but she made sure that it was done, and she talked more often with my teachers. I submitted to the discipline and survived the embarrassment of repeating sixth grade; my work became regular, if only average; it wasn't until eighth or ninth grade that I felt any excitement about going to school. But the experience of failing sixth grade was pivotal. Miss Greenstein had recognized that I wasn't ready to move on—I was immature and unmotivated, I needed a kick in the pants—and her justified action provided it. The jolt of letting down my family, the shame I felt as my friends moved on, the embarrassment I felt in front of my neighbors, the message my retention sent to my parents: all forced me to take my schooling, and perhaps my life, more seriously. At the time I was humiliated; I thought my life was ruined. Today I know the truth: I would not be where I am today if Miss Greenstein hadn't had the courage and love to do what she did.

I say courage and love because that's exactly what it took. It took courage and love to look my parents in the eye and tell them—just as it takes courage and love to do the other things a school system must do if it wants to do what's best for its children. It takes courage and love to say to teachers, "You must put aside your adult concerns." It takes courage and love to remove a teacher, secretary, or principal who has been a member of your team. It takes courage and love to say to a child, "You will not graduate unless your work improves." I think back to Miss Greenstein and wonder, "What would have happened to me had my teacher not loved me? Our school districts need this kind of courage and love because without them, we will never graduate children who are prepared to thrive in the competitive, knowledge-based world they will inherit. If *we* can't do what is difficult now, we subject them to far greater difficulties in the future.

I talked that night with parents, teachers, and the community, about achievement, safety, accountability, and fiscal responsibility, and in the 2½ years I've been here, we've been making good on those issues. Our administrators, teachers, and parents are working together to make Seattle a world-class system. We have created unparalleled partnerships with the community to bring additional resources into the schools; we have taken measures to raise the academic achievement of *every* child; we have generated tremendous excitement both inside and outside our city about the future of public education.

This book is not designed to denigrate previous administrations. I was handed a fine school district. My observations and changes are the direct result of an effective leadership style applied to a new profession.

We are doing what I told the community we would do that night. We are writing a new future for Seattle's children. We are writing the story of an entire city's collaboration with and excitement about its public schools. We are creating a blueprint for success in education that can transform the lives of *all* children.

The board made a gutsy choice and we're on our way to greatness!

John Stanford
April 1998

INTRODUCTION

> *"If you want to transform an institution that has been stagnant for decades, the last place you look for a leader is inside that institution. We needed a noneducator."*
>
> —DON NIELSEN, Seattle School Board

I am not an educator. I am a leader of educators. That is the reason I was hired. When the Seattle School Board brought me on board in the summer of 1995, I needed to learn as fast as I could about the business of education. So I immediately did what anyone would do if he or she were entering a new field: I asked a million questions. I spent my first three months as superintendent meeting with teachers, staff people, business leaders, and parents, and asking question after question. How are you advancing achievement for all children? What is the most important thing we do? What are the challenges that get in our way? How can we serve our customers better? And what I found as a result of asking all these questions was something very curious. I found that our school system was filled with paradoxes.

- We claimed that we wanted every child to learn—but we were promoting children who hadn't.
- We claimed that we wanted every child to learn—but we didn't hold teachers and principals accountable for student achievement.
- We claimed that we wanted academic achievement from our students—but we placed teachers in schools based on seniority rather than merit.

I found that our schools were focused on the morale and welfare of adults rather than on the academic, social, and emotional needs of children.

- Why, for instance, when we knew it cost more to teach children who were chronically below academic standards, did we spend the same amount of money to educate every child?

- Why, if we wanted every child to learn, were we busing children to the other side of town when busing didn't improve academic performance?

- Why, if we wanted every child to graduate with a specified set of skills, did we let teachers pick and choose which skills to teach, instead of making them adhere to the district's curriculum?

- Why, when we knew that thousands of children were behind, did every school not offer after-school tutoring, summer school, and other kinds of supports to get every child up to grade level?

- Why, if teachers were the crucial element in our instructional system, did we give them an average of seventeen minutes of planning time a day and only a few days of training annually in which to strengthen their skills?

What I found as I asked these questions was that there really weren't solid answers. Practices that had developed over the years and were contrary to the goal of educating children had, because of politics, or familiarity, or simply because of tradition, become entrenched. Indeed, in any business, inconsistencies can become so entrenched, so *accepted*, that people who have been inside the business for a long time simply stop seeing them, or become unwilling to change them. And in Seattle there were glaring discrepancies between what the district said it wanted for its children and what its children were actually getting.

If we were going to turn the district around, it was clear we'd have to root out these inconsistencies. We'd have to make sure that *everything* we did furthered our number-one goal: raising academic achievement.

People wondered when I was hired how someone with no background in education could possibly fix the schools. But Seattle didn't need an educator—Seattle needed a professional manager to determine whether or not all functions of the school district were working to promote the goals of the district, to eliminate those that weren't, and to refocus the others onto academic achievement. And Seattle needed a *leader* to galvanize the entire city into action—for change of this magnitude required everyone's excitement and energy.

The other reason Seattle needed a noneducator to turn its schools around was that there was a gap of thirty to forty points between white and minority students' test scores, a rising incidence of violence, and a dropout rate of 15 percent. There was so little confidence in the schools that taxpayers often rejected education levies and business groups micromanaged the district's operations. The funding picture was alarming: The budget for the school year that was about to start had expenditures exceeding income by $15 million, over the next two years the state would cut our allocation by $25 million, and the district had an operating reserve of less than a single day, which meant that the slightest unexpected hiccup—a cold snap, snowstorm, fire, backed-up sewer in one of our aging buildings, or a lawsuit from an employee who felt she was unfairly terminated—would require us to cut into programs.

All these problems had a tremendous impact on how we went about educating children—but they were not educational problems. They were *business* problems. The district needed someone who was experienced at leading large, complex, heterogeneous organizations and had a track record of turning them around. It needed someone who had managed multimillion-dollar budgets and kept them consistently in the black. It needed someone who had inspired a burned-out workforce and infused them with a vision of what they could achieve. It needed someone who had taken an organization that had lost the confidence of its customers and brought it back on track. The district already had 5,000 dedicated, hardworking, highly skilled educators who knew all about helping children learn. What it lacked was a leader who could focus the organization on its goals, unleash its potential, get the obstacles out of the way, and empower the educators to do their jobs.

TEN PHILOSOPHICAL SHIFTS

I had been in the district for about a month when I had a rather revealing conversation with a principal. I'd been meeting with him in his office, discussing the problem of children who were chronically behind, when I asked him what he was doing to help those children learn. The principal thought for a moment, then pointed to a textbook on his bookshelf. "We've switched to the Glencoe math curriculum," he said. "But how does that help individual students?" I asked. "Can you tell me names of students who are behind and what their teachers are doing to help them?" The principal looked at me, confused. "Well, I couldn't tell you all their names," he said, "but I'm sure their teachers are working with them in small groups to help them catch up." "You don't routinely talk to teachers about the academic achievement of their children?" I asked. "You don't ask to see a plan for how they'll help each child improve?" For just a second the principal looked at me as if I'd walked in from outer space (and in a sense I had), then cautiously he answered. "I guess I'd see that as interfering. It would be telling the teacher how to do her job, and that's not part of my philosophy."

I left that school and thought to myself, "That's incredible! This principal, the academic leader of his building, doesn't ask his teachers how they're helping all children learn because it isn't part of his philosophy. What is his philosophy? What is his role as a principal? And how does he expect his students to improve?"

Over the next few weeks I met with other principals, as well as with teachers and administrators in the district, and I asked all of them what they were doing to raise academic achievement. To my dismay, I found equally disturbing answers. Throughout the district, people seemed to be guided by "philosophies" that were not in students' best academic interest. There was the philosophy, for instance, that "poor minority children received little education support at home, therefore they shouldn't be expected to achieve at school." There was the philosophy that "poor minority parents wanted less for their children than middle-class parents, so there is little point in expecting them to participate in their children's education." There was the philosophy that "sports and the arts are feel-good frills, expendable in an academic curriculum." There were a host of "philosophies," some voiced consciously, others held just below the surface, that had an enormous impact on how the district educated its students. The philosophies were not meant to be damaging; they were held by people who loved the children they worked with and labored with day and night to help them learn. They were just part of the accepted culture, the result of years of work within a system that had too few resources to deal with increasingly difficult problems.

"THE EDUCATORS WERE SO BUSY INSIDE THE TREES LOOKING AT ALL THEIR LITTLE PROGRAMS, THEY HADN'T ASKED SOME OF THOSE VERY BASIC QUESTIONS THAT SOMEBODY WHO SEES THE FOREST IS GOING TO ASK."
—LINDA HARRIS, FORMER PRESIDENT, SEATTLE SCHOOL BOARD

But the trouble with all these philosophies was that they got in the way of academic achievement! Expecting only middle-class children to achieve meant that thousands of minority children were allowed to fall through the cracks. Holding lower expectations for minority parents meant that those parents weren't encouraged to give their children the help they needed at home. Regarding sports and the arts as frills meant that thousands of children for whom those subjects were the only reason to come to school had no gateway to academic learning. These philosophies were perpetuating the district's biggest problems; they were at the heart of its inconsistent behaviors. And as long as they were allowed to continue, they would undermine any effort to turn the district around.

Seattle's first step was to make ten philosophical shifts that would shape all of our thinking as we reengineered our schools.

Philosophical Shift #1: We would stop focusing on adults and begin focusing on children. Every action and every decision would be measured against a single inviolable yardstick: Is this in the best interest of children? Does this promote academic achievement?

Philosophical Shift #2: We would stop believing that some children would learn and start believing that all children would learn. No children, regardless of socioeconomic status, would be written off. We would expect every child to achieve, and every teacher to promote that achievement.

Philosophical Shift #3: We would stop believing that students alone were accountable for their performance and start holding students, teachers, principals, parents, and the community accountable. We would establish measurable goals for student achievement and hold everyone accountable for helping students meet them.

Philosophical Shift #4: We would stop believing that we could reach all students with our traditional currciulum and start diversifying our curriculum to meet all students' needs. We would expand our offerings in the arts, sports, sciences, technology, language, and careers in order to meet all students' needs and interests.

Philosophical Shift #5: We would stop abandoning teachers and start giving them total support. We would aggressively give teachers the support, training, and recognition they needed to achieve victory in the classroom.

Philosophical Shift #6: We would stop running schools bureaucratically and start running them entrepreneurially. We would give our schools control over their budgets, staffing, and instructional methods and expect them to compete in the marketplace through excellence.

Philosophical Shift #7: We would stop hiding from the media and begin seeing the media as our partner. Schools do a million things right every day. Because we needed the support of the public to do our job, we would work proactively with the media to get our positive stories out.

Philosophical Shift #8: We would stop embracing the status quo and start embracing change. We would stop offering programs that were not in the best interest of children even if eliminating those programs angered groups of constituents.

Philosophical Shift #9: We would stop serving children out of a sense of duty and start educating them out of a sense of love. We would love every child entrusted to our care, because children don't learn from adults who don't love them.

Philosophical Shift #10: We would not expect the public to support us because they ought to. We would make a concerted effort to build the public we needed.

CHANGE AT THE STRATEGIC LEVEL

Over the past several years, these new ways of thinking have become the cornerstones of our operation. Not surprisingly, as we've made these philosophical shifts, we've found that all sorts of other things had to change. If we really focused on children, for example, we could no longer have a hiring system built on seniority; we had to find ways to put the *best* teachers in every school. If we really believed that all children would learn, we could no longer let children play in the back of the classroom or promote children who weren't ready; we had to change the teaching regime to meet each student's needs and provide extra support to those who were having trouble. If we stopped holding students solely responsible for their achievement, we could no longer exonerate teachers when their children didn't reach their potential; we had to develop measurable goals for student performance and then hold teachers accountable for meeting them.

This book is about how we are making these changes. It is about "scaling up" reform so that it affects an entire city's schools. In the past, most school reform has happened at the level of individual schools. By working one school at a time, reformers have created many model programs, many excellent schools. But for true reform to happen, it has to happen at the district level. That's what we are doing in Seattle; this book describes that process. Each chapter describes an old way of thinking that derailed the district from its mission, the philosophical shift we made in order to redirect our efforts toward achievement, and the strategies we are putting in place so that *everything* focuses on helping children learn.

We have made a tremendous amount of change in our district—and change is never easy. But if some people are unhappy because we have changed the status quo, thousands more are feeling invigorated! Teachers stop me in the halls to say, "I'm working harder than I ever have, but we're moving in the right direction and I'm excited about what we're doing for the children." Principals who have been educators for twenty or thirty years tell me that the pressure on them to perform is higher than it's ever been, but they feel empowered by the focus on achievement. Parents come up to me on the street to say, "I can feel the excitement of the schools through my children." Change is hard, but when it is focused, when it is in the service of a vision, it is also tremendously exhilarating.

I don't mean to suggest, in writing this book, that we have all the answers, or even that everything we're doing is right. It is way too early to declare victory in public education. But we *have* made significant improvements in the way we run our schools, and we've removed many of those damaging inconsistencies from our operation.

- We have negotiated a radical new contract with our teachers' union, one of the first in the nation in which teachers have agreed to be held accountable for student performance.

- We have changed seniority as a factor in assigning teachers to schools and given schools the ability to hire the most qualified, rather than the most senior, teachers.

- We have stopped mandatory race-based busing at the elementary level and enabled all children to choose a school close to home.

- We have changed the way we finance our schools so that children with greater educational needs receive additional dollars.

- We have developed a training program for principals that teaches them academic leadership, organizational development, financial management, and other business and leadership skills.

- We have created "individual learning plans" that tailor academic instruction to the needs of every child performing below grade level.

- We have raised over $15 million in private investments, which is targeted to programs focused on academic achievement.

- We have doubled the number of community volunteers who tutor in the schools.

- We are bringing the arts, the environment, foreign languages, technology, and school-to-work experiences into our curriculum through partnerships with business and nonprofit groups so that we can meet the interests and needs of every student.

- We have rekindled the community's faith in and excitement about the public schools:

  - voters have approved three operations and capital tax levies in the last two years;

  - the state legislature sustained the amount of money school districts could raise through local tax levies;

- the middle class is returning to our schools: for the first
  time in a decade, Seattle has outpaced the suburbs in the
  sale of homes, a change realtors attribute to excitement
  about the schools.

We have also seen an improvement in student performance. Since
1995 our standardized test scores have risen from one to four percentile
points in every subject for every group of students; the gap between minority and white students' test scores has begun to close; the number of violent incidents has reached a ten-year low; and the dropout rate has slid,
for the first time in five years, to under 12 percent. Will long-term trends
bear out these improvements? It's too soon to know for sure, but we believe they will. We believe they are the logical consequence of focusing
everything we do on getting achievement in the classroom.

I am writing this book because, while Seattle, with 47,500 students, is
smaller than some of our nation's urban school districts, its problems are
the same, and I believe that the solutions we are creating here will work in
every community. If, in every community, outsiders—whether a business-
trained superintendent, or simply parents, business leaders, and other concerned citizens—push their districts to change, then they, too, can begin
the transformation required. We all must realize, however, that change is a
two-pronged process. Schools *cannot* educate their children alone. They
need partnerships with parents; they need financial and curriculum support from businesses; they need tutoring and volunteer time from retirees,
religious congregations, ethnic organizations, and social-service groups.
They need their communities to understand that the "war" in public education is not a war about test scores or curriculum standards. It is a war
about the future of our children and our communities, for nothing shapes
the future of a city as much as its children. Our children will be our future
employers and employees; they will choose our elected officials; they will
determine our social, environmental, and economic policies. If our schoolchildren cannot read or think clearly, if they cannot use technology, if they
cannot value the differences in our many cultures or the environment they
will inherit, what kind of future will we have? The public schools are everyone's schools—and it is everyone's job to keep them vital.

Fortunately, when communities rally to support their schools, they can
be a tremendous force for change! Seattle's citizens are extraordinary in
that regard. Seattle wants its public schools to succeed. If parents everywhere read to their children at night, if they request a syllabus from their
teachers and discuss their children's schoolwork daily, if they hold their

children to the highest standards and demand that their schools do the same, they will be boosting their school's academic program. If business leaders ask their schools, "What can we do for you?", if they contribute money and resources to enhance school programs, if they give employees an hour off each week to tutor children who would otherwise fail, they will help create schools that meet the needs of *all* students and enable *all* students to pass. If concerned citizens—artists and grandparents, laborers and clergy, athletes and social workers—vote for school levies; if they "adopt" a student whose grades are falling; if they ask *every* child how he or she is doing in school, they can help ensure that our schools are adequately funded and that all children go to school ready to learn.

Education is not just a matter for the politicians and professionals; it is a matter for all of us. For we are the public in public education. When we work together, we can do it. We *can* make public education work.

CHAPTER 1

THE VICTORY IS IN THE CLASSROOM

QUIZ:
WHAT SHOULD BE THE NUMBER-ONE PRIORITY OF A SCHOOL DISTRICT?

(a) personalizing education

(b) student and teacher safety

(c) maintenance

(d) parent concerns

(e) academic achievement of all children

(f) public perception and support

(g) managing and increasing the budget

Answer on page 10.

A school district's number-one priority is children, right? Surprisingly, no.

When I came to public education in Seattle, I came to participate in our nation's greatest children's system, to work for parents, teachers, principals, school staffs, the school board, and the city who worked so hard for children. I knew my learning curve would be steep, but I came anyhow. It never occurred to me that we would not succeed. The reception I received from the city of Seattle and the school system was magnificent, an exciting sign that Seattle was ready, even anxious, to provide the support needed to make public education work for our children.

But there were many surprises ahead. Perhaps most serious of all, I found a school system that was focused not on children's learning, but rather was focused on the issues of adults. Women and men who were devoted to children, who had entered education because they were "on fire" to help children learn and achieve, were being defeated by a system that had its priorities wrong and that did not celebrate them, their work for children, or children's achievement. The school system and people in it had turned inward to protect themselves. And the children were left outside of the equation.

THE TEACHER WHO COULDN'T BE FIRED

In the opening weeks of school in Seattle, I visited several schools a day, meeting principals and talking to teachers, learning as fast as I could about the district. At one of the schools I visited, a teacher told me a remarkable story.

Mary Kant* was a third-grade teacher who had apparently lost her love of children. She was dour and impatient with them and had been heard on more than one occasion to say, "You're too stupid to learn." Children who had flourished in earlier grades seemed to wither in her class. Time and again parents had complained to the principal, but each time he refused to remove her, claiming that "the system" wouldn't let him. The process of removing a teacher from a school was simply too difficult and disruptive.

After two years of complaints and inaction, another teacher spoke to the principal about Mary's unprofessional conduct. Word of the meeting got back to Mary, who then organized a "freeze" against her fellow teacher, convincing half the teachers in the school not to talk to the "complainer." For the remainder of the year the teacher community was paralyzed: Teachers couldn't work together on curricula, they couldn't discuss their students, they could barely plan the spring play. The "complaining" teacher, who had a stellar record and was loved by parents, threatened to quit. And still the principal refused to move or fire Mary. The children and their education had been abandoned by the warring factions of adults.

Now, had this been the only such story I heard, I might have blown it off, assuming that the incident was an aberration. But it wasn't. In the next few weeks I heard other stories about teachers who had lost their passion to teach children: I heard about teachers who were so distracted by disagreements with the principal that they could barely concentrate on the

* Not her real name

class work; I heard about "unsatisfactory" teachers who had been given "satisfactory" evaluations so they could be transferred to another school; I heard about teachers who had given up on students and let them play in the back of the classroom. Regrettably, the small percentage of teachers who were not performing reflected badly on the vast majority of teachers who were bringing our children love, support, and a bright and hopeful future. Why were these teachers allowed to remain in the system?

As the weeks went by I discovered the answer. In part it was our contract with our union, which made it almost impossible to remove teachers from their jobs. In part it was the leadership of principals, who chose to keep teachers in their schools rather than face the disruption caused by trying to remove them. In part it was teachers themselves, who often rallied behind colleagues whose jobs were in jeopardy for fear of endangering their own jobs. These individuals didn't mean to be self-serving, but they were trapped in a system that made it easier to act in the interest of adults than in the best interest of children.

THE SCHOOL SYSTEM THAT WASN'T A SYSTEM

This sense of misplaced focus was corroborated everywhere I went. At every school I went to, I asked the principal to show me how he or she accounted for the academic achievement of every child. Few of them could do it. Most didn't routinely compare each child's performance to his or her performance during the previous quarter or the previous year. Most had no measurable performance goals for students, no standardized test scores they wanted the children to reach. Most had no systematic method of changing the learning regime when children fell behind.

Equally surprising was my discovery that the evaluation of teachers and principals didn't include academic progress. Teachers were evaluated for such things as classroom management (Could they control the behavior of twenty-eight children?) and the integration of curricular requirements into their teaching (Were they teaching the things they were supposed to?). Principals were evaluated based on the climate in their schools (Was it clean and cheerful? Did the teachers work well together?) and on the number of expulsions and suspensions they'd had. But neither group was evaluated for how much their children had learned. I was astonished. Here was a school system where learning was supposed to be the bottom line, yet fundamental mechanisms that could ensure that learning was happening were missing!

Learning was happening, of course. The district's standardized test scores were slightly above the national average. There were advanced-placement and gifted programs and magnificent music and drama programs on par with those in the city's most respected private schools. But these successes seemed to stem from the individual efforts of many highly skilled and dedicated teachers rather than from the functioning of an organized educational system.

As I walked the halls with principals and talked with teachers in their lounges, my sense of misplaced focus only grew. All were eager to talk to me and were open with their concerns. But the things they wanted to talk about surprised me. Instead of exit exams, or standards, or closing the gap between white and minority test scores—academic issues I had already raised for the district—they wanted to know why some schools got more money for supplies than others, or whether we would be switching to uniforms, or whether the school's site council had the right to direct their curriculum. These were important issues, of course; they affected the staff's quality of life in school. But the fervor with which the staff addressed these and other ancillary issues, and the priority these took over issues of learning and achievement, concerned me. These adult issues, I realized, were distracting us from the classroom. They had sidelined the focus on children.

> Can you imagine working at Microsoft and not focusing on software, or at General Motors and not focusing on building cars? That's what the schools were doing. We had forgotten that academic achievement is the core of our business.

CREATING AN ACHIEVEMENT *SYSTEM*

The directive of the Seattle School Board was clear: Raise academic achievement. I suppose every superintendent goes about the task differently, but coming as I did from a military and county-executive business background, I naturally thought about my task in terms of creating an achievement *system*.

Systems thinking was a built-in skill for me after thirty years in the military. In one of my last assignments I'd been the CEO of a $4.5 billion business, the Military Traffic Management Command, which is responsible for moving soldiers, sailors, airmen, and their families and equipment all around the world. We had facilities in eighty-eight ports, an information system that could locate an individual item at a moment's notice, and a worldwide staff of 5,000 to manage the complexities of the endeavor.

Later, as the director of Plans, Policies and Programs for the United States Transportation Command, I played a role in the logistics planning for the Persian Gulf War. Moving 450,000 troops plus their supporting equipment was the equivalent of moving the entire city of Seattle—infrastructure, hospitals, housing, restaurants, transportation facilities, warehouses—to the middle of the desert, and then supplying it for an indefinite period of time. Neither of these jobs would have been possible without the development and operation of systems: logistics systems, budget and acquisition systems, human resource systems, programming and planning systems, that were all focused on the organizations' goals. The Department of Defense had trained me and thousands like me to develop, operate, and sustain complex, heterogeneous systems under pressure and stress.

It was precisely this kind of systems capability that the Seattle School Board was seeking when they hired me. They made a courageous move by hiring a noneducator; they were opening themselves to the charge that they were experimenting with Seattle's children. But they also knew that they needed a fresh approach from the outside. What they wanted was someone who would do something different; someone who would not *reform*, but rather *transform*, the public schools. What they needed, they believed, was a leader with a solid business background.

Given their charge and my orientation, I did the first thing any businessperson would do on taking the reins of a corporation. I asked the most fundamental question: What is our mission? The answer was fairly obvious: We were trying to build an achiever. Our product takes thirteen years to build and costs about $5,000 per year. That's a cost of $65,000 per student by the time of graduation. What an expensive product! There aren't many products in society that cost that much to build. Were we meeting our objectives? It costs private schools approximately $7,000 per year to produce their achievers, and they have more parental help and students with fewer educational challenges. How could we be expected to do the same job for so much less? Based on what I was hearing from parents, educators, business and civic leaders, we were not doing the job as well as we should: too many of our graduates were leaving our schools ill-prepared for the future. Clearly there were problems somewhere in the production system.

My early discoveries had shown that the district's academic systems had become sidelined from their focus on children. So, too, were many of the systems necessary to support academics—transportation, finance, teacher training, and so on. When I asked, for example, why we didn't have more after-school tutoring and activities, I was told that it was because the school bus cost and availability didn't allow it. The school bus schedule was determining the academic schedule, rather than the other way around. When I asked about teacher training I learned that the average age of our teachers was forty-eight, and that most hadn't been trained comprehensively in over twenty years, despite the fact that students, society, and our understanding of learning and the human brain had changed dramatically in that time. The teacher training system—or lack thereof—was determining our academic program, rather than the other way around. When I asked why we were busing children to schools across town when busing didn't seem to improve their performance, I learned that the district had considered dismantling the program in the past, but hadn't because it was favored by some constituencies. The system we used to assign students to schools was determining their academic regimens rather than the other way around.

What we had was a system in which the components were not focused on the system's goals, where blame and passing the buck flourished. The system had become distracted; it was focused in a thousand different departmental directions. Without a unifying vision—children's academic achievement—pulling everything in one direction, the school district was not a well-functioning system and it was certainly not a system operating in the interests of children.

As I traveled around the country that year, meeting other superintendents, going to every conference to learn as much as I could about this business of education, I realized that these problems were not unique to Seattle. Public education had allowed its systems to lose their focus. I heard stories about districts that had delayed the opening of school to fix boilers and finish painting, taking time away from the classroom to do repairs that could have waited until winter break. I heard stories about districts that kept ineffective programs going because they were afraid to anger certain parents, penalizing children because of adults' political concerns. I heard stories about districts where school boards and superintendents engaged in battles that demoralized everyone.

If we were going to fix public education, I realized, we would have to refocus our school districts on the student in the classroom. We would have to move away from a focus on blame and negativity. And we would have to do it not by tinkering with reforms in our individual schools, but by fixing the systems with which our school districts run. If we could fix the systems—get them focused on achievement—we could affect what happened in every classroom in the district. We could effect citywide change.

BUILDING THE COMMUNITY WE NEED

At the same time I was visiting schools at home and around the country, I was also spending time in my new city. I was learning the neighborhoods, the culture, the politics, and the businesses, because I knew all of that would have an impact on the schools. It was natural for me to look at those things because I had come to Seattle from Atlanta, where I had been the manager of Fulton County. As the executive of a 5,000-person, $750 million county government, I had worked with health and human services, school districts, and recreation departments. We had streamlined the tax system and made the government "user friendly." We had managed budgets for building libraries and senior centers, police stations and fire stations. We had even built a $150 million court complex, which I had called a "monument to the county's failure" because if our county resources had adequately supported the schools, there would have been far less need for such a campus. Managing all these services had given me an understanding of the myriad systems involved in running a large urban/suburban area. Now, in my job as superintendent, I would have to try to bend those systems toward the schools.

We would need to work with all these services because children spend only 10 percent of their time in school. The rest of the time they are in the community—with their parents, in their neighborhoods, exposed to the media—absorbing the countless influences that shape their values, habits, ethics, and self-images. And if these *outside* systems aren't pointed toward the classroom, toward promoting academic achievement, they detract from what we do in the schools. As superintendent, I would need to work with clergy and ethnic organizations to get them to help instill the value of education in their members. I'd need to work with social-service agencies to encourage them to make it easy for families to access their services. I'd need to work with the media to encourage them to use their tremendous power and influence to broadcast messages that promoted educational values. I'd need to work with businesses to get them to invest money and resources in the schools. And I'd need to talk to the public everywhere—on street corners and on television, in restaurants and in newspapers, in town meetings and in workplace speeches—to get them excited about what we were doing in the schools so that they would support our efforts. There have been so many who believe public schools can't work, but they *can* and *do* work when the entire community becomes involved.

That's my job as superintendent. It's not to get involved in the procedural aspects of curriculum development and assessment. It's to work at the systems level. It's to lead our district and city in fixing our systems so that they lead us toward our academic goals. If we can do that, if we can get every system focused on the classroom, we can have an urban district that *works*: a district where taxpayers pass local bonds and levies to support school building, modernization, academic, and sports programs; a district where parents participate at the 75 percent level, a district where the entire business community joins an alliance to support district academic achievement; a district in which 90 percent of our students graduate, in which standardized test scores average in the sixtieth percentile, in which the gap between minority and white scores is nonexistent. A district in which violence is eliminated, in which teachers are excited to come to work, in which parents feel like partners in their children's learning. A district in which our teachers are celebrated rather than denigrated! If we can get all our systems to put children's needs first—and I believe we can—then we can have a district in which excitement and curiosity are everywhere: a district in which *every* child learns.

> One principal came up to me my second year in the district and looked at me a little sheepishly. "You know," he said, "I've been in this business for thirty years and we have never focused this much on academic achievement."

KEEPING YOUR EYE ON THE CENTERLINE

Back in 1960 when I was in ROTC flight training at Pennsylvania State University, I was thrilled about learning to fly. I couldn't wait for the day when I'd get my chance at the controls. Finally the day of my first flight came and, with the instructor at my side, I clumsily navigated the plane through the sky. My heart sank, however, when it was time to land the two-seat Cessna 150. I could see the runway far below me, a narrow line, impossibly small. How could I ever get back there? As if sensing my insecurity, the plane began to yaw.

The instructor said, "Keep it on the centerline, Stanford. Nose down, sixty knots, land on the runway numbers." He took the controls and showed me how. As we were taxiing to take off again, he looked me in the eyes and said, "Now, this is nothing but a machine. You control it; don't ever let it control you." Those were words to live by.

I've thought about the centerline frequently since then; in every job it's helped me keep my focus. When crises or politics have begun to distract me from the vision, remembering the centerline has helped me steer my actions. For a school district, too, there is a centerline. Buses, roofs, contracts, boilers, and other adult issues may distract us. But if we can keep our eye on the centerline, our children will learn.

THE VICTORY IS IN THE CLASSROOM

Focusing our systems has resulted in considerable progress. Standardized test scores are up for every student group in every subject, and the gap between minority and white students' scores is closing. The number of violent incidents has dropped to a ten-year low and the number of high-school dropouts has declined by 8 percent. The city's excitement about the schools is so high that in the last 2½ years voters have passed four education levies. This year middle-class families have begun returning to our public schools.

We've changed the way we fund our schools so that poor, minority, and bilingual children with expensive educational needs receive additional dollars. We've stopped busing those children who can least afford to spend 275 hours on a bus each year. We've brought millions of dollars of private money into the schools, along with a thousand community volunteers.

We are not declaring victory. Far from it, we are a work in progress. But we feel we are moving in the right direction. We know we will have succeeded when *all* children are challenged, when *all* children are expected to pass, when *all* children feel loved and believed in by their teachers. In the meantime, we are keeping the momentum going. We will achieve that victory in our classrooms.

QUIZ:
WHAT SHOULD BE THE NUMBER-ONE PRIORITY OF A SCHOOL DISTRICT?

(e) academic achievement of all children

Schools should have one single driving priority: the academic achievement of their children. Unfortunately, many other concerns distract districts from that focus. It is easy to be seduced by all these adult issues, but until schools make student achievement the focus of all they do, they will not produce significant gains.

CHAPTER 2

WE CAN ACHIEVE THE VICTORY WHEN ... WE SHARE A COMMON VISION AND A PLAN FOR GETTING THERE

> ### QUIZ:
> #### WHAT IS THE MOST IMPORTANT COMPONENT OF A SCHOOL DISTRICT'S STRATEGIC PLAN?
>
> *(a) lofty goals that will inspire people*
>
> *(b) inspirational messages that will motivate people*
>
> *(c) measurable objectives that tell people what they must achieve*
>
> Answer on page 28.

Once, two men shared a hospital room. The man in the bed by the door was gravely ill; doctors questioned his hold on life. But the man in the window bed was stronger and often passed the time by describing the scene outside. "There's a park," he would say, "I see children playing." Or, "Look, the ice cream truck is coming!" Or, "Ah, two young lovers walking hand in hand." As the sicker man in the bed by the door grew stronger, he would nod and smile; the vicarious contact with the outside world cheered him.

After a week the man in the window bed went home and the sicker man was moved to the bed by the window. The following morning, as soon as the nurse had opened the curtains, he raised himself and looked out. There, to his surprise, was a parking lot—barren concrete with a few randomly parked cars. No children. No lovers. No park. At first he was furious; how could his friend have misled him? Then disappointed—he had so anticipated the view! But as the hours ticked by he realized what a gift his friend had given him. The images the man had painted had reminded him of all that was good about life; they had renewed his sense of hope and possibility. More than the medical care he was receiving, those images had strengthened him.

Today I am the man looking out the window for the children of Seattle. I must paint a similar vision for our citizens and school employees. They, too, must see the possibilities in the schools—and believe that the possibilities can be realized. How else will they inspire our children every single day? For the sake of the children, for the sake of our city, we must all share a common vision of what our schools can be: safe places filled with love where all students learn.

THE CULTURE OF THE PURPLE HEART

Unfortunately, what I've found in the world of education is that most school districts don't have a vision that lives. Instead, after years and years of trying, and being beaten up, most school districts have essentially become dormant. They no longer believe that change is possible. They no longer believe that every child can learn. My first year in the district, I went to several education conferences, and at every one a superintendent took me aside. "You know, John," he or she would say, "you are new and too naive about the business of education. You must understand two things: One, that the school board hired you to fire you; two, that you better start looking for someplace to fall." What they meant was that no one—not my school board, not my staff, not even my community—expected me to succeed. They seemed to share a common belief that there are no solutions for public education.

Now, I don't mean that those superintendents didn't want their children to succeed. They did! They and their administrators, principals, and teachers were working incredibly hard to make that happen. But their strenuous and well-intentioned efforts were being sabotaged by an undercurrent of defeat. It was as if they were bound by a "culture of the Purple Heart," a culture in which they expected to fight hard and get wounded rather than fight hard and win.

This culture is endemic in public education. Educators have been persuaded that a child's social condition is a determinant of learning, and they carry this belief into the classroom. As a result, when homeless, or poor, or single-parent children begin to fall behind, they are allowed to slip rather than be held to the higher standards that have been set for their more advantaged peers. This isn't intentional; no qualified teacher would knowingly let his or her students fail. But given the bleak circumstances of the children's lives, given the fact that many of these children fail time and time again, given the appallingly limited resources available to teachers in our public schools, it's easier to accept that the fault is in the child, or in the family, or in society as a whole, than to believe that the responsibility and power to make change is in the schools.

NOTHING STARTS WITHOUT A VISION. NOTHING HAPPENS WITHOUT A PLAN.

The only way we can defeat the culture of the Purple Heart is with vision backed up with belief. When educators stop believing that change can't happen and start enthusiastically envisioning how it *will*, we will begin turning our schools around.

A WORLD-CLASS, STUDENT-FOCUSED LEARNING SYSTEM BY 1999

When I arrived in Seattle I found a district in which the culture of the Purple Heart was fairly well entrenched. The community had driven the schools there. In school after school I saw wonderful things happening: teachers kneeling lovingly next to children, patiently helping them rise to the challenge of an assignment; children gathered around teachers in heated dialogue—whether about the anatomy of a frog or about current events; principals making phone call after phone call to parents, talking warmly about the children, inviting the parents to school, offering suggestions on raising school-smart young adults. But riding just below the surface in almost every school I visited was a sense of demoralization. And it was understandable: As in most school districts, a combination of societal problems, a pounding, critical press, and shrinking funds had created a host of problems. Of our 125 buildings, two-thirds were in need of major repairs; the maintenance backlog totaled $185 million. Thanks to the excellent work of my predecessor, staff, principals, and teachers, standardized test scores averaged in the fiftieth percentile, right at the national average, one of the best urban performances in the country, but the gap between minority and white students' scores was appalling. In nine of the twelve content areas measured, the gap between African-American students and white students was over forty points. The high-school dropout rate had been slowly coming down, but was still almost 15 percent. The rate of suspensions and expulsions had been climbing steadily. And overall confidence in the district was low. Within the district there was a sense of resignation, as if the staff were powerless to correct these problems. The district needed a vision.

Seattle is hardly unique in having significant, and costly, building maintenance problems. Across America, approximately one-third of our public schools need extensive repairs or building replacements. According to a 1996 report by the General Accounting Office, it will cost $112 billion just to bring our nation's school buildings up to federal mandates.

Since I knew nothing about the education business, I'd made a point of looking at other districts' visions. (I was looking for one to copy!) These visions said things like "Through restructuring we will support and maintain an environment in which every student is a self-directed and interactive learner," or "In partnership with our community we will help all students learn successfully," or "We will meet our students' diverse educational needs in a way that is nurturing, challenging, and effective." These statements reflected admirable intentions, but they described processes. They weren't galvanizing pictures of what the district could become. None was the kind of dream you could get excited about, and want to work toward. The poet Robert Browning said, "Let your reach exceed your grasp, or what is Heaven for?" That is what an organization needs to do: It must dream the impossible dream. And then it must use that dream to inspire its people to strive. School districts, especially, must reach for the dream because their children depend on them to do so. And those children—not administrative processes—must be the center of their dreams.

So with that in mind we began to develop a vision. Again, we began by asking lots and lots of questions of principals and teachers, of parents and students, of businesspeople and retirees: What are we trying to achieve? How will we know if we've succeeded? What are the problems that get in the way? Why aren't we focusing on the core of our business? What resources do we have to work with? What resources do we need?

Fairly quickly the answers shaped themselves into a pattern. We needed to create the highest possible standards for students, teachers, and principals—and then hold our people to them. We needed to focus our entire operation on our children because they were the core of our business. And we needed to get the community involved in making our district successful; we couldn't do it alone. With these three principles, I had the outline of our vision: *to be a world-class, student-focused learning system by 1999.* *World class* because that implies that we will be among the best, because we are home to 115 cultures and 80 different languages, because our students will have to compete in a global society when they leave our schools. *Student-focused* because everything we do has to focus on the children: how we spend our money, how we build our schools, how we hire and train our teachers, how we make decisions every day. *Learning system* because our school district would be focused on learning, not on teaching; because the operative question would be, Did the student get it? not, Did the teacher teach it?; because every business, every nonprofit organization, every individual who knows a child, must understand that they are part of a citywide learning system, that they have a role in raising our children. These words are our statement of what we believe: that we *can* make change, that every child will learn, that it is not too late, as some people believe, to create truly excellent public education.

WHERE THERE IS NO VISION, THE PEOPLE PERISH.
—PROVERBS, 29:18

MAKING THE DREAM REAL

But the vision was only words, and rather abstract ones at that. We needed goals that would give us concrete targets to reach for, objectives that would enable us to measure our progress, and timelines that would keep us glued to the track. We needed a strategic plan.

I had learned about planning in the army, where nothing happens without a plan. As a logistician, creating—and then carrying out—strategic plans was the core of my job. I started as the First Lieutenant operations officer for an armored rifle battalion of 750 men when I was right out of ROTC. I studied advanced planning at the Command and General Staff College and later at the Industrial College of the Armed Forces. In my last job in the army I worked for all four military services, developing plans that would take units from all corners of the globe and send them at a moment's notice, prepared to fight and win, to a conflict anywhere in the world.

What I had learned in my thirty years of military planning was that successful plans have four essential elements.

1. *Every element of the plan must be focused on the single most important goal: achieving victory in the field.* Like any organization, the army has many competing priorities. Every choice of action must be weighed against its cost, its degree of political support, its military effectiveness, and a host of other factors. But first on the list of priorities was the question, What must we do to ensure that our combat soldiers are prepared to win? They'll be crossing rough, muddy terrain at about fifteen miles per hour? Then we had better have refueling tankers stationed every "Y" miles because asking combat troops to waste an ounce of unnecessary energy on a task other than the objective defeats our priority. They'll be in battle conditions; daily mail delivery would boost morale; we'd better try to deliver mail daily with the rations. Nothing was included because "it was convenient" or because it had "always been done that way." Every item in the plan contributed to the combat readiness of the troops.

2. *The plan must have measurable goals and objectives.* Unless the expected outcomes are measurable, there's no way to know if they have been achieved. So when we planned to support the Sixth Air Cavalry Combat Brigade in the field, we didn't plan "to have aircraft at the highest operation readiness rate possible." We planned to have 90 percent of our aircraft combat ready at all times. We planned to have our supply of repair parts at 90 percent. We planned to have a fuel reserve of five days. We needed numeric goals like these to be able to guarantee our combat units that the support would be there when they needed it.

3. *The organization's budget must be tied to the plan.* In order to "operationalize" a plan—that is, to turn it into action—the organization must spend its money on the activities that have been planned. This happens only if the budget and the plan are made in tandem. In the army we made our plans, determined what they would cost, reviewed all the plans for an operation against each other to eliminate any duplication, then costed the whole package out. Since there was never as much money as we needed to accomplish everything we had planned, we then prioritized our plan items and retained the top priorities. We then worked our way down the list of priorities, assigning dollars to priorities until we

ran out of money. As a result, the final budget was tied, line by line, to the plan.

4. *People must be held accountable for achieving the plan.* The best plan in the world is meaningless if people aren't held accountable for following its strategies and achieving its goals. Therefore, the plan must include the names of people who are responsible for achieving the objectives, and timelines that specify when the objectives will be met. And the people named in the plan must be held accountable by their superiors for achieving the objectives on time.

Our army plans weren't long; they weren't complex—they were purposely kept simple to make them easy to follow. But by consistently containing these elements, they became blueprints for success. In the last two decades, the United States Army has proven time and again—in Haiti, in Panama, in the Persian Gulf, in Somalia, in Bosnia—to have a superior record of readiness, weapons development, training, mobility, and will. It truly has realized its vision of having the finest men and women of any country, and the world's best-trained, best-equipped fighting force. That success is due in large part to its ability to plan, from the manufacturer to the foxhole.

IN THE SCHOOLS: SOLID GOALS— BUT NO PLAN TO BACK THEM UP

These were the planning expectations I brought with me to the school district. What I found when I got there, however, was a very different kind of planning operation. The district had gone through a lengthy planning process, including a citywide education summit and work with a loaned executive, and as a result they had chosen a vision, a mission, and five goals:

- Increase academic achievement
- Attract, develop, and retain an excellent multicultural workforce
- Maintain a healthy, safe, and secure learning environment
- Vigorously seek to assure stable and adequate funding
- Increase the district's flexibility to meet diverse student/parent needs and to attract and retain more students

But when I looked at the plan they had developed to achieve these goals, I found it was missing three of the four essential elements.

- *It wasn't focused on its most essential goal, the academic achievement of children.* The hiring of teachers, the deployment of buses, the maintenance of buildings, and so on should all have been determined by how they affected children's ability to learn. But that wasn't the case. Schools were slated to be reroofed based on which principals had asked first or which buildings were simply the oldest. The district didn't consider which buildings would be needed for summer school and then build their maintenance plans around the summer-school schedule. Special ed and advanced placement programs were put in buildings where principals wanted to have them—and were kept out of those schools where the principals said they didn't want them. The availability of these vitally important programs was held hostage by the whims of individual principals. Every spring, hundreds of teachers were laid off because the district feared it wouldn't have enough money for their salaries in the fall, when the state allocated its budget. By fall, however, school enrollment had invariably risen, and because the state grants money on a per-pupil basis, the district always received enough money to rehire the teachers who had been laid off. No one bothered to ask, "What is the effect on academic achievement of creating such instability in the workforce?" And whose interests were being served by these decisions? Not the children's.

- *The budget wasn't tied to the activities in the plan.* Because the plan wasn't focused on academic achievement, neither was the budget. The budget was made in response to tradition ("This is the way we've spent money in the past") and in response to politics (various constituencies lobbied for a share of the pie). But line items in the budget were not tied directly to the goals and activities specified in the plan.

- *People were held accountable for meeting the plan's objectives, but . . .* Within the district, the planning process had been led not by the superintendent, but by a strategic planning department comprised of members from the state legislature, city government, and the business community. The superintendent himself didn't take strong ownership of the plan. Since he didn't hold his department heads responsible for meeting the plan's objectives, no one used the plan as a guideline and it became little more than a dust-collector sitting on people's shelves.

The plan did have one of the four strategic plan essentials: It had many measurable objectives. But even these objectives were not helpful; there were simply too many of them in too many disparate areas, and without a focus on achievement, they measured the wrong things. Without accountability and money to back them up, they were unlikely to be achieved.

SUPPORTING THE SYSTEM IN PLACE

The board and I decided to keep the five goals of the district's previous plan because they reflected some of the most important aspects of our operation. (Remember, the previous goals were good; it was the strategic plan on attaining these goals that was lacking.) They had also been developed as a result of community input. Changing them would have required months of process—months I didn't have. The tenure of an urban superintendent was two to three years; the pressure was on from all corners for us to make change. But the old goals needed two improvements. One, several goals lacked a focus on children, so we changed the wording to give them that all-important element. Two, we were missing a critical component. The school board had charged us with closing the achievement gap between white and minority students. That could be subsumed under "increase academic achievement for all students," but I felt that it was such an important goal—and such an intransigent one—that it deserved special attention. So I added it as a sixth goal and bumped it up to second place, right behind raising academic achievement for all students. I placed those two goals first because they were of a different magnitude from the others. They were what our district was all about. The other four goals were supporting goals, things that had to be in place in order to get the achievement we needed. I then asked every department to focus on supporting our two primary, critical targets, and coached them with questions.

- In the Department of Curriculum and Instruction, what must you do to increase student learning? Develop an "exit decision" system to determine who is ready to be promoted so we can stop passing children who can't do the work? Refine our process for intervening in schools whose performance is declining so we can begin turning those schools around? Create a district-wide reading campaign so we can increase the time our students spend reading?

- In the Department of Logistics, what must you do to support academic achievement? Maintain buildings and develop security procedures so students have a safe environment in which to learn? Acquire funding for capital projects so students have buildings with warm classrooms, adequate space, wiring for the Internet, and other amenities that enhance their learning? See to it that the buses run on time so that children arrive at school in time to learn? See to it that quality meals are served on time?

- In the Department of Human Resources, what must be done to promote academic achievement? Train teachers to teach to the new curriculum guidelines we're developing? Teach them to use the new methods of student assessment we're creating? Train them in multicultural awareness so they can understand the values and attitudes of the children in their classrooms who come, literally, from all over the world? Hire a multicultural workforce to support learning? Provide a teacher contract that will support other academic goals? Arrange for teachers to get the training they need to be the best teachers possible?

- In the Department of Communications, what must you do to support academic achievement? Increase the number of news stories about the schools so that the community understands our efforts to raise standards, provide meaningful assessments, and measurably improve student learning? Improve communication with teachers so teachers feel informed and consulted, and like valuable members of our team when they go into the classroom? Increase public understanding of our need for funding so that citizens will support levies that pay for student learning?

Seattle's school district is divided into seven departments, like Curriculum and Instruction or Affirmative Action, and twenty-two offices that provide direct and support services. The head of each department was appointed as goal manager, and was responsible for developing a four-year strategy within their department for increasing academic achievement. After working with their departments, they brought their strategies back to me. Some were clear, focused, on target: "Develop and implement 'student exit system' using multiple types of assessment to measure student performance." Others were murkier and needed further refining. These were sent back to the drawing board. Soon every office had defined two to four strategies that it would use to promote the district's two most important goals. We met again as a group to make sure that each office's strategies meshed with every other's; the plan needed to be comprehensive and mutually reinforcing.

The next step in the process was to determine our expected outcomes. "Once you implement these strategies," I asked, "how will you know if they're successful? What measurable results will you expect to see? What tools will you use to measure? And what tasks will you do to achieve those results?" The goal managers went back to their departments. Again we went through a process of refining. We wanted every student to rise to grade level—but how much improvement was reasonable to expect? Could we raise 100 percent of failing students? Fifty percent? We settled on 10 percent a year as a reasonable expectation. We wanted to measure the performance and effectiveness of every school—but could all schools improve on every indicator? Could they improve on five out of fifteen? We agreed that 75 percent of our schools should show statistically significant gains on one or more indicators (test scores, dropout rates, disciplinary incidents, etc.). In every area, department staffs hashed out their measurable goals and enumerated the tools they would use to measure. And again, as they worked on their plans, we convened whole-group meetings to make sure that all the plans were meshing.

Once the measurable outcomes were established, our plan was halfway finished. Only two critical elements remained: assigning names to each of the tasks the departments had outlined, and developing the timeline by which each task would be accomplished. The goal managers went back, worked with their departments, and by the spring of 1996, six months after we'd begun the process, we had our completed strategic plan. It was not a long document—three or four pages per department—but those pages were bibles by which our departments would live for the next four years. I promised that when I met with the department heads I would check on how well they were doing in accomplishing their goals—and as any of them can tell you, I have kept my word.

"ONE OF THE BEST THINGS ABOUT THE STRATEGIC PLAN WAS HOW QUICKLY WE DEVELOPED IT. JUST THE FACT THAT WE DID IT SO FAST WAS A MORALE BOOST. PEOPLE FELT WE WERE REALLY GOING TO MAKE THINGS HAPPEN—WE WEREN'T JUST GOING TO *TALK* ABOUT MAKING THINGS HAPPEN."
          —SUSAN BYERS, EXECUTIVE DIRECTOR, HUMAN RESOURCES

BUT WHAT WILL IT COST?

At the same time the departments were preparing their plans, they were also preparing their budgets. How else would they know if they had the money to do the things they were saying they would do?

We had begun the budget process by establishing a list of principles that would guide our budget decisions. Like the strategic plan, the budget would need to be focused on academic achievement. You can tell what an organization believes in by how it spends its money, so we needed to be spending our money on things that would directly contribute to student learning. Our list of principles went like this:

- Budget cuts will happen as far from the classroom as possible.

- Financial priority will be given to the *schools* rather than to central administration.

- We will limit our administrative expenses to 5.8 percent of our total budget.

- We will freeze administrative hiring.

- We will cut programs that don't work well rather than continue to pay for them.

- We will use our resources as if they were our own, seeking out efficiencies in transportation, utilities, and other expenses in order to save money.

- If an outside agency cuts money for particular programs, we will cut the programs commensurately rather than take money from other sources to make up the difference.

- We will pay only for programs that are covered in the strategic plan.

The departments were asked to keep these principles in mind as they prepared their budgets.

The departments prepared their budgets by costing out every program articulated in their plans, then they turned their budget requests in to the finance office. Our CFO and his staff compared the requests to anticipated revenues, then sent the budgets back to the departments for cuts. Three or four times, the budgets passed back and forth between the departments and the CFO in the effort to make our expenses match our anticipated revenues. Of course, each time the budgets changed, the departments' plans changed as well: we could do only what we had money to pay for. So every department faced hard decisions: What would we *not* do because we didn't have the money? Following the principles we had outlined, we knew we had to take the cuts as far from the classroom as possible. Expenses that had a direct bearing on how children learned had to remain intact. Among other things, we cut twenty-six school custodians and seventeen curriculum advisers. We cut the district's in-house television studio and the teacher recruitment center. And we switched to a just-in-time inventory system for supplies and decreased our use of water, gas, and electricity, which enabled us to save almost $1 million annually.

We also convened the "stakeholders' committee," made up of representatives from every group that needed input into the budget. The teachers' union, the principals' union, the union of custodians, security personnel, and food service workers, the union of building trades (electrical workers, plumbers, ironworkers, and so on), the PTSA, the major department heads, the chief of staff, the chief financial officer, and others were all represented on the committee. Once we had a balanced budget assembled, we presented it to the committee. They gave us their comments, we altered the budget to reflect their input, then sent it back again, never losing sight of the objectives: academic achievement and students. Three times it went back and forth, changing slightly each time. When we arrived at a plan and budget we could all agree on, they went as a package to the school board. The board approved them in July 1996, seven months after we'd started the process, in time for the 1996–97 school year.

BRINGING THE PLAN TO LIFE

When I had first come to the district and asked to see the strategic plan, I'd noted that people had had to search for copies on their bookshelves, and that the ones they'd handed me were absolutely pristine. This was a sharp contrast from the army, where plans had sat open and dog-eared on everybody's desk, margins filled with handwritten notes, pages interlaced with typed addenda. Because our plans were being continually updated, and because they were continually right in front of us, they were part of our daily lives. The more information we had about how the plan was being operationalized, the better the next version of the plan would be.

Updating was a continual process. Each time we completed a task or a strategy, it would come off the plan and be replaced with a new one. Each time timelines shifted—because things took more or less time than we'd expected—new timelines were drawn in. Each time a change in one area of the plan necessitated a change in another, that change was added. These changes were made, as necessary, by the people responsible for each plan. As a result, the plans were fluid, ever-changing documents that both guided and responded to our actions.

We have created the same fluid planning system in the school district. Today each of our goal managers is responsible for updating his or her department's plan multiple times throughout the year. He or she has to; each department isn't standing still, it's making progress, and that progress has to be reflected in its plan! The Department of Curriculum and Instruction, for example, as part of its strategy to develop and implement an exit-decision system, planned to revise and present the system to the community between March and October of 1997. They did that. But what they heard from the community caused them to extend that revision and communication period longer. The community felt that if we were going to hold students back, we needed to offer more support than we had planned: more summer school, more after-school tutoring, more "Saturday Academies" for catching up. They were right—and we agreed to do so—but that meant we had to go back to the budget and look for areas where we could make cuts in order to shore up those extra supports. We cut back on hiring outside evaluators, we postponed buying some textbooks, and we found some cost savings in our logistics and information services departments. We would have preferred to keep our expenses as they were, but given our focus on academic achievement, those expenses had to take a back seat to getting our at-risk students up to par.

"THE REASON WE'RE MOVING IS BECAUSE THE SUPERINTENDENT IS
ALWAYS OUT THERE FOLLOWING UP WITH US ON EVERYTHING!"
          —DAN GRACZYK, DIRECTOR OF LOGISTICS

These plan adjustments are made continuously by the goal managers. There's probably not a department in the district that hasn't crossed out completed tasks, extended timelines, revised expected outcomes, and added subtasks as it implements its strategies. The staff does these things rather than put their plans on bookshelves because they know that I will check them. Principals know that I will ask them about their strategic plans when I visit their schools. Staff know that any day I'm apt to leave a "See me" note in their mailbox, or drop by their office with my copy of their plan, and that I'll want to know how they're doing on implementing their strategies and tasks. They know that I'll be pointed in my questions: "You've said you're going to revise high-school graduation requirements by June 30, 1997. How are you doing relative to that deadline? What changes are you making? Who are you coordinating with in the schools? Have you sought community input? Will the new requirements be feasible for students to attain? Are they consistent with our curriculum frameworks?" And they know that my expectations for their answers will be not unreasonable, but high. It is these checkups that keep each department focused and on schedule in attaining its goals.

In addition to these occasional meetings, every April all the goal managers come together to update the entire plan. At these meetings, the chief operating officer and I review all the department plans. We check to see that people are accomplishing what they said they would, and we review the new tasks and outcomes they have established. We look to make sure their goals are realistic and aggressive, and that the goals of the entire organization are coordinated. Once the plans are approved, each department is asked to produce a budget, and the budget process, as described earlier, happens again. By July we have the district-wide budget and strategic plan for the next school year ready for the school board for approval.

This highly systematic process, and the strategic plan that it produces, make the school board's job of governing the district relatively easy. Our priorities and goals are clearly spelled out. Our expected outcomes are measurable. Our expenditures are tied to our goals. At its quarterly retreats the board can review the plan, ask me the same kinds of pointed questions I ask my staff, and gauge how well we are doing what we said we would do. And because board meetings are open to the public, parents, taxpayers, the business community, and other interested parties can also come and make the same comparisons. Through the clarity and measurability of our strategic plan, we've created a system that not only permits me to hold our department heads accountable to our objectives, but that also permits our entire community to hold the district—and me—accountable for building world-class schools.

SUMMARY OF THE SEATTLE SCHOOL DISTRICT STRATEGIC PLAN

GOAL #1: INCREASE ACADEMIC ACHIEVEMENT FOR ALL STUDENTS.

Expected Outcomes:
- Standardized test scores will increase district-wide by at least four percentile points.
- The number of students judged by the Direct Writing Assessment (a standardized writing test) to be either Proficient or Exemplary will increase by at least 10 percent.

GOAL #2: CLOSE STUDENT ACHIEVEMENT GAPS.

Expected Outcomes:
- Ten percent of students in the fourth quartile (the lowest quartile), grades 2 through 11, will move to the third quartile on the standardized test.

- Fifteen percent of students in the third quartile, grades 2 through 11, will move to the second quartile.
- Five percent of students in the second quartile, grades 2 through 11, will move to the first quartile.

What do "quartiles" mean?

Standardized tests are graded in percentile points. The grades are "norm-referenced," which means that students are graded not against a body of knowledge, but against each other. A score of 60 percent means that 60 percent of the students who took the test got fewer right answers. Students who score between 75 percent and 100 percent are in the first, or highest, quartile, students who scored between 50 percent and 75 percent are in the second quartile, and so on. The tests are calibrated so that the national average score will be 50 percent. Students who score above 50 percent are scoring above the national average.

GOAL #3: ATTRACT, DEVELOP, AND RETAIN AN EXCELLENT MULTICULTURAL WORKFORCE TO PROVIDE STUDENTS WITH SUCCESSFUL ROLE MODELS.

Expected Outcomes:
- By the spring of 2001, our annual "parent satisfaction survey" will show that at least 80 percent of district parents are "definitely satisfied" with teachers, principals, and with the respect shown for all individuals, races, and cultures.
- Twenty-five percent of the teachers hired each year will be minorities.

GOAL #4: PROVIDE STUDENTS WITH A HEALTHY, SAFE, AND SECURE LEARNING ENVIRONMENT.

Expected Outcomes:
- Parent/student satisfaction with school safety and security will be increased.
- The number of K–12 suspensions and expulsions will decrease; the number of weapons in the schools will decrease.

- The number of buildings that provide state-of-the-art educational spaces and meet current building codes will increase.
- An updated Facilities Master Plan that identifies future building needs will be developed.
- A plan for developing future levies and bonds to fund identified needs will be created.

GOAL #5: PROVIDE STABLE AND ADEQUATE FUNDING TO ASSURE THAT STUDENTS WILL RECEIVE A HIGH-QUALITY AND CONSISTENT EDUCATION.

Expected Outcomes:
- The schools will have more money to spend per student.
- The district's unobligated funds will increase and will become a larger percentage of the general budget.
- The maintenance backlog will decrease.

GOAL #6: MEET DIVERSE STUDENT AND PARENT NEEDS TO ATTRACT AND RETAIN STUDENTS.

Expected Outcomes:
- The level of customer satisfaction will increase by 10 percent as measured by our customer satisfaction surveys.
- Student enrollment will increase by 2.5 percent (1,175 students) at the elementary and secondary school levels.
- The number of volunteer hours contributed by parents, community members, and businesspeople will increase by 15 percent.

QUIZ:
WHAT IS THE MOST IMPORTANT COMPONENT OF A SCHOOL DISTRICT'S STRATEGIC PLAN?

(c) measurable objectives

Lofty goals and inspirational messages are very important! They enable people to share a common dream of what they can achieve, and motivate them to get there. But without measurable objectives to back them up, vision statements are worthless. People must have measurable targets, and must be held accountable for meeting them, if a school district is going to meet its goals.

CHAPTER 3

WE CAN ACHIEVE THE VICTORY WHEN . . . WE TURN OUR SCHOOLS INTO ACHIEVEMENT SYSTEMS

QUIZ:
IS IT UNREALISTIC TO EXPECT EVERY CHILD TO ACHIEVE?

(a) The effects of poverty are so severe that it is almost impossible to overcome them.

(b) All children can achieve. It is the schools' responsibility to make that happen.

Answer on page 60.

When the Seattle School Board hired me as superintendent, their mandate was very clear: Raise academic achievement for all students and make public education work for Seattle. As tools, they gave me a four-year-old scathing report about the district, a $35 million deficit, and all the encouragement and teamwork for which a superintendent could ask. One out of three wasn't bad, and encouragement was all I needed. So in my first weeks in the district, as I visited several schools a day, I tried to learn as much as I could about how our "achievement enterprise" worked.

I was so new to education, and I had so much to learn, that in every school I asked the same, most basic, questions: What are you teaching? Why are you teaching that? What are your goals? How do you know if the students have achieved them?

One of my first visits was to a second-grade class where the students were busy reading. They were seated in pairs around the room, books open in front of them. As one student read aloud, the other followed along in the text.

"What are the children working on in reading?" I asked the teacher, who had gotten up from where she'd been kneeling next to two children and come over to join me.

"Right now we're practicing reading aloud. They're working on fluency."

"And why are you doing that right now?"

"We use the Macmillan reading series, and that's what this lesson focuses on."

"I see they're using different books."

"Yes, those are the different reading groups."

"What are your goals for the children this year?"

The teacher laughed. "I hope that every group will get all the way through their books!"

"What if they don't?"

"Well, then they'll pick up where they left off when they get to third grade next year. See that group over there?" She pointed to four children seated at a round table. A boy was leaning across the table, drawing on another boy's paper while a girl and another boy looked on. "They're still working on first-grade skills."

"So you're teaching first grade and second grade at the same time."

The teacher looked at me oddly. "Well, they're all in second grade," she said. "They just work at different levels."

The teacher and I talked a little longer, then she went back to the children, kneeling next to every pair to listen and comment on their reading. I was impressed by the devoted attention she gave each child, but her comments concerned me. When I had asked why she was working on fluency, she hadn't said it was because the district had decided that was an important skill; she'd said it was because Macmillan had made it a focus. When I'd asked what her goals were for the students, she hadn't told me what skills she wanted them to learn; she'd said she hoped to finish the book. And when I asked what would happen if students didn't meet the goal, she said they wouldn't stay back to master the work; they'd go on to third grade anyway, and the third-grade teacher would deal with it.

I left the classroom and went next door to another second-grade class.

Here, too, the children were reading. But they didn't have Macmillan readers in front of them; each child held a copy of a book called *The Chick and the Duckling*, and up in the front of the room two students were acting out the parts.

"It looks like you're putting on a play," I said to the teacher.

She smiled. "After we finish a book the children like to act it out."

"I noticed the class next door is using Macmillan. Do you use Macmillan too?"

"I use parts of it," the teacher said. "But I also use a lot of other materials."

"The children next door are working on fluency. Is that something you're working on too?"

"We'll do some work on fluency later in the year, but we focus mostly on decoding and comprehension. They'll do more with fluency in third grade."

Again I was surprised. Here were two second-grade teachers teaching two different sets of skills! I thought back to my own experience as a teacher in the army. I had taught one small area—the principles and repair of aircraft electrical-instrument hydraulic systems—but my course objectives were identical to every other instructor's.

At the back of my classroom my book of lesson plans was open on a table, outlining exactly what I was teaching that day, that week, that year. Each plan stated the learning objective for the lesson, along with the methods and materials I'd use to teach. Each plan described the assessment tools I'd use to measure my students' learning, and explained how the lesson supported the training objectives to follow. At defense training centers all across the country, similar lesson plans were open on the table, and they all taught the material in the same way. The books wouldn't be identical: the army gave us lots of leeway in developing our style and lessons. But our lesson plans were aligned *horizontally* from school to school and *vertically* from class to class to make sure that everybody who graduated as a helicopter and aircraft mechanic had mastered the same material.

The more I visited classrooms in our district, however, the more I found that kind of horizontal and vertical alignment missing. Teachers in every grade were teaching their students different material, and teachers in the following grades were having to make up the work from the preceding grade as well as teach their own. In fact, there seemed to be very little communication from classroom to classroom about what our students needed. The district was functioning as a series of autonomous classrooms instead of as a cohesive teaching *system*.

This didn't make sense. Our mission was to make sure our children learned, yet we'd relinquished control over how the learning happened—

and, indeed, over what was being learned. We'd given control of our curriculum to textbook publishers, we didn't have clear performance goals for our students, our curriculum wasn't aligned from class to class, and we were passing students who couldn't do the work! I thought, What are we doing to our students? Will this fulfill the school board's mandate? Is this the loving thing to do? Is this in the best interests of the students?

Obviously, the answers were no. If we were going to be an achievement enterprise, we would need to create a four-part achievement system throughout the district.

This new achievement system would need to:

- STANDARDIZE THE CURRICULA so that all children in each grade learned the same material;

- EMPLOY NEW METHODS OF ASSESSMENT so that we could more accurately gauge what each student had learned;

- INCLUDE EXIT STANDARDS so that students who had not mastered the material for their grade would not be promoted; and

- INCLUDE A SUPPORT SYSTEM that would provide remedial help *as soon as* a student began to fall behind.

STANDARDIZING THE CURRICULUM

The first step in building our achievement system was determining what we wanted our children to learn. As I'd seen in the schools, the existing standards seemed to vary from class to class. Moreover, our curriculum and assessment specialists had been talking about the importance of higher-order thinking skills: helping children *use* the information they were learning, not just absorb it and parrot it back. We needed a stronger curriculum, which would encourage children to *analyze* information, *evaluate* it, and *apply* it to their lives.

Our curriculum was also quite segmented. Several decades ago, the American philosopher John Dewey pondered the best ways to combine what children learned in school with what they experienced in their lives; in other words, how to make education meaningful to them. Since Dewey's time, Renate Caine, Geoffrey Caine, and other researchers in the field of brain-based learning had found that since the brain searches for patterns and connections, and since understanding is enhanced when a lesson is presented in many different ways, an interdisciplinary curriculum helps to improve children's academic achievement. In laymen's words, this means that an English class can complement a history class; the student will learn both subjects better if the curriculum is integrated, if teachers know what other teachers are teaching. But in Seattle, our language arts, math, science, and social studies courses were being taught independently, as if the disciplines bore no relationship to each other, or to our students' lives. For instance, students studied the First World War in eleventh-grade social studies and might read *A Farewell to Arms* in twelfth-grade English, but wouldn't use the learning from one to inform the learning of the other. We needed to move away from a blind, segregated curriculum. We needed to incorporate math into science, science into history, history into language arts, and reading and writing into everything.

THE OLD WAY OF LEARNING FRACTIONS

Teachers taught the fraction units in the textbook. Students learned and practiced by doing the textbook exercises.

THE NEW WAY OF LEARNING FRACTIONS

Teachers do not start with the textbook. They have as their goal to teach students to understand the concepts of one-half, one-quarter, and one-eighth. To get these concepts across, they may use a variety of materials. They may start by having a pizza party, with students dividing the pizzas into fractions. They may follow that hands-on activity with a unit from the textbook. Then they may do a science experiment where they make lemonade in different strengths: ½ water, ½ lemonade powder; then ¼ water, ¾ lemonade powder, and so on. Later they may record the weather for the week and make a pie chart using fractions to show how many days were rainy, sunny, or cloudy. They may follow these activities with worksheets that give students repeated practice at working with fractions. This blend of activities gives students multiple opportunities to learn the concept. It enables students to learn using a variety of learning styles. It enables students to do real-world problem-solving using fractions. And it focuses on a specific skill rather than on covering the textbook.

Of course, excellent teachers have taught this way for years. The new curriculum frameworks are designed to bring this way of teaching to all classrooms district-wide.

Aware of the deficits in the curriculum, the district had begun to develop new curriculum materials several years before in the areas of math and language arts. These "curriculum frameworks" defined precisely what students needed to know and be able to do in every grade. But they left the "how" of teaching—what materials to use, how to present ideas, what projects the students would do to practice and demonstrate their learning—up to the individual teachers. That meant that teachers would be free to develop their own teaching style and lessons, but that our autonomous classrooms would all be part of a cohesive teaching system.

DEVELOPING ONGOING STUDENT ASSESSMENT (INSTEAD OF ONE-SHOT TESTS)

Of course, if the district was going to change its goals for students' learning, it would also need to change the way it *assessed* that learning. The old assessment tools were primarily the ones that came with the textbooks—the "unit tests" that followed every chapter. Like the curricula, they focused on lower-order skills. But that was just part of the problem. Even more problematic was the narrow way the unit tests worked. It was a conversation with one of our elementary school principals that pointed up the full extent of the problems for me.

This excellent principal had recently moved to a new school and, in an effort to track the progress of every student, had asked her teachers to give her all their unit-test scores. But the scores were slow in coming in.

"What's the problem?" I wondered.

She sighed. "A lot of the teachers don't give the tests, which I understand: They don't want to overtest the children. Also, they feel the tests are unfair—some kids freeze the minute you say you're giving a test. And the tests themselves are so narrow; they're fine for kids who are good linear, verbal thinkers, but they really don't let the rest of the kids show what they know." She paused. "And the other reason they don't like giving the tests is that the tests bring bad news. They show that a lot of children haven't learned the material, and teachers don't have time to teach it again because we want them to get through the whole curriculum."

What we needed were tools teachers could use daily or weekly in the process of teaching that would paint a constantly evolving portrait of what their students could do. Tools that wouldn't penalize kids who aren't strictly linear thinkers, tools that would gauge students' strengths as well as their weaknesses, their learning styles as well as what they'd learned. We needed tools that would let students use different kinds of intelligence to demonstrate their learning, and that would help teachers customize their teaching to every student's needs.

What kinds of tools would do that? The things teachers were already doing! Projects, reports, homework assignments, class participation: Virtually everything that happened in the classroom could be a tool for assessing students' learning.

All of these routine classroom practices gave teachers opportunities to assess students' learning. But unlike one-shot tests, which caused children to freeze and which gave an artificial picture of what a child could do, they would paint a detailed, up-to-the-minute portrait of precisely what the students could do and where they still needed work. The challenge would be to educate teachers about how to use these everyday activities for formal evaluation.

We would also need to help them assess the higher-order thinking skills. Many of the homework assignments, quiz questions, and project ideas that teachers were accustomed to using were designed to assess the lower-level skills. A fifth-grade math quiz, for example, might ask students to interpret a diagram in order to compute the perimeter of a square. But the kind of teaching and assessment we were switching to would require students to use those skills to solve a real-life problem. We would want them to look at a price list and a simple blueprint, for example, and then compute the cost of building a doghouse, or to look at a diagram of a bedroom and a list of variously sized carpet remnants and then determine whether they had enough carpet to cover the floor. And we would want them not to just give us the answer, but to explain how they got the answer by describing their thought process in words or illustrating it with a picture. Teachers would need help in designing assignments, homework questions, quizzes, and other tools that both taught and assessed these higher-order skills.

The district had neither money nor time to develop new assessments. However, Washington state, like many other states in the last few years, had developed its own set of curriculum frameworks that were about to become required learning for all students. These "essential learning requirements," as they were called, had been released shortly after we brought out our district's new frameworks in math and language arts, and like ours, they emphasized higher-order thinking skills and integrating disciplines. They also contained sample assessments teachers could use to determine how well their students had learned the required skills. Their assessments were exactly the kinds of things we were looking for. They were activities teachers could do in the course of daily teaching to determine what students could do and where they still had challenges. The state had created a "tool kit" of teaching aids and sample assessments to help teachers begin to use the essential learnings and assessments in their classrooms. So we distributed the tool kit to each of our schools and asked teachers to begin incor-

porating both the learnings and the assessments into their teaching. Teams
of teachers and subject specialists went to work in every curriculum area,
using the state frameworks as a baseline. By the spring of 1998 we had
brought out standards and assessments in math, reading and language arts,
science and social studies, preschool and kindergarten, library and technology, school-to-work, PE, and the arts. It was a lot of work to accomplish
in under two years. But we had to work that fast: We'd promised world-
class schools by 1999; our students didn't have time to wait.

Teaching the Teachers
"You know, for the last ten years we've been telling teachers that the test
is the thing. 'Give the unit tests. Teach to the standardized tests,' we've
been saying. Now we're telling them the opposite. It's going to take them
a while to get used to that."

The counsel came from Dr. Jill Hearne, our director of assessment. She
was right, of course. With our decision to emphasize *ongoing* assessment,
we'd be reversing decades of pressure and training. We believed that the
teachers would agree with our decision, that the new frameworks and assessment methods would support the kind of teaching they wanted to do,
emphasizing problem-solving, higher-order thinking skills and relevancy
to life outside the classroom. But like teachers in most districts, our teachers had seen so many educational theories come and go over the years that
they were rightly skeptical about change. How could we reassure them that
this was, in fact, a long-term direction? How could we give them the training and support they needed to implement the new procedures? Teacher
training is a tremendous job; it takes a lot of time and a lot of money. We,
of course, had neither.

Since we couldn't afford the time or money to train every teacher in
workshops, we decided to use a grant from Washington state to create a
"train the trainer" program. Under the program, each school would send
us two teachers who would become our teacher trainers. The trainers
would work in small groups with our curriculum and instruction specialists, then go back to their schools to train the rest of their staffs. Follow-
up training would be given by the specialists.

Most of our teachers had already been trained in multiple intelligences and in tailoring teaching to individual students' needs; therefore,
we didn't need to focus a lot on that area. The frameworks would require
more attention, however, and the new assessment methods would require
the most attention of all. Not only would we be asking teachers to alter
radically what they were doing; we'd be asking them to switch to a much
harder assessment system. With the old curriculum, teachers were focusing on material that had one or two right answers. With the frameworks,

on the other hand, they'd be encouraging children to apply, analyze, and evaluate information. Answers would be more complex, and grading would be far more challenging. It would also be prone to subjectivity: what one teacher considered acceptable, another might consider weak. So we would have to provide "anchor papers" defining the standards for "beginning," "developing," "proficient," and "exemplary" work, and teachers would need to be trained in how to judge their students' work against those standards.

We began the training in the fall of 1997, training "teacher trainers" in groups of twenty to thirty at a time. Most of these teachers were excited by what we were presenting: In listening to Dr. Hearne they saw how the frameworks and assessments together would help them know exactly what skills their children had mastered, where the children needed help, and what they needed to do to take their students to the next level. The teacher trainers went back to their schools as eager spokespeople for the changes, and now are leading workshops in what they learned for their colleagues.

Out in the schools the change to the new frameworks and assessments will happen slowly. We're asking our teachers to make a major transition, and as with any significant change, they are experiencing a spectrum of emotions—from resenting the changes, to wondering how they will handle them, to understanding them and putting them to use. We believe it will take three to five years before the new frameworks and assessments are fully implemented in every school. But even while teachers implement these elements slowly, they acknowledge that they appreciate the reasons for the change. They agree that assessing children by observing their performance is far more accurate than giving one-shot tests (even as they struggle to change long-set ways of thinking). And they like the emphasis on higher-order thinking skills (even as they express reluctance at having to give up some of their more familiar curriculum units). Today when I walk into two second-grade classrooms, I'm still apt to see teachers using different materials and working on different skills, but now I know that the teachers have read the curriculum frameworks, studied the new assessments, and are devising ways to incorporate those elements into their own teaching. And I know, because I hear it in their comments and in their conversations with their principals, that while they feel the challenge of altering long-familiar practices, they also feel a sense of excitement. Our teachers have gone into teaching because they love children and want to help them succeed. They have been teaching a less thought-provoking curriculum and testing with one-shot tests not because they wanted to do those things, but because that was what *we* expected them to do. The new frameworks and assessments will free them from those constraints. Along with the other elements of our growing "achievement system," they will empower them to be the kind of teachers they truly want to be.

"EDUCATION IS A VERY ISOLATING PROFESSION. FOR A HUNDRED YEARS TEACHERS HAVE GONE INTO THEIR CLASSROOMS AND DONE THEIR THING. NOW WE'RE SAYING THAT DOESN'T WORK. YOU HAVE TO BE ALIGNED WITH THE GRADES BEFORE AND AFTER YOU. YOU HAVE TO PLAN COLLABORATIVELY WITH OTHER TEACHERS. IT'S A BIG ADJUSTMENT. IT TAKES TIME. BUT NO ONE'S SAYING THIS ISN'T IMPORTANT. THE TEACHERS BELIEVE THESE THINGS ARE NEEDED."
—JOANNE FRANEY, ELEMENTARY-SCHOOL COORDINATOR

A Tool for Bringing Parents On Board

At the same time we asked our teachers to switch to the new curriculum frameworks and assessment methods, we placed yet another request on them: We asked them to produce syllabi. A syllabus is an outline of what a teacher plans to teach in a course, and I had been astonished to find out that teachers didn't routinely file them. Without syllabi from every teacher, how could the principal know what each teacher was teaching? How could the principal make sure the frameworks were being followed? We wanted to save money by conserving resources whenever possible. Buses for field trips, supplies for special projects, textbooks, were all things whose costs could be reduced if they were shared among classes. But without syllabi, the principal wouldn't know if two classes were planning a similar project or field trip. How could he or she encourage sharing and resource conservation? For all these reasons, syllabi seemed essential.

And there was yet another vitally important reason for having teachers create syllabi. Like most school districts, we claimed that we wanted parents involved in their children's education. But, in fact, we were doing little to involve them actively. We gave them report cards three times a year and held annual parent-teacher conferences, but these were only brief and cursory communications. They did little to give parents the kind of information they could actively use to help us educate their child. We didn't tell parents, for instance, what we planned to teach their children week by week so parents could discuss the material at home with their child. We didn't tell them what we expected their children to learn by the end of their current grade so parents could reinforce the importance of meeting those goals. We didn't tell them how, or when, we planned to assess their children's learning so parents would know that our assessment measures were fair and comprehensive and genuinely representative of their children's abilities. Considering that parents gave us their children, with few questions asked, for thirteen years, we gave them remarkably little information. How could we really expect them to be our education partners?

The syllabus, we felt, would bring parents inside the education circle. It would show them, week by week, what their children were expected to know and when they would be given major assessments. Parents now had a document they could use to talk with their children about the classroom experience, and might even see places where they could make a contribution. If they laid all the syllabi side by side, they would see the sequential progression of skills we expected their children to achieve, and where we expected them to be on the day of high-school graduation. By giving parents this most basic information about how we were working with their children, the syllabi would begin to remove some of the sense of mystery that parents feel about school.

So we asked every teacher to prepare a syllabus and turn it in by the first week in October. Some of the teachers were not pleased. Most missed the October deadline. But principals upped their leadership, and the syllabi dribbled in. By February, we'd gotten them all.

We sent the syllabi home to parents. Although none of the schools surveyed parents to get their feedback, the informal response was positive. "I feel more connected to school," parents reported. "Now I know what to ask my child at night." At parent conferences more parents had specific questions about their children's course work and performance; some even brought their syllabi with them to discuss.

The following year, of course, we required syllabi again. This time the quality of the syllabi was better: The first year they had been very sketchy and filled with jargon ("We will be using math manipulatives to help children learn one-to-one correspondence") and they focused on what the class would be doing rather than on what skills the children would be learning ("We will be using the Macmillan/McGraw-Hill reading series" rather than "Using the Macmillan/McGraw-Hill reading series, we will work on predicting events in a story, understanding the main idea, and summarizing what we've read"). The second year the syllabi were more detailed, and tended to be more specific about what skills the children were learning. They also came in more quickly. That was partly because teachers now had experience at doing them, partly because they'd anticipated the request, and partly, I believe, because they knew our demand for the syllabi wouldn't go away: They were part of our effort to create a district-wide achievement system.

MOST ELEMENTARY SCHOOLS FILL THEIR HALLS WITH CHILDREN'S ARTWORK. BUT AT VIEWLANDS ELEMENTARY SCHOOL, PRINCIPAL CATHY PROFILET HAS FILLED THE FRONT HALL WITH HER TEACHERS' SYLLABI. SHE HAS STAMPED EACH ONE WITH THE WORD "BRAVO!", MOUNTED THEM ON BLACK AND GOLD PAPER, AND SURROUNDED THEM WITH GOLD STARS. THERE, FILLING BOTH SIDES OF THE THIRTY-FOOT HALL, THEY FORM A BEAUTIFUL TESTIMONY TO THE SCHOOL'S MISSION, A CONSTANT REMINDER OF WHAT ITS TEACHERS AND CHILDREN HAVE COME TOGETHER TO DO.

DO YOU NEED A SYLLABUS?

How many times have you asked your child, "What did you do in school today?" How many times has he or she answered, "Nothing"? How can you help your child in school if you don't know what he or she does there? That's what a syllabus is for. It should tell you:

- what the school expects your child to know and be able to do by the end of the year;
- how and when they will assess progress;
- how and when the school will communicate with you about your child's progress; and
- how you can help your child at home.

IMPLEMENTING EXIT STANDARDS

But the best curriculum frameworks, assessment methods, teacher training, and syllabi in the world wouldn't mean a thing unless we held our students accountable—unless we refused to pass them until they met the standards. So at the same time we were developing standards for what children should know in every grade and working with the teachers to change the ways they measured how well the children had actually learned it, we needed to develop *exit standards*, concrete measures that would enable us to determine whether a child was prepared to transition to the following grade.

As with the new assessment methods, we knew we didn't want a test. A test would be far too narrow, the antithesis of what we were trying to achieve. Instead, we wanted a "profile" of the student, a set of data collected throughout the school year that would indicate whether or not the child had the skills to move ahead. So a team of teachers and specialists from our Curriculum and Instruction Department began to develop a system of "exit profiles." The profiles would evaluate each student using three types of evidence. They would use classroom work: in-class assignments, class participation, homework, tests, and projects. They would use formal assessments made by the district: the standardized Iowa Test of Basic Skills and a test of writing proficiency called the Direct Writing Assessment. And they would use assessments mandated by the state: a standardized test called the Comprehensive Test of Basic Skills and a new exam that tests higher-thinking skills and the state's "essential learnings." But this evidence would not be weighed in a formulaic way. Rather, a team of people at the school and the students' parents would look at each child individually and determine his or her readiness for advancement. Some students, for example, might have strong classroom work, yet do poorly on standardized tests. The team would be free to agree that those students were prepared to move ahead. Other students might do well on the tests but have less than proficient classroom work. The team would then evaluate each child's class work to make sure the child had the skills to thrive in the following grade. Children whose work was clearly proficient (met the standard as determined by the teacher) would not need team evaluation; they would pass.

The system of using the three types of evidence combined with a team evaluation seemed as if it would allow us to make solid exit decisions. But there was still a question: What if the team made a bad decision? What if they passed a child who was genuinely not ready to move? In that case, the principal of the receiving school and the principal of the sending school would discuss the decision and examine the evidence used to make the decision. If the principals could not reach agreement, the Department of Curriculum and Instruction would examine the evidence and make a final decision. This meant that for the first time, receiving schools would no longer be required automatically to accept every child sent to them. The burden of accountability would now be on the sending school to exit its students prepared.

At the same time the team was deciding how exit decisions would be made, they also considered when such decisions were necessary. They believed that students didn't need to be held back in every grade because grade groupings are somewhat artificial; children mature at different rates and learn at different paces. That's why several of our schools, like school districts and private schools across the country, had eliminated single-grade classrooms and adopted mixed-age groupings. There were points, however, by which it seemed essential that certain skills be developed. Research showed, for instance, that while not all children will learn to read fluently by the end of second grade, children who aren't fluent by the end of third grade fall behind in subsequent years, as substandard reading impairs their ability to take in new material. The transition years from elementary school to middle school, and from middle school to high school, are also pivotal. Students with marginal performance who are able to survive in the intimate setting of elementary school often lose ground in the larger, multiclassroom environment of middle school, and those who barely "make it" in middle school fall farther behind in high school as the pressure intensifies yet again. The end of junior year in high school is also a pivotal time: Students who haven't mastered the eleventh-grade skills are rarely able to graduate on time. For these reasons the committee decided to create four exit-decision points: the end of third, fifth, eighth, and eleventh grades. Children would not be passed beyond those grades if their profiles and their team evaluations suggested that they didn't have the skills to go on.

Of course, if we were going to create stringent exit requirements at the lower grades, we would also need to hold students accountable at graduation. Our goal was to graduate students who were truly prepared for the world, and we couldn't do that if we let them exit with skills that were less than proficient. We had already established new curriculum standards for seniors. With the adoption of the frameworks, the requirements for what twelfth-graders should know were rising sharply in almost every area. To graduate, students would now be required to show that they had read, understood, and evaluated a minimum of twenty books over the previous four years; they would need to write a comprehensive, well-researched paper, which they would have to present and defend orally; they would need to write effective directions, letters, summaries, and instructions for performing a variety of procedures; and they would need to demonstrate proficiency in our five basic mathematical "strands" (numbers and numeration, algebraic concepts, probability and statistics, measurement, and geometry). Because we had made citizenship an essential component of our academic plan, they would also have to perform sixty hours of "service learning" (also known as volunteering or community service) over their school career.

But at what level would students have to perform these requirements? At present, seniors were permitted to graduate with a .83 grade point av-

erage (out of 4.0), less than a D. How embarrassing for an academic institution. I thought, If students need a 2.0 to join the football team,
shouldn't they need a 2.0 to graduate from our schools?

So we began to talk about raising the grade-point-average graduation
requirement. As I traveled around the district and talked to parents, I
found that reaction was largely positive: Most families liked the idea that
their children would be held to a higher standard. Some were opposed,
concerned that their children wouldn't graduate on time. "You mean to
tell us that your child can't get a C?" I responded. "We think he can! We
believe in our students, and they can make the grade if we push them. And
what's more, we need your help to make it happen." Some parents were
skeptical: "What if teachers give out C's for D-level work just so students
can graduate?" they asked. "C's alone won't enable students to graduate,"
we answered. "Students with marginal performances will be assessed by a
team, just as in the lower grades, to make sure they're on target for graduation. Those who aren't will stay until they are." But these concerns were
in the minority; the vast majority agreed with our plan. So in September
1997 we took it to the school board, and the board agreed. They unani-
mously approved the higher GPA and it went into effect for that year's
freshmen, the class of 2001.

We knew we couldn't introduce all of our new exit requirements immediately, however. That wouldn't be fair to students who had already progressed through the system under the old rules. So we decided to phase
them in. At the end of the present school year (1997–98), promotion from
fifth grade would be made according to exit profiles. Eighth-grade and
third-grade profiles would go into effect in the 1999–2000 school year, and
high-school students would be affected by the exit standards beginning in
the year 2000–2001.

We are introducing these exit standards to ensure that we do what
we've promised to do: graduate children with the skills they need to succeed in the world. But I am hoping that these standards will achieve another result as well. I am hoping that they will serve as a rite of passage, a
sign to the community *and to the child* that the child has achieved something momentous. These exit standards are not easy for everyone to meet.
For some children they would be a daunting challenge. I want the attain-
ment of those standards to carry with it all the pride—and all the em-
powerment—that come with real achievement.

ONE DAY I WAS WALKING THROUGH A SCHOOL AND A FIFTH-GRADE
BOY CAME UP TO ME. "MR. STANFORD!" HE SAID, "I'M REALLY WORK-

ING ON YOUR GOAL." SINCE I ALWAYS TALK TO STUDENTS ABOUT READING, I ASSUMED THAT THAT WAS WHAT HE MEANT. "THAT'S GREAT!" I REPLIED, "WHAT ARE YOU READING?" "NO," HE SAID, IMPATIENTLY, "I DON'T MEAN READING. I MEAN I'M GOING TO GET OUT OF FIFTH GRADE!" THAT CONVERSATION REINFORCED FOR ME THE RIGHTNESS OF WHAT WE'D DONE. THIS BOY WAS *MOTIVATED* BY THE EXIT DECISION.

CREATING A SUPPORT SYSTEM

Not too long ago, I described our exit-decision system to an attorney whom I'd met at a function. "Oh, you'll be holding so many children back," she said. "No!" I replied quickly. "We won't be. If all we'd done was put this exit system in place, then you're right, we would be holding hundreds, maybe thousands, of children back. But we want to raise the bar for every child and get every child up to meet it, so we've done more. We've also created an early-warning system that tells us when students need help, and we've created an individualized instruction system that gets them the help they need."

This woman, of course, had raised a critical point. Once we put our exit standards in place, unless we created a companion system that raised students to the standards, we'd be sentencing many to fail. What could we do to prevent that? Two things. One, identify early the students who were not on track to meet the standards while there was still time to boost their performance. Two, find a way to get extra help to every child who needed it.

The idea of identifying students who were not working at grade level wasn't new, of course; teachers did that every time they filled out report cards. What was new was the idea of identifying students *early*, before it was too late to take corrective action. If we could identify students as early as the fall and then again midyear, we would be able to get them the attention they needed before the end of the year. So we decided to institute quarterly reports. Three times a year we asked teachers to file a report with the superintendent's office on every student, indicating whether the student was on target to meet the curriculum standards for the grade. That meant that by as early as December we would know which students needed extra help and could begin finding ways to get it to them.

The teachers didn't exactly embrace the idea of quarterly reports with open arms. Although the form we'd created was purposely simple, most viewed it as extra work. Some teachers wondered how accurate it would be to predict early and midyear whether children would be ready for promotion in the spring. And as with the syllabi, some teachers lagged at getting their reports done. But principals used their leadership skills and got the "bubble sheets" in, and by the second year, the reluctance to do them had vanished. They'd become a fact of life in the district, one more example of how we had placed our focus on academic achievement.

Extra Help for Every Child Who Needs It

Now we'd created an early identification system for finding the children who needed extra help. But how could we get them the help they needed? That would be far more challenging. One way would be to bring in tutors. We'd already begun to recruit volunteers; the media attention surrounding our annual district-wide reading campaign had brought in several thousand. But tutors wouldn't be enough. We would also need to change the way the children were taught. Throughout the district (in fact, throughout public education) there was a tacit belief that if a teacher taught something it was the student's responsibility to "get it." Students who didn't get it were considered at fault because the system placed the entire burden of learning on the child. But that wasn't fair! Not all students learn the same way or at the same pace. It was unreasonable to expect a teacher to teach material one way to an entire class and to expect every student to pick it up the first time. If we really wanted every student to learn, then the responsibility for learning would have to be shared. Students would have to agree to pay attention, work hard, and try their best to learn, but teachers would have to bend their teaching methods to individual students' needs.

Would that be possible? We believed it would. We would need to look closely at every child who was at risk to determine his or her instructional needs; then we would need to craft an *individualized academic plan* for every one.

Key to the individualized plans would be looking at each child *fully*— not just at his or her academic performance, as we were used to doing, but at the total child. What were his strengths? What turned her on? Who were his friends? Who were the meaningful adults in her life? We would then use this information to craft a learning plan. James is behind in reading? Well, let's think: How does he learn best? Is he a kinesthetic learner; is he always moving and touching things, does he use his body to learn? Then let's let him move around while reading instead of confining him to a seat; let's free up the energy he's using just trying to sit still so he can apply that energy to the book. Is he friends with Peter, who is strong in reading? Let's make a reading group of two and ask Peter to be his helper. Are his auditory skills stronger than his visual skills? Let's get him books on tape so he can hear as well as see the words and build his vocabulary while he practices word recognition. Let's work with James's strengths and interests to bring him up to speed.

But simply making adjustments in the classroom would not be enough for many of the children, so the individualized plans would also need to marshal outside resources. Tutoring, help with homework, summer school, mentoring: We'd have to offer those kinds of interventions for every child at risk. And we'd have to bring in the students' parents. Parents were our students' first and most influential teachers; without their participation the effectiveness of everything else we did would be lessened. Could schools create this kind of comprehensive support net for every at-risk child?

We believed they could. We ran the numbers: How many students in a midsized elementary school were at risk of not exiting fifth grade? Ten. How many adults in the school? Thirty. Surely thirty adults, along with other district specialists and parent volunteers, could develop and monitor plans for ten children. To help them, we created a form called the Accelerated Learning Plan, which suggested criteria for evaluating each child. It asked about the child's strengths and weaknesses, about her strongest forms of intelligence, about her relationships with others, and about her own feelings and dreams. Inside, the form coached school staff on building an individual plan. It asked them to define goals, strategies, and activities they would use to help the child, as well as ways they would assess the child's progress. The forms were not mandatory; they were meant as a guide for the planning process, a spur to encourage schools to think comprehensively and strategically about their at-risk students.

If we expected the schools to be overwhelmed, we were pleasantly surprised. For the most part, instead of seeing the plans as yet another burden, they embraced them as a way to get children the help they needed. When we had first begun talking about the exit decisions and the individualized plans, many of our educators had expressed consternation. They were fundamentally opposed to holding children back; they believed that children who were at risk of failing needed boosts, not blows, to their self-esteem, and that many would suffer long-term damage if they were forced to repeat a grade. As one principal said, "For so many years we've focused on the emotional and social implications of holding children back, it's hard now to see it as positive." But this isn't about holding children back, we had explained. It's about catching them early and giving them the help they need so they can exit on time. It's about recognizing that all children learn and mature at different rates, and that some simply need more time to master a set of skills. When teachers stopped me in hallways or stood up in meetings to question the policy, I'd ask, "Are we building a child's self-esteem if we let her move to middle school unable to read, or let her graduate from high school unable to hold a job? Will her self-esteem grow as she slips farther behind her peers? Will it rise when she's twenty-three, living at home, unemployed, on welfare, and raising a child? Or do we do her a *favor* by delivering a setback now, while she's surrounded by teachers who can help her learn, and by giving her the skills that will make her successful for life?"

Every school wrestled with the issue. They talked about it in teachers' lounges and held whole-staff meetings to discuss it. Some asked me or Gary Tubbs, our director of academic achievement, to come out and talk with their staff about it; some used part of their training budget to get outside help with how to handle the policy at their school. Fifth-grade teachers, who would be the first to implement the exit-decision policy, admitted that they had long promoted children who were at risk of failing in middle school; perhaps this *was* a way of ensuring children's future success.

Against this backdrop, the individualized plans were seen as critical. Through all the discussions, teachers came back over and over again to the fact that the plans were the children's lifeline, the tool that would get them the help they needed, that would diminish their chances of being held back. Even teachers who remained opposed to the exit policy appreciated the value of the plans: Children who might previously have slipped through the cracks would now get extra support. By the time the time came to implement the plans, support was strong. As one principal said, "We'd talked about it so much that by the time we had to do it, we really believed in the possibilities and opportunities it offered."

Finding ways to provide extra support for so many children at risk of nonpromotion was, of course, a challenge. No school had the money to hire tutors for every student or to buy special learning materials to meet children's individual needs. But the schools became creative at finding ways to get students additional help.

- Most schools had a volunteer coordinator (usually a parent) who became tremendously resourceful at getting parents and neighborhood volunteers to come in and tutor.
- Some also hired tutors using money from their budgets.
- Some formed relationships with organizations in their neighborhoods—churches, Masonic lodges, senior centers, nonprofit social service organizations, and so on—which sent in volunteers to tutor.

- Some found college or community-college interns.

- Some found high-school interns.

- Some used their paid instructional assistants, often scheduling the IAs to stay later in the day so they could work with students after school, or using IAs to free up classroom teachers so they could give extra attention to an at-risk child.

- Some created buddy programs in which older students tutored younger ones at lunchtime.

- Some asked adults in the school to mentor an at-risk child, to commit to giving the child special attention for the entire year.

Using these extra people, the schools created after-school tutoring programs (when possible, they arranged for school buses to pick up children later; when that was impossible, some schools had teachers drive children home); before-school tutoring programs during the twenty minutes between bus drop-off and the start of classes; and Saturday Academies, which met for two to three hours on Saturday mornings to go over work from the previous week. Not all schools offered all these programs, but each one determined the needs of its students and developed support activities that worked for them.

At the same time, the schools divvied up responsibility for the children among their staff. One person was made the "case manager" for each child; it was this person's task to see that the plan was followed. Others were assigned other responsibilities: The parent volunteer coordinator was asked to find the child a tutor; the teacher was asked to coordinate with the tutor to make sure he or she taught the right material; the school librarian was asked to find books and tapes at the proper reading level that would appeal to the child's interests; the family support worker, if the school had one, was asked to work with the parents. By dividing the responsibilities this way, everybody had a little more, but no one felt overwhelmed.

The schools also worked hard to bring in parents, since their support would be crucial. Particular emphasis was put on working with parents of fourth- and fifth-graders, since they would be the ones most immediately affected. In April 1997, each elementary school sent letters to the parents of all fourth-grade students telling them about the exit-decision policy. They explained that the following year their children would be the first in the district to be subject to the policy and explained how exit decisions would be made.

A month later the schools sent a second letter. This one went to the parents of the fourth-graders who, based on test and classroom evidence, were not on target to exit fifth grade the following year. The letters specified the areas in which the children were having trouble, explained that the children would be getting extra support in school, and asked parents to speak to their children's teacher about summer school, after-school tutoring, and other remedial services.

This time reaction was far more mixed. Many of the parents appreciated the warning. They'd never gotten this kind of official notice before— or this kind of concrete plan for remedial action. They called immediately to arrange for remedial programs. More parents, however, were angry. "It isn't fair!" they protested. "How do you expect my child to make up this work in one year?" "You're putting too much weight on standardized tests!" As we reviewed the feedback we realized that we hadn't done our homework; we hadn't adequately explained the dimensions of the program. Parents didn't understand that exit decisions would be made by weighing the student's complete profile, not just test scores, and they didn't understand the safety net we were creating to get students up to speed. So the following fall we held fifteen community forums in schools across the district. Gary Tubbs, director of academic achievement, and I attended the forums and explained the policies more fully.

At the same time, the staffs in the schools worked overtime to bring in the parents. Parents were asked to help develop the plans for their children. Principals, teachers, and counselors explained the positive, rather than punitive, intent of the programs and stressed the variety of strategies the schools would use to help the children catch up. They also emphasized the importance of parental participation if the program was going to succeed, and worked with parents to develop ways they could support their children at home. Nightly reading and nightly checking of homework, frequent parent conferences, daily or weekly phone calls and notes from teachers to parents, and contracts, monitored by parents, between the child and the school, were some of the strategies schools and parents agreed on.

I'm sure there were some parents who disagreed with the exit-decision policy even after these meetings. But the vast majority left the meetings believing we were right. They saw how the schools were mobilizing to help their children and how fervently the teachers wanted the plans to succeed, and they realized that what we'd said all along was true: Despite the seeming harshness of the exit policy, when combined with the individualized plan, it truly operated in their child's best interest.

The 550 fourth-graders who received "early warning" letters in the spring of 1997 are now finishing fifth grade. Over the past year they've attended more after-school tutoring sessions and more Saturday Academies than this district has ever held; their parents have had more contact with their schools than any of those parents had had before. The children, their teachers, and their parents have all worked extremely hard—and their efforts are paying off. As I write this, we are one month shy of the day when this year's fifth-graders will graduate. All but fifty of the 550 will join them.

"TELL ME: HOW CAN WE HELP OUR CHILDREN ACHIEVE?"

THE QUARTERLY REPORTS, THE SYLLABI, THE EXIT DECISIONS, THE INDIVIDUALIZED PLANS . . . THESE THINGS WEREN'T MY IDEAS: I GOT THEM FROM TEACHERS.

The field of education is full of stories about superlative teachers, teachers who pull remarkable performances from every student year after year. Every school has at least one of these teachers. Many schools are fortunate enough to have several. How do these teachers do it? It isn't really a mystery. They love every child, they see each one's strengths, they find ways to work with each child individually, capitalizing on his or her strengths to overcome areas of weakness. They do whatever it takes—making materials at home, calling parents at night, staying late to give extra help after school—to help their children succeed. The individualized plans haven't turned every teacher into a superlative teacher, but they have *systematized* the superlative teachers' methods. They have enabled us to give every student who can't succeed without it that kind of individual attention.

The individualized plans have also changed the way schools look at what they are doing. Instead of monitoring their performance solely in the aggregate—by looking at average test scores, overall attendance, overall dropout rates, and so on—schools now need to monitor the performance of each individual student. We still expect them to raise their averages, but, just as important, we expect them to raise the performance of every child. The individualized plans enable them to do that. The quarterly reports, which are sent to my office, are the measure of their success.

SANISLO ELEMENTARY SCHOOL: PARENT INVOLVEMENT PLAN

Sanislo Elementary School has developed a wide variety of avenues to get parents involved in their children's education:

- *Nightly reading:* Each student is required to read for twenty minutes a night, and children in grades K through 3 must have their reading sheets signed by a parent. The school encourages reading further by turning nightly reading into a contest:

  - They track the number of nights of reading by each student and class.
  - They hold biweekly drawings and give special rewards based on nightly reading.
  - They post a giant "Reading Thermometer" to track the school-wide goal of 50,000 nights of reading.
  - If the goal is reached, the school takes students on a special trip in June to celebrate their 50,000 nights of reading.

- *Weekly homework packets:* Teachers at each grade level (beginning in kindergarten) jointly develop weekly homework assignments, which go home with students on Friday or Monday and must be returned by the following Thursday. The teachers also write letters to parents about how the assignments fit into the grade's curriculum, and offering suggestions on how they can help. Each week teachers write a letter telling parents what they are working on in the classroom and suggesting enrichment activities parents can do at home.

- *Family reading night:* Once each year families come to school bringing books to read, sleeping bags, blankets, stuffed animals, even pajamas, and spread out on tumbling mats in the gym to read. Afterward, everybody celebrates with an ice-cream social sponsored by the PTA. Some years the school uses Title I funding (federal money to help serve low-income families) to give each child a free book to encourage reading at home.

- *Parent-teacher conferences:* Regular conferences are scheduled in November, but the school holds them more frequently with families of children who are in danger of not meeting the exit standards for their grade. For some students, parent contact happens daily or weekly.

- *Family fitness night:* Several times a year Sanislo invites families to come join in a fun physical-fitness activity. Past events have included an evening of jump roping at which parents practiced double dutch, speed jumping, and other jumping techniques with their children, and an evening at a roller rink. The school's SCAT team of student acrobats, unicyclers, and jugglers, who have been trained by the PE teachers, also performs for families (as well as in locations around the city!).

- *Multiethnic dinner and open house:* An annual event during the first week of school when families are invited to come share in an informal potluck get-together with the school staff to welcome everyone back to school. Families get to meet teachers informally without the pressure of discussing student performance and everyone enjoys the dishes from the school's thirty different cultures. There is always a huge turnout.

- *Curriculum night open house:* A night in the fall when teachers distribute syllabi and discuss grade-level exit standards, curriculum content, and the school's expectations of students.

- *Class letters to parents:* Regular bulletins updating parents on activities in the classroom.

- *The School Connection Hotline:* A telephone message system used by schools across the district (funded by Washington Mutual Bank). Parents can call a number, punch in their teacher's extension, and hear a recorded message about homework, classroom events, special events, and any other information he or she wants parents to know. Some first-grade teachers let their Readers of the Week record a short reading passage.

- *Translations:* Communication with non-English-speaking parents is provided by translators and bilingual staff.

- *Parent workshops:* Occasional workshops are offered on subjects such as "How to Help Your Child with Reading."

- *Books on tape:* Cassette players and tapes are available in the school library for checkout by families to increase family access to literature.

- *Postcards:* Teachers communicate daily or weekly with parents of at-risk children regarding their children's progress.
- *Parent corner in library:* An area of the school library is devoted to parent resource materials. Families also have access to all library materials.
- *Half-time parent volunteer coordinator:* This position, filled by a parent, actively encourages and facilitates parent involvement in the school.

Keeping the Airplane Flying

When I was the commander of an aviation unit in Vietnam, one of my pilots once took an airplane up with one of its two fuel boost pumps broken. The crew chief had told the pilot about the deficiency before the flight, but the pilot had been so mission-oriented—he was fighting for democracy!—that he'd taken the plane up anyway. Since the second pump is used for backup in case the first pump fails, he'd felt he could fly the plane safely without it. But when he came back I was waiting in the hangar for him with a reprimand. Under *no* circumstances, I said, did we permit pilots in our company to jeopardize their safety, and the safety of their crew, by flying planes that were not operationally ready.

I wish we could have the same policy in the schools. Imagine if we could delay our mission until we'd fixed everything that was broken! While we repaired all the leaky roofs, revised our entire curriculum, retrained all our teachers. What an ideal system we would have. But of course we can't. We have 47,500 children who need to be educated *today*, and we have to serve them even while we're improving our methods of doing it. Once school opens in September, a school district is like a big wheel rolling—rolling day by day, week by week, until school closes. Repair in flight is possible, but difficult. Shutting down is *not* an option.

These last two years have been years of extensive repairs. We've asked teachers to change the way they teach and the way they monitor student performance. We've asked them to change their most fundamental attitudes—about whether students can learn, about holding students back, about how to assess their students' abilities. We've changed the long accepted practice of "social promotion" in which students are promoted when they cannot do the work, and we've required schools to bring parents into the loop when children are at risk of failing. We have taken almost every comfortable, accepted district practice and turned it on its head in an effort to help our students achieve. And as if each of these changes would not have been difficult enough when made sequentially, we have done them simultaneously—because the longer we fly with broken systems, the longer we jeopardize our students' ability to fly.

Undergoing this amount of change is hard—for teachers, for students, for parents. People have chafed, some have grumbled, a few have tried to stir up discontent. But the vast majority have rallied to the effort because they know the change is serving a vision that focuses on children. They know that if we weather the discomfort now, we will soon have the schools we truly want: schools in which all students are taught with methods tailored to their needs; schools in which every average student is pushed to become above average; in which every above-average student is in challenging courses; in which a troubled student is caught early and given extra attention; schools in which all students are promoted on time, having mastered the work for their grade.

I'm sure that if our changes were not yielding improvement, people would be less supportive—but the changes *are* working! Since we've begun redesigning our achievement system, every performance measure is up. Standardized test scores have risen from one to four percentage points for every student group in every subject. The gap in test scores between white and minority students has diminished by four to six points in nine of the twelve areas measured (in the remaining three areas, eighth-grade reading, eighth-grade math, and eighth-grade science, it has remained level). Parent satisfaction, as measured on surveys, has risen, as have teachers' ratings of their school's cohesiveness, leadership, climate, and curriculum.

Change is hard, of course, but when it propels an organization toward its vision, it is also exciting. Not long ago one of our principals told me about a meeting he had attended where a group of principals had discussed the district's many changes. They'd talked about the extra work involved in developing individualized plans, in pushing teachers to do the quarterly reports, in working with teachers to teach to the new curriculum frameworks and adopt the new methods of assessment. The conversation had focused on the challenges involved, and there had been a lot of head nodding and consensus. But after a while one of the principals had said, "You know, we're all grumbling here about the extra work we have to do, but isn't this what we got into education for? Don't we *want* this kind of focus on achievement?" And all around the room the principals had nodded in agreement. Like most of our teachers, most of our parents, and most of our students, they were proud to be part of an achievement system.

Most important, our graduates will hold their chins high and proclaim loudly, "I am a graduate of the Seattle Public Schools."

BUILDING ACHIEVEMENT FOR CHILDREN OF POVERTY AND CHILDREN OF COLOR

Margie Lyons looks up from braiding a child's hair. The teacher and her student have been talking quietly in the almost empty classroom as Ms. Lyons's fingers deftly twist the dark strands, inserting a rainbow of colored beads. The child has been telling Ms. Lyons about something troubling that happened at home last night, but as the school bus unloads outside and children begin bubbling into the classroom, she grows quiet. Ms. Lyons finishes the last braid, gives the girl a hug, then greets the rest of her children. "Hello, Rex! How's your baby brother?" "Krystal, did you get your reading done last night?" "Ping, what a beautiful dress! Did your mother make that for you?" Ms. Lyons greets every child individually, touching many of them gently on the head or shoulder, looking every one in the eye. It is clear she loves these children.

A few minutes later, when all the children have hung up their coats and settled into their chairs, Ms. Lyons writes a sentence on the blackboard: *We's supposed to bring the childrens lunch today.* "What's wrong with this sentence?" she asks. Immediately, a flurry of hands shoots up. "Kenneth?" A small boy in a starched-looking white shirt says, "It says 'we's.' " Ms. Lyons nods. "Angelina, what's wrong with that?" The girl whose hair the teacher braided says softly, "You're not supposed to say 'we's.' " "Why not?" Ms. Lyons looks around the room. "Because it's not good English." "That's right. Why not?" No one seems to know for sure so Ms. Lyons explains that "we" is plural and therefore needs the plural verb "are." She fixes the sentence on the board, then leads the class in a discussion of what else is wrong in the sentence. They find and correct the missing apostrophe in "childrens."

Every morning Ms. Lyons's class starts with two sentences of oral language practice. It helps them learn the rules of grammar, spelling, and punctuation, but, just as important, it's part of the school's strategy to have children explain their thinking out loud. Listening to their peers explain how they found the answer to a question helps the children who didn't know the answer learn to problem-solve themselves.

After the oral language practice Ms. Lyons asks the class to take out their readers and turn to "The Shimmershine Queens." It's the story of a young black girl from a single-parent home who gains self-confidence when she's asked to play a part in a play. Ms. Lyons selected this story because it reflects her children's lives: many of them, too, lack self-confidence and come from single-parent homes. As the children open their books she sets up a challenge. "I'd like you to write down one thing that happened in this story. Just one thing." The children think for a moment, then bend over their papers and write industriously. One boy looks out the window. "Can you think of one thing that happened, John?" He shakes his head. "You can't remember anything from the story?" The boy thinks for a minute, then lights up. "When the girl was on the stage!" "Yes." A few moments later every child has written a sentence and Ms. Lyons calls on a girl to read hers aloud. "When the aunt talked to the girl." "Good. Can you put that in a whole sentence?" The girl thinks for a moment. "I liked when the aunt talked to the girl?" Ms. Lyons nods. "Who wrote down something that happened *after* that in the story?" A flurry of hands goes up. Ms. Lyons calls on a boy, who says, "When the aunt talked to the girl." "No! no!" rises a chorus of voices. Ms. Lyons looks at the class. "Let's give Calvin a chance to explain his thinking." And once again she gives the children a chance to explain their thought process out loud. As they answer, she reminds them to phrase their answers in complete sentences, and to be sure they are written down that way as well, because familiarity with full sentence structure is important to their success.

As Ms. Lyons leads the class in this discussion one boy sits at the back of the room with his tutor, a University of Washington student who comes once a week, specifically to work with Xavier. Today Xavier has read a story to her and she is asking him questions from a set of cards she holds in her hand. "What is the main idea of this story?" she asks him. "How do you know?" The cards, which contain close to seventy-five questions grouped by reading skill, have been prepared by the school for just this situation. They help the 250 volunteer tutors who come in once or twice a week tailor their tutoring to the specific skills the children need to learn.

Just outside the classroom, at a table in the hall, another university tutor is working with a girl in math. As the girl looks at her eagerly, the tutor slowly reads a list of directions: "Take the number four . . . multiply it by itself . . . divide it by two . . . add six. . . . What do you get?" The girl seems to stop breathing as she concentrates on each task. Finally she announces, "Fourteen!" The tutor gives her a high-five. Asking the girl to follow these directions in her head is reinforcing a number of important skills: listening, concentrating, following directions, organizing material in her mind, and, of course, basic computation.

This scene is taking place at Bailey-Gatzert Elementary School, a high-poverty school in Seattle's inner city. But more and more, similar scenes are taking place at schools across our district because we have begun to pinpoint the factors that boost achievement in children of color and we are working to institutionalize those factors district-wide. Here are the factors we are aiming to address:

1. *Teachers' attitudes:* Teachers *must* believe that every child will learn because children rise to the level of expectations that are held for them. To encourage our teachers to have the highest expectations of all their children, we hired an organization called the Efficacy Institute, based in Washington, D.C. The institute specializes in helping schools recognize that they often hold subtly different expectations for different groups of students. Over a two-year period, trainers from the institute conducted a series of daylong workshops for all of our teachers. At the workshops the teachers were challenged with questions: Do you believe that children of color are inherently inferior? Do you treat them as if they were? Do you put them in the back of the classroom and let them play around? Do you pass them with lower-level work? The answers were startling. Teachers and principals who hadn't considered themselves biased recognized the subtle ways they'd held minority children to a lower standard. They came away with a new sense of what it meant to say that *every* child would learn.

2. *Establishing a relationship of love and respect:* Children need to feel that there is someone in their corner who really wants them to succeed. They need a stable relationship with an adult they can count on and to whom their success means a tremendous amount. Teachers must play this role *overtly* for their children, as must the principal, the counselor, the family support worker, and other adults in the school.

3. *Tutors:* Children who are below grade level need the extra attention of tutors in order to catch up—not just for academic support (which is essential), but also to provide the kind of stable, nurturing relationship described above. Therefore, schools must be very aggressive in mining their community for volunteers, and if at all possible, must provide weekly or biweekly sessions where one adult tutors one child for the course of an entire year. This sounds undoable—but it isn't. Bailey-Gatzert, which does not have a stable of parents who can come in to help, has found 250 tutors through other organizations in the community. They have used all the sources listed on pages 47–48, and in addition have found tutors through special programs that operate district-wide.

- *The Pipeline Project* is a joint project between the Seattle schools and the University of Washington funded by the Coca-Cola Foundation. The project matches university students with students in our schools for one-on-one instruction. The first year of the program, 1997–98, the university supplied 140 tutors; by the year 2000, when the project is at full capacity, we will have 2,500.

- *Team Read:* With a million-dollar grant from communications pioneer Craig McCaw, we implemented a program in which high-school students tutor first-, second-, and third-graders at four high-poverty schools. The McCaw program focuses on reading in an effort to ensure that these mostly minority children are reading at grade level by the end of third grade.

To ensure that the tutors' time is used effectively, all of our schools have volunteer coordinators who schedule volunteers and make sure their needs are met. Many also provide "coaching cards" with tips to tutors that help them structure their work with students.

4. *Tailoring the instruction to the child's learning style and needs:* All children need to learn the same material, but they won't all learn it the same way. That's why we've given our schools total discretion over their budgets and instructional materials. They are free to purchase the materials that will work best for their individual students. At Bailey-Gatzert, teachers rejected the kindergarten reading textbook that is used by most other schools in the district and selected instead a program that they felt bore more relation to their children's lives. They've brought in computer software programs that help children hear the middle and ending sounds of words so the children can learn to pronounce and spell them correctly. And they've culled material from numerous other sources to find materials that respond directly to their students' diverse needs. We've made it a little easier for them to purchase a variety of materials by changing the way we fund our schools. Thanks to the "weighted student formula" (see Chapter 9), schools like Bailey-Gatzert that serve large numbers of low-income children now have more money to serve their students' greater educational needs.

5. *Addressing children's basic needs:* Many children who live in poverty come to school unable to focus because they are worried about

adult problems: what they will eat for dinner, where they will sleep that night, who will be there when they get home from school. Before we can help children learn, we have to address these most basic issues. Therefore, each of our high-poverty schools has a family support worker whose job is to connect families with outside resources such as job-training programs and social-service agencies, and to provide support and guidance for families who need it, and the principals, counselors, and teachers in these schools are careful to look behind the children's surface behavior for signs of home problems that the school can help address. Often our schools provide food, clothing, and a washer and dryer to their families when those items are needed to help their children learn.

SEEING RESULTS

Improving the achievement of poor, minority students is a long, slow process. It will be five years before we can say with certainty that we have reversed the gap in performance between white children and children of color. However, in the meantime, this constellation of measures seems to be producing positive short-term results. In Seattle, scores are broken out into three categories: by ethnic group—American Indians, African Americans, Latinos, Asians, and whites; by grade—fourth, eighth, and eleventh; and by subject—reading, language, math, and history/social studies. With just two exceptions, between 1995 and 1997, student scores rose on the state-mandated Comprehensive Test of Basic Skills for *every student group, in every subject area.* The two exceptions were the scores of eleventh-grade Latinos, which dropped two points in language and history/social studies. All other grades, all other ethnic groups, in all subjects—including Latino fourth-graders and eighth-graders—rose. The gap has begun to shrink.

QUIZ:
IS IT UNREALISTIC TO EXPECT
EVERY CHILD TO ACHIEVE?

(b) All children can achieve!

But until schools believe that, and act on their belief, it will not hap-
pen. We must stop promoting children who cannot do the work, and
instead find ways to teach and support them that will enable them to
achieve.

CHAPTER 4

WE CAN ACHIEVE THE VICTORY WHEN ... WE HOLD OUR PEOPLE ACCOUNTABLE

QUIZ:
WHICH OF THE FOLLOWING IS NOT USED
IN MOST SCHOOL DISTRICTS AS A CRITERION
FOR EVALUATING SCHOOLS?

(a) number of disciplinary incidents
(b) building maintenance
(c) student performance
(d) parent satisfaction

Answer on page 86.

It was October 1997, and I was standing in the hallway of our central administration building talking to Ron Jones, our director of curriculum, about the recent surge in demand for copies of the new math, reading, and language-arts frameworks. In an effort to strengthen our curriculum and standardize it across the district, we had distributed the new curriculum frameworks to teachers two years before. These frameworks detailed specific learning objectives for students in every grade. In the intervening years, however, we'd received only sporadic requests for additional copies. What was triggering the sudden demand?

Ron smiled. "I think part of it is that the principals are putting on pressure. Ever since we announced that fifty percent of a principal's evaluation would be based on how well students have learned and on the principal's performance as an academic leader, the principals feel they better make sure the teachers are teaching the skills delineated in the frameworks. And I think the other part has to do with the new union contract. If teachers are going to be held accountable for having their students learn the frameworks, they feel like they better start teaching them!"

I was sure Ron was right. With teachers' evaluations tied directly to how well students had mastered the new learning objectives, the frameworks had taken on a new importance. I couldn't say I was surprised. It's a truism that people do well the things they're held accountable for. We'd decided to hold people accountable for the things that really mattered.

What did surprise me was that teachers and principals across America hadn't been held accountable for student achievement all along. In our district, as in school districts across the country, the superintendent was the only person evaluated based on how much the children learned. Teachers were evaluated for how well they managed their classrooms and for whether they knew their subject matter. Principals were evaluated for the cleanliness of their buildings and for how many suspensions and expulsions they had had.

That didn't make sense! Our mission was to ensure that every student learned. But if we weren't holding our educators accountable for their learning, how could we ever meet our goals? It is amazing to watch what happens at Boeing when the company establishes a production goal of 415 planes for the year and then is short by five. Accountability becomes very clear very quickly. Any organization that wants to achieve its goals *has* to have a system of accountability, or else the goals will never be met. Therefore, the district had no choice. If we wanted to produce the kinds of achievement gains our school board and community wanted, we'd have to start holding our teachers and principals accountable for what their students learned.

HOLDING PRINCIPALS ACCOUNTABLE

One of my earliest meetings in the district was with a man who had been a high-school principal for ten years before moving to a position in central administration. After a few minutes the conversation turned to discipline. He told me a story about a boy in his school who had been caught with a knife in his locker. "Did you suspend him?" I asked, thinking an offense like that didn't deserve a second chance. The former principal shook his head. "No. Principals try to keep suspensions down because they count against you in your evaluation."

What? I thought. Principals are encouraged to let a boy with a knife remain in school because they get penalized for suspensions?

"What else counts against you in evaluations?" I asked, suddenly even more curious.

"The number of violent incidents you've had. A lot of incidents and you're seen as not being in control."

"They look at the number of incidents you've had, rather than how you handled them?"

"Yes." He paused. "So lots of incidents don't get reported."

His answer was so guileless it took me a minute to absorb it. "You don't report them?"

He shrugged. "Oh, you report most of them, but not all."

"What else?" I wondered.

"Dropout rates. Having a lot of dropouts looks bad, so you find other ways to explain them."

"What makes for a good evaluation?" I asked.

"Clean building, no graffiti, toilets work, teacher morale is good." He paused. "Keeping the school free from controversy."

"Test scores? Academic achievement?"

"That too."

That too? As if it were an afterthought?

"You know, of course, what principals do, don't you? To make their schools look good, they test only those students who can pass the test."

I nodded grimly. I had heard that before, from others. "What about minority students, closing the gap?"

The man shook his head in a gesture that seemed half embarrassed, half discouraged. "You know, we've been working on the achievement gap for years. We've had task forces that have produced voluminous lists of recommendations, but the problem hasn't gone away. So our solution is designed to placate the minority communities and pacify the students."

"What's that solution?"

"Social promotion. Frankly, it's been an easy problem to conceal. We didn't report test scores by race, so no one knew how bad the problem was."

I was astounded. This man had described an evaluation system that worked absolutely contrary to what we needed to achieve! No wonder people were losing faith in the schools. We needed to change the way we held our principals accountable so that the system reinforced the goals we were trying to achieve.

I began to think about creating a new accountability system for principals. I knew that principals had tremendous power in shaping the performance and climate of their schools. And I knew that whatever accountability measures we selected would drive the principals' behavior. It didn't take long to come up with a list of three "unrecoverables," three behaviors that, if they formed a pattern, could cause a principal to lose his or her job.

The first unrecoverable would be the *failure to plan for the academic achievement of every child*. A clean building and high morale were important, but unless principals felt personal responsibility for the achievement of every child, achievement would not rise the way it needed to. We didn't expect every child to make tremendous gains; that would have been unrealistic. Nor did I want principals to inflate their test scores falsely; that would have been unethical. But we expected every principal to put a plan in place for helping every child succeed: We expected them to monitor the progress of every child through quarterly reports; we expected them to implement an individualized plan for every child at risk of failing; we expected them to pull in community volunteers so that every child who needed it could be given extra help. And to convey the importance of this effort, I said that 50 percent of a principal's evaluation would now be based on their students' academic progress.

The second thing we needed to do was to change the way we considered the issue of safety. We needed our accountability system to *discourage* violence, not soft-pedal it. That meant we needed to know about every incident, we needed to discipline every perpetrator appropriately, and we needed to encourage principals to root out students who were initiating acts of violence. So I said that my second unrecoverable for principals was *failure to establish a policy or follow a policy designed to prevent the catastrophic injury or death of a student*. We didn't expect every school to be completely free of incidents; that would be unrealistic. But we expected our principals to deal with incidents in a way that would aggressively discourage their occurrence and recurrence.

To help principals keep their schools safe, we also increased students' accountability for their own safety: We enlisted peer pressure as a means of keeping the number of incidents down. Within each school, we offered to pay each middle-school grade $50 and each high-school grade $100 for every month they remained incident-free; but we said we would rescind a month's worth of money every time an incident occurred. At the end of the year, the student body of each grade would be free to spend its money on whatever school-related project it liked. Because the code of silence surrounding teen violence is so strong, we felt we needed a powerful incentive to break through peer pressure. So we also said we would pay $100 to any student who helped us find a knife that had been brought to school and $500 to any student who led us to a gun.

Our announcement of the programs met with a mixed response.

People complained that we were paying students for good behavior when good behavior should be expected, not rewarded. They questioned whether encouraging students to inform on others is appropriate school policy. But our answer was practical: We *must* keep our schools safe, and until students become our partners in that effort, we will not succeed. Statistics bore us out: The first year of the programs, our violent incidents dropped to a ten-year low, down 732 occurrences, or 23 percent, from the previous year.

The third thing we needed to do in changing our accountability system for principals was get them out of the job of *managing* their buildings and into the job of *leading*. The principal's job was to be the academic leader of the school—to make sure the teachers were teaching to the frameworks, that the students' achievement was rising, that the teachers stayed focused on academics instead of on the hundreds of other issues that could easily get in the way. So we made our third unrecoverable for principals' *failure to lead*.

But were the principals ready to lead? I didn't think so. Most had risen to their positions because they'd been excellent classroom teachers, but teaching required an entirely different set of skills. If we wanted our principals to lead their schools successfully toward our vision, we'd have to train them in leadership techniques. So, in partnership with Larry Rowedder of the Mayerson Academy, a principal-training organization in Cincinnati, we developed the Principal Leadership Institute (see box, pages 65–67), an ongoing course that teaches our principals what we need them to know: how to craft a vision and inspire people toward it, how to work collaboratively with teachers rather than autocratically, how to encourage teamwork, how to recruit and develop excellent teachers, how to ensure accountability—in short, how to be an academic leader.

PRINCIPAL LEADERSHIP INSTITUTE

As soon as it became clear that we were going to decentralize our district and give a great deal more operating control to the schools, I realized that our principals would need training in leadership. Each one was already a premier educator. But they needed additional skills: skills in inspiring, motivating, and guiding their diverse communities of students, teachers, and parents. So I began to think about creating a leadership training program.

At first I thought I would teach the classes myself. But I soon realized that while I was equipped to teach a leadership class in the army, or even in the private sector, I was not prepared to teach a class for principals; I didn't know enough about education. So I went to the Alliance for Education, our nonprofit fund-raising/R and D partner (see box on pages 96–97), and asked them to find an individual or organization who could help us develop and teach an ongoing principal leadership course. After investigating several principal-training programs, the Alliance selected the Mayerson Academy in Cincinnati because they incorporated leadership principles from both the corporate and education worlds. Together with Larry Rowedder, founder and president of the academy, we developed the Principal Leadership Institute.

The first PLI training was held in October 1996. Since then, Larry and his associate, Mike Rutherford, have come to Seattle approximately once a month to conduct large-group, small-group, and individual sessions. They offer the following types of training:

- *Advanced leadership development:* Four four-hour sessions for incumbent principals in which participants learn:

  - how to provide clear, positive direction;
  - how to ensure accountability;
  - how to build positive relationships and teamwork;
  - how to select and develop outstanding staff;
  - and other skills that are vital in academic leaders.

- *Leadership training for aspiring principals:* Up to twenty hours of training in the same skills for teachers and assistant principals who want to advance into a principal position and who are selected by their principals to attend.
- *Coaching and mentoring:* Individual and small-group sessions in which principals receive support as they apply leadership-training concepts to specific challenges in their schools.
- *The leadership series:* Seminars with outstanding leaders from other fields in which principals explore the application of ideas from the corporate and nonprofit sectors to education.

Not all the principals were happy, initially, about having to attend the sessions. They were reluctant to spend so much time away from their schools, and longtime principals, especially, wondered what a neophyte superintendent could bring them that they didn't already know. But as the sessions progressed, more and more principals reported that they were finding them highly valuable. They found that the sessions caused them to examine their own behavior and rethink some of their most basic operating assumptions, asking questions like, Do I include teachers in decision-making? Do I encourage teamwork among my teachers? Is everything in my school focused on student achievement? For many, these were questions they had never asked themselves before.

Midway through the first year we made some changes to the program in response to principal feedback. By year two, 90 percent of the principals reported that the training had changed the way they operated their schools. Evidence backs them up: Since the institute began, the degree of trust and teamwork in our schools has increased (the number of conflicts between principals and teachers has measurably declined), and the degree to which principals focus on academic achievement (rather than on bus schedules, maintenance, and other management functions) has grown.

In addition to the monthly sessions of the PLI, principals receive training from me at our monthly administrators' meetings. At these sessions we discuss the business skills that principals need to be the CEOs of their schools:

- how to run a market-based school, which must compete for customers through excellence;
- how to develop systems in our schools (academic achievement systems, parent involvement systems, transportation systems, and so on) that support academic achievement;
- how to do strategic planning and budgeting;
- how to collect and manage data (for example, data about student achievement for different student populations) so that the data is useful for improving school performance;
- and other skills that principals need to lead their incredibly complex organizations.

Leading a school is a very isolating experience. Unlike teachers, who are surrounded by their peers, the principal has no peers in the building. The people with whom he or she has the most in common are in other schools in other parts of town. So one of the most important aspects of both the leadership institute and our monthly meetings is the opportunity to network. At every session principals share problems, transfer ideas, offer constructive criticism, and, perhaps most important, provide each other with moral support. The combination of training and camaraderie has created the powerful sense that our principals are working together to create world-class schools.

We introduced these new standards for accountability—the three "unrecoverables"—during my first year in the district, 1995–96. The principals' reaction was fairly swift. "There are too many factors outside my control that affect my students' performance," one principal said, voicing the concern of others. "I have large numbers of students who come from low-income homes, and the correlation between poverty and low performance is well documented. And I have teachers who don't get great performances from their students, but I can't remove them and hand-pick new ones. Give me control over all the elements that influence performance and I accept accountability. But until then, holding me accountable isn't fair."

I answered their concerns directly. Yes, it's true that low-income students tend to do more poorly than middle-class students. But low-income children can learn! It's your job to make that happen. Work with their parents to create more support at home. Bring in volunteers who can read to children who don't get read to at home. Set up after-school tutoring programs to give extra help to children who are falling behind. Do whatever it takes to help these children learn. I'm not asking you to raise their test scores ten or fifteen points; just to raise them a little bit each year. Every child can show improvement.

To the argument that the principals couldn't select their teachers, I responded: You're right. It *is* difficult to remove ineffective teachers and you don't have the ability to hand-pick new ones (except for a very limited, two-week period in May). But we are going to work to change that; we're going to try to get you the authority you need. (And in fact, over the next two years we negotiated a new contract with our teachers' union, which gave principals and their staffs the ability to select new teachers for their teams. See Chapter 6.)

"BEFORE, WE [PRINCIPALS] FOCUSED ON MAKING SURE THE SUPPLIES WERE THERE, THAT THE GROUNDS WERE MANICURED, THAT THE SCHOOL WAS CLEAN AND MORALE WAS HIGH, THAT YOU TALKED TO PARENTS. THE ASSUMPTION WAS THAT IF YOU TOOK CARE OF THOSE THINGS, THEN THEY WOULD EQUATE TO ACADEMIC ACHIEVEMENT. BUT IT DOESN'T WORK THAT WAY. NOW WE'VE FOCUSED ON ACADEMIC ACHIEVEMENT AND EVERYTHING ELSE FOLLOWS."
—DAVID ACKERMAN, FORMER PRINCIPAL, COOPER ELEMENTARY

Seeing how serious I was about the unrecoverables, the principals felt understandably nervous. Almost immediately they began pressuring teachers to produce their quarterly reports and to identify children who were lagging. They began soliciting their communities for volunteers who could come in and tutor, and began spending more time in classrooms evaluating teachers and talking about why individual children weren't learning. They began delegating some of their management functions (such as bus scheduling and building inspections) to others and began analyzing the performance data of their student groups by class, grade, and ethnic group in an effort to determine patterns.

The new focus on achievement—and the principals' concern for their jobs—also changed the way they treated less than competent teachers. In the past, principals had tolerated ineffective teachers because it was easier to keep them than to let them go. Now that they were being held accountable for student achievement, however, they couldn't afford to keep ineffective teachers; so they turned to a second way of dealing with underperformers: the long-standing practice of giving unsatisfactory teachers "satisfactory" evaluations and then suggesting that the teacher consider transferring to another building.

We didn't want ineffective teachers transferred elsewhere in the district, though. From now on, we said, principals who found a teacher ineffective would have to give an "unsatisfactory" rating and work with the teacher to help him or her solve the problem. The principal could recommend the teacher for the STAR program, a union mentoring program for all first-year teachers and for teachers who were having trouble; the principal could suggest that it might be time for the teacher to retire (the district became more willing to "buy out" contracts); or the principal could be very clear that a second "unsatisfactory" would make termination easier. None of these measures would be easy for the principals. But they had no choice: For the sake of their jobs, they had to ensure that every child would learn.

The principals' reaction to the new accountability measures was one of high anxiety mixed with exhilaration, however. For while the new measures were challenging, they were also perceived as right. Our principals had gone into education because they wanted to help children learn, and, clearly, the measures would support that goal. One principal summed up the sentiment of the group when he said to me, "I've got to be frank with you. I feel like the pressure is on and it's scary. But I think I'll adjust to that; I think we all will. In the meantime, I have a vision for where we can go in my school and the power to achieve that vision. And I like that."

"WE'RE ALL BEING HELD ACCOUNTABLE NOW. I BELIEVE THE
PHRASE IS 'YOUR FEET TO THE FIRE.'"

—ED JAMES, FORMER PRINCIPAL,
DEARBORN PARK ELEMENTARY SCHOOL

BUT HOW WELL IS EACH SCHOOL DOING?

If principals were truly going to lead their schools *and* raise achievement *and* increase safety, they would need a plan for how to do it. Before they could begin planning, however, they needed accurate data: detailed records of test scores, disciplinary infractions, parent surveys, and other performance measures either to confirm their impressions or to establish goals for the year. Without that data, they were really only guessing at where they needed to improve.

We needed detailed school data in central administration as well. If we were going to hold principals accountable for improving their school's performance, *we* needed an accurate picture of how each school was doing. So we began to assemble "data packets." We pulled together measures of each school's performance over the previous three years, including student scores on the Iowa test and the state-mandated Comprehensive Test of Basic Skills (with a breakdown of scores by ethnic group so we could chart the discrepancy between white and minority performance). We included the school's figures for attendance, truancy, suspensions, expulsions, and dropouts, and the results of the customer-satisfaction surveys we gave annually to parents, students, and staff. We included data that indicated whether the school was parents' first-choice placement for their child.

As soon as we assembled the data packets we grew excited: For the first time we had a comprehensive but easy-to-use portrait of the district. Our administrators could see at a glance how every school was doing, and the schools had an essential tool for determining where they needed to go. When we showed their packets to the schools, many were surprised. They'd had a sense of how they were performing, but they'd never seen three years of data so clearly laid out, delineating undeniable trends. One principal gasped, "I didn't realize it was so bad!"

Now the schools were ready to plan. They knew objectively in thirty-two different areas whether their performance was weak, strong, or average, and they had hard numbers they could use for setting goals. Equally important, the district had data it could use for holding schools accountable. In the spring, when we updated their packets, we could use the new data to monitor their achievement.

EACH SCHOOL CREATES A PLAN

We began the planning process by mandating that each school plan in six broad areas, the same six areas we had targeted in our goals as a district:

1. Raising academic achievement
2. Closing the achievement gap between white and minority students
3. Teacher training
4. Improving school safety and climate
5. Strengthening financial management
6. Improving customer satisfaction

Within each area we wanted the schools to define a single broad goal, measurable objectives they hoped to achieve, and strategies for achieving the outcomes. We also wanted to know how and when they would assess their progress. And we wanted these elements developed not solely by the principal, but by a team of people, including the principal, teachers, and parents. If the plan was going to be followed, it needed to be shaped and supported by the entire school community.

Many of the schools, however, had no experience doing this kind of planning. So we decided to provide a structure that would guide them, step by step, through the planning process. We asked them to answer each of the following questions for all of the six major goals. Goal #1 is given as an example.

Goal #1: Student Academic Achievement: Raising academic achievement for all students.

1. *Targeted Outcome:* What do you expect to achieve? (This should be written in terms of the number or percentage of students you expect to reach a higher standard.)
2. *Strategies:* What will you do to make it happen?
   a. What will students need?
   b. What will teachers need?
3. *Time and Action Plan:* What steps will you take to implement these strategies? When will each of these steps occur?
4. *Assessment:* How and when will you assess your progress?

The planning process began in August. Each school used parent and teacher committees to review their data packets and hash out answers to the questions. Because the data in the packets was so detailed, and because the schools now had autonomy over their budgets and staffing, their plans could be carefully tailored to improving school performance. A school in which reading scores were down, for example, could:

- ask every teacher to devote more time to reading;
- set aside a twenty-minute reading period each day when everyone sat down to read;
- cut back a specialist (such as a PE teacher) in order to add a reading specialist to their faculty;
- train math, science, and social studies teachers to incorporate reading into their course work.

The solutions were up to them, based on what they felt best served their students' needs.

"THERE'S BEEN A LOT TO ADJUST TO IN THE LAST TWO YEARS. I THINK AT FIRST PEOPLE RESISTED SOME OF THE CHANGES. BUT WE TALK ALL THE TIME, EVERYWHERE, ABOUT HOW WE'RE FOCUSED ON KIDS AND ACADEMIC ACHIEVEMENT. WE NEVER BUDGE FROM THAT. EVERYONE KNOWS IT ISN'T GOING TO GO AWAY; IT'S HERE TO STAY. SO NOW THEY PUT THEIR ENERGY INTO DOING IT, NOT FIGHTING IT."
—JOAN BUTTERWORTH, HIGH SCHOOL COORDINATOR

When the plans were done, each one was reviewed by the department of academic achievement. Some required minor improvements, a very few needed substantial rethinking. But by October the process was finished; each school had a comprehensive strategic plan. The following summer, when we updated our data packets with the latest test scores, disciplinary and attendance records, and student, teacher, and parent surveys, we would find out how effective those plans had been.

HOLDING SCHOOLS ACCOUNTABLE

Of course, a carefully constructed plan with clear objectives and strategies was meaningless if the schools weren't held accountable for following it. So we needed a method of both monitoring and coaching the schools as they put their plans into action. We gave primary responsibility for doing that to our five school coordinators. (Most large school districts have "coordinators" or "zone administrators" who supervise clusters of schools.) We asked them to ask each school every time they visited, "How are you doing on your plan? Have you done all the incremental steps you said you would do by now? How are the assessments going? Where do you need help?" These were not idle questions. The coordinators write principals' evaluations, and the number-one criterion on which principals are evaluated, their school's academic record, rests on their adherence to their plan. We gave additional monitoring responsibility to the director of academic achievement. He reviews each school's quarterly reports to see how many students are working at grade level. When the numbers are lower than expected, he meets with the school to find out why and helps them plan mid-course corrections.

The final piece of monitoring is provided by me. When I visit schools, which I do unannounced several times a week, the first thing I do is sit down with the principal and ask to see the plan. Principals tell me that since I've been making these visits there is a noticeable difference in the classrooms. "We never know when you'll walk in," one principal said, "so now there are very few times you'll see a teacher behind a desk without students around her. There's much more focus on learning."

That focus is paying off. When we updated our data packets after the first year of the schools' new plans, we saw a noticeable difference in the trend lines. Most schools had either stopped or narrowed the gap between white and minority test scores, most had succeeded in boosting overall student performance.

ONE TEACHER TOLD ME, "THE LAST TIME YOU WERE HERE I WENT HOME AND TOLD MY HUSBAND I'D TALKED TO THE SUPERINTENDENT. HE SAID, 'YOU TALK TO THAT SUPERINTENDENT MORE THAN YOU TALK TO ME!' "

HOLDING TEACHERS ACCOUNTABLE

Key to making the plans work, of course, was the teachers. Without their hard work and dedication, the best-conceived goals would not be met. But if we were truly going to hold schools accountable for improving student performance, we had to bring accountability down to the classroom, where the actual teaching was done.

But could we do that? Our contract with the teachers' union stipulated the ways we could hold teachers accountable, and academic achievement was not among them. Could we introduce a new accountability measure without violating the contract? I didn't know, but the notion that teachers could argue successfully that they shouldn't be held accountable for children's learning seemed like an unsupportable proposition. In any event, regardless of a possible challenge, we had to try to institute the practice—because if we didn't try, we certainly wouldn't achieve it.

Therefore, we told teachers that from now on, a portion of their evaluation would focus on whether or not they had raised their students' performance in two areas. We expected them to raise each child's classroom performance, that is, performance on assignments, tests, projects, homework, and class participation. And we also expected them to raise each child's performance on the Iowa Test of Basic Skills.

Immediately we heard complaints. Interestingly, the complaints were not about the notion of being held accountable; as I had suspected, the teachers recognized that accountability was a reasonable component of their jobs. Rather, the complaints centered on fairness. They argued, as the principals had, that it was unfair to hold the same expectations for teachers in low-income and high-income schools. We responded as I had to the principals, by saying, "We don't expect all children to rise to the same level. We just expect all children to rise."

The teachers also objected to our emphasis on the Iowa test. It didn't measure higher-order thinking skills, the skills we'd chosen to emphasize in our curriculum, and the test itself, they felt, was unfair since standardized test scores tend to correlate with socioeconomic status, with low-income children doing less well than children from higher-income homes.

"There is no question," we agreed, "that standardized tests have serious limitations. But they also serve a purpose. The outside world still measures school districts by their test scores, particularly the Iowa Test of Basic Skills. If we want to prove to the world that we are doing what we promised, making every child an achiever, we need to hold ourselves to the same measure that the outside world is using."

We also reassured teachers that they would not be expected to raise the performance of low-income children immediately to the same level as that of middle-class children. But the concerns didn't go away. The fact that teachers would now be held accountable for student learning created a palpable sense of tension in the district, which was only magnified by the fact that principals were now giving unsatisfactory evaluations. The accustomed sense of job security was gone.

The tension was not all bad, however; I knew that the majority of teachers were excited by what we were doing. It was nervous-making, yes. It forced them to work harder and differently, yes. But in their hearts they knew that accountability was right and they were motivated by the vision of a district where every student learned.

HOLDING PARENTS ACCOUNTABLE

We had been working hard to encourage parents to become part of our accountability system—by asking them to read with their children and check their children's homework, by making syllabi available to them so they knew what their children were learning, by scheduling more parent conferences and increasing the communication between home and school. All of those measures were essential if we wanted to boost academic achievement, but they wouldn't be enough, because there were too many parents who couldn't, for a variety of reasons, provide the healthy, stable, nurturing environment their children needed in order to do well in school. If we really wanted to turn all of our children into achievers, we would first need to help their parents. So I developed a long-range dream. I began to imagine a seamless social-service net for families. In Seattle we had dozens of public and private agencies providing services to families—but they were not well connected. A family that needed help in one area often needed help in another, yet there was no easy way to access the full range of services. Nor were the agencies easy to find. What we needed, I believed, was a seamless family support system that could be accessed through the schools, a system through which a teacher could recognize that a child was having problems, call the family, and then, with a single phone call, register the family for all the services they would need.

I knew this was a plan that would take years to develop. There would be tremendous hurdles to getting a network developed: Funding, tradition, caseloads, and government regulations all currently kept social-service agencies apart. But creating such a system would alleviate so many of the problems that now challenged us in the schools. So I went to the Alliance for Education, our partner in developing new ventures (you can read more about the Alliance in Chapter 5), and asked them to help us begin a dialogue between the agencies and the schools. The Alliance convened a working group of executives from Seattle's major social-service agencies— the YM and YWCA, the Human Services Policy Center at the University of Washington, Seattle Children's Home, the United Way, the federal and county departments of health and human services, and many others—and this group has begun to discuss the issue. Their discussions are in the earliest stages. It will take months for them to determine the best ways they can work together and months more to agree on ways their agencies can successfully overlap. But the discussion has begun. All the players are excited. They see the need for a seamless system and they share the vision of what we can achieve.

These services outside the schools will help families send us their children more ready and able to learn. But if we wanted to turn their children into achievers, we'd also need families to support our efforts in the classroom. We'd need them to read to their children at night, to check their homework daily, to come to parent conferences, to send their children for tutoring. We'd need them to turn off the TV until the homework was finished, and to talk to their children about what they were learning. We'd have to bend over backwards to get our parents involved, we'd have to make our expectations very clear, and we'd have to make our schools vital centers of their communities by meeting other parental needs.

We began by beefing up the communications from the schools. We made it hard for parents not to know how and what their children were doing. We required teachers to send home syllabi, outlining what they were teaching, week by week, throughout the year, so parents could discuss the learning at home. We informed parents as early as November if their child was falling behind his or her grade and put them on notice a year in advance when their child was at risk of not being promoted. We increased the number of phone calls and conferences at which teachers talked to parents about their children.

We also gave parents clear and concrete assignments. We told them that they had to read with their children for twenty minutes every night, and sign a paper showing they'd done it. We told parents whose children were falling behind that we needed their help to design their children's "individualized learning plan." We created numerous support options to help children succeed—after-school tutoring, Saturday Academies, expanded summer-school programs—and told parents they had to make their children attend if they wanted them to be promoted. We carved out a specific, unequivocal role for parents in helping their children succeed, and made it clear that their children would not be promoted unless the parents did their homework.

But giving our parents homework would not go far enough toward ensuring their participation in our schools. Too many of our parents had had bad school experiences themselves. The idea of talking to a principal, of meeting with a teacher to design an individualized learning plan, was intimidating. The only way to get these parents into school was to make school seem less threatening, to create nonacademic programs in the schools that parents would *want* to attend. So our principals began to develop ways to bring their families into the schools. Using money raised by their PTSAs, several of our lowest-income elementary schools were already doing monthly family dinners. In neighborhoods where families' idea of eating out was going to McDonald's, these schools were serving white-tablecloth, sit-down dinners at which their parents were the guests of honor. After dinner the children would perform, reading aloud or showing off new skills, and the principal would talk to parents about what they could do to bolster their children's learning. Other schools were offering technology classes for parents, classes in job seeking and résumé writing, and classes in English as a second language. Others held classes in parenting. These classes brought parents into the schools for skills they wanted to learn, but also gave the schools a chance to talk to parents about their children's education. Now we are asking our principals to continue these programs and to develop more ways to bring families into their schools. We've encouraged them to think of their schools as community centers; to open their buildings for meetings, to rent their gymnasiums for functions, to use their art rooms and music rooms for community classes. We've encouraged them to create summer programs that offer instruction in sports and the arts as well as in academics, and that serve parents as well as students. As an incentive, we've told them they can keep the money they earn. These, and other programs our principals will dream up, will give parents reasons to come into the schools. They'll give parents a chance to rub shoulders with principals and teachers, a chance to explore their children's classrooms, a chance to become comfortable in a place that for some is frightening and foreign. At the same time, they'll give our educators a chance to talk with parents about how they can support their children's education.

Wooing parents into schools and getting them to adopt unfamiliar behaviors is a tremendous challenge. Progress is necessarily slow. But we believe our efforts are paying off. In the last two years the number of parent volunteers in our schools has nearly doubled. More children are attending after-school tutoring and Saturday Academies than ever before, and the numbers of parents attending parent conferences has risen. Our annual reading campaign, a year-long program designed to produce measurable gains in students' reading skills (see Chapter 5), has encouraged many more parents to read to their children at night, and thanks to leadership training, many more principals are taking the lead in calling parents and making their schools inviting. Our students' performances have risen steadily in that same amount of time, and while many factors are responsible, certainly part of the credit goes to parents—because we cannot fully educate their children without them. When our communities begin to *hold themselves accountable* for promoting the attitudes and behaviors they want, then—and only then—will we have excellent public schools.

WHAT HAPPENS WHEN A SCHOOL DECLINES?

In Eddie Reed's Pre-Integrated A math class at Washington Middle School, Jesse and Caitlin are trying to figure out how much money they can spend to buy a new car. Mr. Reed has given them each a "family profile." Jesse knows that he's the head of a two-parent, two-income family with two children in public school. Caitlin knows that she is a single mother of a high-school-age son. Jesse earns $60,000 a year and Caitlin earns $27,000. They also know, because Mr. Reed has given them these "parameters," that they spend one-quarter of their income on housing, 20 percent on food, and that the ratio between their monthly income and expenses is 4:3. Now they have to use this information to determine how much they actually have to spend on a new car. Before this class project wraps up four weeks from now, they and the other twenty-eight students in their class will have used algebra skills to convert the fractions, decimals, percentages, and ratios into hard numbers in order to compute how much money they have to purchase the car. They will have comparison-shopped for cars in the newspaper and called or visited actual showrooms to see what kind of car they can actually afford. They will go to a real bank to discuss a loan for their car (since that, too, will determine what kind of car they are able to buy), and they will use their monthly loan payment as part of their calculation of the annual cost of owning and operating their car. They will also use formulas Mr. Reed supplies to calculate the depreciation of their car over the first three years of its life. And as if that weren't enough, before they finish their research, they will talk to a human resources person in a corporation or to a counselor at the state employment office to learn about seven types of jobs they could have that would enable them to earn the money necessary to purchase the kind of car they have selected. When they have accomplished all those tasks, they will record all their findings on a poster.

If the students are daunted by the enormity of this task, they don't show it. Right now this class of mixed seventh- and eighth-graders is busy sharing ideas about how to proceed. The class, which is approximately half students of color and half white, reflects the school's population:

Approximately 49 percent of Washington students are African Americans and are in the "regular education" program; the remaining 51 percent are white and are in the district's gifted program. These distinctions seem meaningless now, however, as this eager crew of students in their oversized sweatshirts and jeans brainstorms with each other.

The students are used to these "real-life" projects. Every quarter they are asked to do something on a similar scale, just as they were last semester when, among other projects in Mr. Reed's Number Sense B class, they had to use what they had learned about scale, proportion, drawing diagrams, working with geometric shapes, and recording data to design a floor plan for their dream house. Their house plan had to employ four different shapes (*not* including the square, rectangle, triangle, or circle!), had to be between 3,500 and 4,000 square feet, had to include furnishings and landscaping and be architecturally correct, and had to be drawn on graph paper to scale.

But even the students who didn't have Mr. Reed last semester were not surprised to find themselves tackling challenging real-world problems in order to rack up points because these assignments are a standard part of the curriculum at Washington. Down the hall from Mr. Reed's room, Jennifer Rosenthal is also teaching Integrated Math I, and the students in her class are doing exactly the same thing.

This would not have been the case a few years ago. Back in the "old days," before the math team at Washington jettisoned their old curriculum and developed a new one, the scene in Mr. Reed's classroom would have been very different. In those days the class would have been made up almost entirely of white students (since few students of color advanced to upper-level courses), and there would have been far fewer girls than boys (for the same reason). The class would have been far rowdier, as well. Like all the classes at the school, it would have contained students at varying levels. Those who were ahead or behind the rest of the class were likely to have become disruptive as they either lost track of the material or grew bored. The pace of learning in the class would have been far slower as Mr. Reed tried to accommodate every student's progress, and the learning would have consisted primarily of paper-and-pencil practice sessions, not real-world problems that challenge students to apply what they are learning.

What has triggered these changes in the math department at Washington? In 1995 Washington became a Focus School. The Focus School program is a two-to-three-year program in which the district provides extra money, resources, and attention to schools whose performances are sliding. The schools have one year to reverse their multiyear decline or the district will step in and make decisions about how the school is to be managed. Washington was one of the first schools to go through the Focus School program.

Washington is an enormously complex school. Home to nine separate programs—four special-education programs, two gifted programs, one bilingual program, a program for homeless children, and a regular education program—the school has an excellent principal and a tremendously dedicated staff, but by 1995, the performance of the students in its regular education program was in serious decline. The problem had been masked by the fact that the district didn't disaggregate standardized test scores by student group; they reported scores for all ethnic groups and all academic programs as a single score for each school. The gifted students at Washington (who made up half the student body) caused the school's scores to look very high, masking the fact that students in the regular program had been dropping. In fact, scores for the regular education students were very low. So Washington entered the Focus School program with well-delineated one-year goals: raise the test scores of the regular education students to the forty-third percentile and stop the white/minority gap from growing wider.

By virtue of being a Focus School, Washington had the luxury of doing long-term, "big-picture" planning. Instead of making small refinements in the way they delivered instruction, they had the freedom—indeed, the imperative—to rethink everything about their program. As the first step in their "rebuilding," the staff committed themselves to employing "standards-based instruction." Standards-based instruction is a method of teaching where students are told very clearly before any lesson or assignment what skills they will be learning, and then have to meet a standard of performance in those skills in order to pass.

The first department to implement the new standards-based approach was the math department. No one objected to the idea of radically changing what the department was doing. Students in the "regular" program had some of the lowest math scores in the district, and the teachers had wanted to change their program for some time. In fact, six years before they had proposed to the principal that they restructure the department, but their proposal had been denied: At that time individual schools didn't have the flexibility from the district to engage in such restructurings. So now as the teachers all sat down together, the enthusiasm and the ideas began to flow.

They began by setting new goals for the department. They wanted to:

- close the gap between their white students and their students of color;
- create a curriculum that would not hold students in place but rather challenge them to go as far as they could;

- increase the number of students of color in the upper-level math classes; and

- ensure that all students mastered the skills required in the district's curriculum frameworks and arrived at high school prepared to do high-school-level math.

All that year the math teachers met almost every day after school. Sometimes their meetings went until 8 or 8:30 at night. By the end of the year they had created an entirely new way of teaching middle-school math. The old grade groupings were gone; so were all the old courses. Now, instead of seventh- and eighth-grade regular math, seventh- and eighth-grade honors math, and Integrated I for the really bright students (all year-long classes), they had:

- Number Sense A and B (which covered basic arithmetic and pre-algebra skills);

- Pre-Integrated Math A and B (beginning algebra); and

- Integrated Math I, II, and III: (high-school-level coursework).

Each of these courses was designed for seventh- and eighth-grade students only (the math team decided to leave sixth-grade math as it was in order to ease the transition of sixth-graders to the middle-school environment; they felt it was difficult enough to adjust to multiple teachers, classrooms, and assignments without also having to compete in classes with seventh- and eighth-grade students). And except for Integrated I, II, and III, the courses were only one semester long.

The courses were designed specifically to teach the skills required in the Washington state essential learning requirements (which matched the district's new curriculum frameworks). Students would take each of the courses in succession, taking a placement exam at the end of every semester to determine if they were ready to advance. Students who weren't ready would repeat the course again. Because the teachers had no way of knowing until the students took the placement exam every semester how many sections they would need of every course, the seventh- and eighth-grade teachers agreed that they would teach any course at any time, in order to accommodate the students' needs.

Over the course of their meetings, the teachers had developed lesson plans for every course, emphasizing real-world projects as well as paper-and-pencil practice, and had developed scoring rubrics for every assignment based on the standards, or skills, they wanted the students to learn. They had also developed the lengthy two-part placement exam.

Doing all that work had been draining; the teachers had had to fit it in on top of all the regular planning, grading, and teaching they were already doing. But they had also found it exhilarating. For the first time, they had felt they were focusing as a team on what they were in school to do: help children learn math. In the past there had been lots of meetings, but those had always dealt primarily with nonacademic issues—schedules, absenteeism, when reports were due. Now the meetings were about the substance of the teachers' professional lives. And by fall 1997 the new lesson plans, the placement exam, and the in-class assessments were in place. The new math program was ready to go.

HELP FOR AT-RISK STUDENTS

At the same time the math team was restructuring their offerings, the rest of the staff was looking at how they could increase their teaching of math and reading. Since math and reading were the school's priorities, it made sense to give students as much exposure to and practice in them as possible. Why not incorporate them into classes in science and social studies? The science and social-studies teachers felt they needed help to do that effectively, so Washington asked curriculum specialists from the district to help them develop themes, activities, and assessment tools that would effectively blend the disciplines. Normally that kind of help is hard to come by because the district's specialists have limited time and the demands on their time are great, but because Washington was a Focus School, the school was assigned specialists immediately.

The sixth-grade teachers, meanwhile, decided that they were losing valuable teaching time at the beginning of the year while they helped their students get used to life in middle school. So they decided to beef up the new-student orientation they offered each fall. Instead of a two-hour meeting where students did little more than witness a parade of teachers and learn how to use a combination lock, they designed a four-hour orientation where students would learn more about the school and engage in bonding activities with teachers and fellow students. That way, they felt, when students arrived for the first week of school, teachers could actually begin *teaching*.

All of these changes, the staff believed, would help improve student performance. But these were big changes that wouldn't take effect until the following year. What could they do in the meantime to push student achievement upward during the current academic year? After a series of brainstorming and discussion sessions, the staff developed a list of strategies that they hoped would improve student performance on both an immediate and an ongoing basis:

- *They scheduled two parent-conference periods*, one at the end of the first quarter, the other at the end of the third. Most middle schools did not hold parent conferences, but the staff felt that if they were going to help their students improve, then parental participation was vital.

- *They began to do frequent progress reports on every child.* Prior to that year, Washington had sent home progress reports every five weeks. Now they decided to send them weekly, or even daily, for children who were falling behind.

- *They began to telephone the parents of children at risk of nonpromotion* to discuss their children's performance and involve them in helping their children learn.

- *They created a mentoring program* in which teachers "adopted" a handful of children for the year and monitored their homework and performance.

- *They began to work with students on study skills* as part of the regular course work.

- *They created an after-school tutoring program* that met every Tuesday and Thursday afternoon. Teachers were paid to staff the sessions (using part of their Focus School money from the district). In addition, volunteers were recruited from Seattle University, the University of Washington, the Coast Guard (which had signed on as a school partner several years before), and the parent body. To make it easier for children to stay, the school used money from a city "Families and Education" levy to pay school buses to take the children home after the tutoring sessions.

- *They created twice-a-month Saturday Academies*, also staffed by teachers and volunteers, to tutor at-risk children.

- *In January they added an extra session of after-school tutoring* specifically for eighth-grade students who were at risk of not graduating from middle school.

All of these strategies were implemented during the 1995–96 school year. That spring, after students took the standardized tests, the staff waited with bated breath to see how they would score. Under the terms of the Focus program, the school didn't have to meet its ambitious goals of averaging in the 43rd percentile to avoid intervention by the district, but they did have to reverse the downward trend. Of course, for their own sense of accomplishment, the staff wanted to see their goals met. In June the scores were released. Students in the "regular education" program averaged in the 40th percentile. The scores of students of color lagged whites by the same number of percentage points as the year before. For the first time in four years, the gap hadn't widened. Washington had stopped the slide.

YEAR TWO

In September of 1996, Washington began its second year as a Focus School. Under the parameters of the Focus program, if a school has not made significant improvements during its first year, central administration will become more involved in setting goals and strategies. In the case of Washington, however, no such intervention was necessary; we needed only to support them in carrying out their second-year plans.

Their second-year plans were to get further increases in performance. They aimed to get their test scores up to the 43rd percentile, and to begin to *close* the white/minority gap. Achieving these changes would be hard. First-year reform usually enables a school to make the easy improvements, to up the performance of students who are most amenable to change. Improving the performance of those who haven't budged the first time around is far more difficult.

They began the year by introducing the new math program. Guidance counselors were trained in how to explain the program to parents and made plans to rework the school's schedule at the end of the semester to accommodate the anticipated changes as students were promoted to next-level courses. The school held several forum nights for parents at which they explained the change. The parents, they found, were quite support-ive of the restructuring; they appreciated the focus on specific skills, the grouping of students who were at the same level, and the emphasis on real-world problem-solving. Best of all, they liked the fact that the school was taking a bold, constructive action to strengthen student achievement.

It didn't take long for the math teachers to sense that they had made the right decisions. They found that they loved teaching classes in which they could move smoothly through the material because their students were all at the same level, and they loved the variety of activities each of the courses included. The students seemed to enjoy the classes as well. Students who had asked in their previous math classes, "Why do we need to learn this?" were now intrigued by the unusual "real-world" projects and saw, through them, the relevance of math to everyday life. Students who had been bored in math before now found themselves more involved be-cause the classes were at their level and because the work was far more in-teresting.

The sixth-grade team conducted their new orientation and felt that it made a significant improvement in their classroom productivity during the first few weeks of school; as early as the first week they were able to focus on teaching and were giving students substantive assignments. All the extra support activities that the staff had initiated the year before—the weekly progress reports and parent conferences, the tutoring and mentoring programs, the time devoted in class to learning study skills—began again. This time students had the benefit of those programs for the entire year, not just for the second half of the year.

That spring, when students once again took the Iowa Test of Basic Skills, anticipation about the scores was tremendous. As it turned out, the staff needed not have worried. The students in the "regular" program posted the highest standardized test scores in math of any school in the district, students of color scored at or above the fiftieth percentile. Combined scores (for math, reading, and language arts) for students in the "regular education" program had risen to the 43rd percentile, and for the first time ever, the gap between white and minority students had shrunk.

At the end of 1997, Washington was officially "graduated" from the Focus School program. They had met their goals and no longer needed extra help or attention from the district. Leaving the program meant little to the staff, however. The move toward standards-based instruction continued—and does today. Principal Bruce Hunter hopes that soon the language arts department will do the same kind of restructuring the math department did, and that the social-studies and science teams will follow. He envisions a school in which grade groupings, gifted programs, and regular education programs cease to exist and are replaced by one-semester courses that students move through at their own pace as they demonstrate that they have learned the skills. He envisions a school in which all students are given the level of extra help they need, and in which parent involvement through frequent conferences and home/school communication keeps every family focused on academics. He envisions a school that is recognized across the country for its excellence, and whose staff is recognized as leaders in their fields.

What if Washington hadn't turned its performance around in those two years? It would have undergone a major district intervention. We would have rescinded the school's authority to self-govern and would have sent in specialists to make curriculum, scheduling, staffing, and budget decisions. We would have transferred staff, and perhaps the principal, to other positions, or recommended that they be released. If the school had been seriously troubled for many years and had lost the confidence of its community, we might have closed it, reorganized it, and reopened it as a new school with a new staff and focus. So far, in our Focus School program, we've had very few schools where we've had to take strong intervention measures. On the contrary, we've found that most schools are eager to take advantage of the Focus School program because they desperately want to improve. Schools don't want to watch their children's performances decline; they don't want to feel their community's censure. Teachers and principals love their children and want to see their children improve. They simply have not determined how to turn their school's performance around. In almost every case, we've found that a little help from the district is all it takes to get them back on track.

QUIZ:
WHICH IS NOT USED IN MOST SCHOOL DISTRICTS AS A CRITERION FOR EVALUATING SCHOOLS?

(c) student performance

Schools measure many variables—but student achievement, their single most important goal, is usually not among them. Shocking, isn't it?

CHAPTER 5

WE CAN ACHIEVE THE VICTORY WHEN ... WE MAKE SCHOOL MORE EXCITING THAN THE STREETS

QUIZ:
WITH LIMITED BUDGETS, WHICH IS THE BEST INVESTMENT A SCHOOL DISTRICT CAN MAKE TO FACILITATE LEARNING?

(a) athletics
(b) basic academics
(c) foreign languages and cultures
(d) technology
(e) visual and performing arts

Answer on page 109.

Elvin is an energetic boy. He's small for five, but he's got the whirlwind energy of someone on a mission. He lives in the projects two blocks from Van Asselt Elementary School, where he is in Sheila Mae Bender's kindergarten class. He lives with his mother and older brother, and these days Elvin is flying high because he knows he's going to college. He knows because Ms. Bender told him so. She told him that if he keeps practicing reading the way he has been, nothing will stand in his way.

Elvin has been working on reading as part of our district's annual, year-long reading campaign. Every night he takes home a piece of paper that says "I'm a Reader Leader" and asks his mom to read with him for twenty minutes. When she does, she signs off on the form and Elvin brings it back to school. Elvin has had perfect compliance since the program began. If he can maintain that record, he'll become a Reader Leader and win prizes: a slick white water bottle from Washington Mutual Bank, a basketball or jersey from the Seattle Supersonics, a chance to go to a concert and magic show featuring the well-known band Pearl Jam. Elvin's mother likes the program too. She says she particularly likes the quiet time they get together; those are some of the nicest moments in her day.

We began the reading campaign my first week of school. As a new superintendent, new to education, I was casting about before school began for a bold first initiative, a program we could use to kick off our revolution in academic achievement. One day a retired school librarian, Elaine Quan, dropped by to see me. She entered my office, made a slight bow, looked me in the eye and sat down. "Mr. Stanford," she said, "I know that you are new to education. Let me tell you what I think is the key to succeeding in our schools." She then delivered an hour-long lecture that ranged over many different subjects, but mostly she talked about reading. I listened quietly, utterly mesmerized by her experience and wisdom. When she was done, she bowed to me again, and left.

And as soon as she was gone, I realized that she'd given me the idea for the program: *a massive, district-wide reading campaign*, a campaign that would get the entire city focused on the skill that, more than any other, affected children's success in school. But I knew we couldn't do a reading campaign on our own. Love of reading isn't just a schools issue: It's a cultural issue that requires community reinforcement. If we were going to get our kids to read, we'd need their parents and the community to help. Parents would have to be enlisted to read to their children every night, and to make sure their children did their reading homework. Radio stations would need to broadcast messages encouraging children to read. Local heroes—the Mariners, the Supersonics—would need to come to schools to talk to children about the importance of reading. And volunteers, thousands of volunteers, would need to come to the schools to tutor children one-on-one and read with them in small groups.

But how could we generate such community involvement? Where would we find so many volunteers? Would businesses agree to lend us their employees in an effort to boost the literacy of our city? Would they underwrite the creation of campaign materials? Would they provide prizes for our contests? I believed they would. I also knew we had an ally who could help us recruit sponsors.

Just a month or two before, the business community had formed a non-profit organization called the Alliance for Education, whose mission was to recruit community resources for the schools. With its ties to business, the Alliance was the perfect partner to help us find sponsors, so I approached them with the idea. They loved it. Immediately they pulled together a committee of community representatives, including executives from Boeing, Washington Mutual Bank, Cole & Weber—a local advertising agency—literacy groups, and the library, and the committee helped us plan the campaign and recruit corporate partners.

In addition to the committee members, KING-TV, the Northwest Bookfest (an annual bookfair), the Northwest Booksellers Association, the Seattle Supersonics, Golden Grain, and BP Oil signed on as sponsors. All these organizations liked the idea of working on a highly visible campaign that touched so many sectors of the city. They felt it would build name recognition for their companies and would make a long-term difference in children's lives. Each sponsor agreed to send employees into the schools, supply prizes, and fund special events that promoted reading.

Meanwhile, each school designed a strategy for boosting reading. Some added a daily period for sustained silent reading, others created reading incentive programs that offered prizes to students who read to certain levels. All schools emphasized reading in every subject area and asked students to do more reading aloud. To help the students who needed remedial work, we began a massive drive for volunteers. Schools recruited from their parent communities; I asked for volunteers in my daily speeches to business and nonprofit groups. Years before, Seattle had created a program called PIPE, Partners in Public Education, in which corporations "adopted" an individual school. Now the Alliance for Education sent information about the reading campaign to the eighty businesses that had become PIPE partners, asking them to send their employees into the schools to read. Cole & Weber created public service announcements for the campaign, and with funding from Boeing and other companies, these PSAs ran on TV and radio stations, encouraging people to help out in the schools. Between September and June of that year (1995–96), the number of volunteers in the schools rose from 450,000 to 670,000.

At the same time, we campaigned on the home front. We sent newsletters home to parents describing the campaign. "You taught them to talk; now help us teach them to read," we urged, and asked them to read with their children nightly. We gave a book to every kindergartener to begin her own home library, and with the help of KING-TV we held a book drive to collect "gently used" books for families who couldn't afford them. TV and radio stations reminded parents to read with their children at night, and that winter, when snowstorms shut the schools for a day, instead of the usual storm closure announcements, the radio stations ran this announcement every twenty minutes: "The Seattle Public Schools are closed today. Please stay home and read."

By the end of the year students had spent more hours reading in school and at home than ever before. Chains of paper cars and airplanes snaked through the hallways of the elementary schools advertising the names of every book the children had read. Principals, who had promised to sit on the school roof for a day or to come to school in crazy costumes if students read to a certain level, did so; I kept my promise to arrive at an elementary school in an army helicopter. (I'd hoped to pilot it myself and rappel out, but army regulations wouldn't let me.)

The real reward, however, was the students' academic performance. Teachers reported gains in reading comprehension. Students' writing improved (we did formal writing assessments for the first time that spring so we had no baseline against which to measure improvement, but teachers said they saw a blossoming of students' ideas and an increased ability to express them. The following year, when we did both the campaign and the writing assessment again, 4.5 percent more students met writing standards for their grade than had the previous year). Teachers noted that students' vocabularies had improved and that their interest in reading had risen. School librarians said they had trouble keeping enough books on the shelves. That spring when we administered the Iowa Test of Basic Skills for the first time (we switched that year from the easier California Achievement Test), scores remained on a par with where they'd been the year before. Because test scores commonly drop when a district switches tests, these scores reflected an *improvement* in performance. (The following year, after we held the campaign again, students' scores did rise in every area.) We believe this overall gain in academic achievement was directly due to the emphasis on reading.

Reports from parents were favorable too. We heard stories about children who had asked their parents to buy them books instead of toys, about children who after years of struggle had suddenly blossomed into readers. One of our school-board members went to a friend's home for dinner. Midway through the evening, the young son turned off the TV and headed upstairs. "Where are you going?" his mother asked. "I'm going upstairs to read," he answered. "The superintendent says I have to read twenty minutes every night." Another mother said she thought she'd heard every excuse under the sun until her daughter came up with a new one: She refused to take the garbage out because she had to do her reading.

Since its inception the campaign has grown. New sponsors have come on board and we've increased the number of programs. And last fall we received our biggest reading contribution yet: Craig McCaw, the telecommunications pioneer, donated $1 million to create a program in which high-school students will get paid to tutor elementary students in reading. It is the excitement, visibility, generosity, and impact of the campaign that made this contribution possible. We've now made the campaign a permanent part of our operations.

ENABLING LEARNING

By three months into the reading campaign it was clear that it was working. Schools were excited about seeing the reading message in the media; it made them feel supported. An unprecedented number of volunteers were coming into the schools. Students were excited about becoming Reader Leaders and were reading twenty minutes every night to do it. The chains of paper cars and airplanes were growing. We began to realize how powerful an educational campaign could be when the community got involved.

At about that same time, my staff introduced me to the ideas of Howard Gardner. Gardner is the developmental psychologist at Harvard University who believes that all people learn in different ways using seven different types of intelligence. Some people learn visually and spatially, for example, processing information by drawing, building, and imagining. Others learn kinesthetically, processing information through movement, dance, and touch. Still others learn interpersonally, processing information through talking and sharing information with others. Gardner maintains that if schools want to reach all children and make it possible for all to learn, they need to offer rich and varied learning experiences that enable children to learn in their own way.

These ideas resonated with me. I had no formal background in education, but my observations, just since coming to the field, seemed to bear them out. I'd been spending time in the schools, and everywhere I went I saw children who were not turned on to learning. They sat at the back of the room, laughing with friends, oblivious to the books and the teacher in front of them. They were barely keeping up, or were falling behind in academics—yet it was clear that they had tremendous talents and interests in other areas. I saw children who sketched fantastic drawings while their teachers lectured at the blackboard. I saw students whose faces lit up as they sang impromptu choral harmonies in the school yard. I saw one boy who had failed ninth-grade algebra throw a football fifty yards with the perfect arc and perfect force so that it landed exactly where it needed to go to be caught. I'd thought at the time: If we can only keep him hooked on football while working with him in math, who knows? Eventually something might click!

That boy reminded me of *me*. I was a late bloomer in school. I didn't apply myself. It was far easier to play with the boy in the neighboring seat than to listen to the teacher at the blackboard. As you already know, I failed sixth grade.

In junior high things changed a bit. I joined the choir, I was in school plays, I fell in love with sports. The excitement of basketball and football kept me interested in school.

But it wasn't until eighth grade that I had my first flirtation with academic success. I took a French class and, to my surprise, I liked it. French came easily and nurtured confidence that gradually spread to other subjects. At the end of eighth grade my algebra teacher, Miss Lippman, prophesied, "When you come back next year, you'll be older and wiser and it will all be simple to you." And it was true.

Now, as I watched these children I thought to myself, I "turned on" to academics because school kept me hooked through sports, but our children today don't have that option. Even the football game where the boy was throwing was not part of a school-based athletics program because, twenty years before, voters had rejected two school levies in a row and as a result, sports, art, music, and drama had all but disappeared in an effort to focus on academics. Yet despite this narrowed focus, academic achievement had not improved! Now I thought, We're moving in the wrong direction! We can't just focus on the basics. Despite our financial problems we have to *add* to every school! We have to bring back art and music, sports and language, to keep our children hooked on school.

I knew from the army that all people don't excel in the same way. Time and again I'd seen soldiers in training for one specialty moved to another if they didn't have the skills to make it in their chosen field. The army found a way to work with the individual's strengths in order to help that person succeed. Well, I thought, schools need to be encouraging, flexible, and accommodating too. All our children can excel at something; our job is to find their strengths, and then work with them until they succeed.

There was also another reason I believed we'd have to offer more than the basics. As I watched the children in our district, with their expensive sneakers and their logo-emblazoned clothes, as I listened to their conversations about computer games and MTV, as I thought about the world that some of them came from, a world of gangs and drugs and the illicit excitements of the streets, a world of twenty-four-hour-a-day entertainment, I realized that for our schools to be successful, we would have to *compete* for our students' attention. If we wanted to reach them, we'd have to offer subjects they found meaningful and relevant. We'd have to use computers, videos, and the Internet to create dynamic learning environments that matched the high-tech pace they were used to. The burden was on us. If we wanted all our children to learn, then we would have to change the way we taught.

What I began to imagine was a different kind of school; not a school that focused on the basics with a sprinkling of art, music, and sports on the side, but a school where a wealth of nontraditional experiences was *integral* to what and how the children learned; a school where students would study painting, music, dance, and drama, and then use those skills to demonstrate their understanding of history and literature.

How could we offer such a range of programs? Obviously we couldn't if we had to do it by ourselves; it would cost a fortune and we were losing $35 million. But we didn't have to do it by ourselves! The reading campaign had shown us that we could use the community to bring excitement and relevance to the schools *and* have an impact on student performance. Why not engage our community's strengths to make this expanded curriculum possible?

A NINE-PART ACADEMIC PLAN

I began to muse on how we could mobilize the kind of effort necessary to bring the entire community into our orbit. I had searched far and wide for examples and had discovered a wealth of interesting programs. There were high schools with advanced technology labs. There were magnet schools that featured arts and science. Across the country high-tech companies were wiring schools for the Internet, and artist-in-the-schools programs were bringing painters and sculptors into classrooms. I discovered that my idea of bringing the community into the classroom wasn't new—but as far as I could tell, no district had created the kind of partnerships I was imagining *district-wide*. No district had made these kinds of experiences available to every child in every school. Clearly, the challenges would be enormous.

The first challenge would be establishing our learning objectives. What subject areas would our expanded curriculum need to address? We wanted to tap our students' strengths and interests; we wanted to give them the skills they would need to succeed in the world. But what subjects should we offer to meet those goals?

A second challenge would be developing the partnerships. The district already had approximately eighty business partners as a result of the

PIPE program. But most of these partnerships were insufficient and few of them were tied directly to academic achievement goals.

A third challenge would be the planning. Once we determined our areas of focus, once we located our potential partners, figuring out the specific contributions we needed would be a monumental task. What kinds of programs, what kinds of materials, what kinds of pairings between the community and the district would serve our students best? Then we'd need to work with our partners to help them shape their contributions in ways classroom teachers could use.

A fourth challenge would be the expense. Even with our partners providing time and materials, we'd have tremendous costs of our own: transporting students, training teachers, creating classroom materials, and on and on. The development budget would be in the millions, with hundreds of thousands of additional dollars needed every year. How could we raise the money?

All of these challenges were significant, but we felt we had no choice. Our students needed these programs if they were going to stay, and thrive, in school. So with a collective deep breath we took the first step and established learning objectives for a new, expanded curriculum. After meetings with people both inside and outside the district, we chose six areas of primary importance on which the curriculum should focus:

- *Academic achievement* because that is the focus of all we do.
- *Visual and performing arts* because research shows that experience in the arts enhances students' ability to problem-solve, persevere, and work cooperatively in teams.
- *Sports* because the lessons learned in sports—about competing and practicing, winning and losing, striving individually and working on a team—are lessons students need for life.
- *International language and culture* because our district is home to 80 languages and 115 cultures, and because our students will need multicultural skills and sensitivities to succeed in a globally connected world.
- *School-to-work* because all students, regardless of their aspirations, need to be prepared to succeed in the world of work.
- *Special education* because 10 percent of our students had special needs, yet the programs we were offering were deficient.

We also added three additional areas where we felt skills must be built into every student:

- *Technology* because all students graduating from our schools would need to be masters of technology in order to integrate the world of information that surrounded them.

- *Citizenship* because we couldn't assume that our graduates would become good citizens; we had to teach them the importance of contributing to their community and of some day giving back to their public schools.

- *Environmental education* because our graduates would be the future stewards of our planet; we needed to teach them to respect it, conserve it, and use it wisely.

These nine areas became the basis of our new academic plan, the focal areas in which our community partnerships would be developed. Each area was assigned a director whose job was to oversee curriculum development in that area and to help each school implement the curriculum in its building.

THE ALLIANCE FOR EDUCATION

Having defined our areas of focus, we were now ready to tackle the other challenges that stood in the way of the expanded curriculum. Clearly, there was no way we could meet those challenges on our own. What we needed was a partner, an organization that was imbued with our vision and values, that truly understood what we were after, that had links to the business community and could broker partnerships and dollars, and that had a full-time staff that could devote itself to the effort. We found that partner in the Alliance for Education.

The next question was how to structure the staff and operation of the Alliance in order to accomplish this herculean task. The answer, we felt, had to do with alignment. If we wanted the organization to develop resources in our nine focal areas, it seemed logical to structure it according to those nine. So the Alliance hired managers for each of the areas, and in each one it convened "compacts," or groups of businesses and nonprofit organizations that agreed to work closely with us to develop curriculum resources for the schools. Our goal was to spend a year planning in each of the areas, and then, by year two of the project, to begin introducing elements of the new curricula into classrooms.

THE ALLIANCE FOR EDUCATION

We could not do all that we are doing without the Alliance for Education! The Alliance is our fund-raising partner, our vital link to the business, government, and nonprofit communities, our purveyor of outside resources, and our research and development lab all rolled into one.

The Alliance is a nonprofit corporation that was formed in 1995 with the mission of supporting the Seattle Public Schools. It is governed by a board of directors that includes the mayor, executives from the area's major businesses, the president of the University of Washington, the presidents of the Seattle Foundation and the school board, the superintendent of schools, and the president of the Seattle chapter of the PTSA. It has its own offices in downtown Seattle, separate from the school district, and a full-time staff of fourteen. The budget of the Alliance is paid by a consortium of Seattle-area businesses.

Many school districts have nonprofit organizations that "adopt" a school, raise money, or help with school district governance. The Alliance differs from those organizations in that its work is broader. Its purpose—like everything else in the district—is to support academic achievement, to ensure that all students learn. It does that in three ways:

1. *The Alliance works to make the community a vital part of the learning system.* It has a program manager for each part of the district's nine-part academic plan (see page 93). These managers work with businesses, nonprofit organizations, institutions of higher education, and government agencies to locate learning opportunities in the community (from the wilderness, to medical and biotech labs, to theaters), to coordinate them directly with the district's curriculum, and to make them accessible to *every* school in the district.

2. *The Alliance raises money from individuals, corporations, and foundations* to pay for programs that supplement the "basic education" services paid for by the state. As of May 1999, the Alliance has raised $14 million in private commitments. This money is being used to fund the development of a tutoring program in which high-school students are paid to tutor inner-city primary students in reading, the training of teachers in integrating the arts into basic education, the Principal Leadership Institute, and numerous other pro-

grams. By serving as a nonprofit foundation separate from the district and governed by both district and community leadership, the Alliance provides an alternative to the "black hole" of the district's general fund, which turns off many donors.

3. *The Alliance serves as an R and D center for new ideas.* We take new ideas to the Alliance and ask them to help us realize them:

- We ask them to find people who can work with us to develop the ideas. (For example, the Alliance found Larry Rowedder of the Mayerson Academy to help us develop the Principal Leadership Institute; it created compacts of Seattle-area businesses, nonprofits, and government agencies to help us develop new curricula in the arts, school-to-work, and environmental education.)

- We ask the Alliance to find the money, volunteers, and material we need to make the ideas happen. (For example, after Larry helped us develop the curriculum for the Principal Leadership Institute, the Alliance created an advisory board of business and education leaders and brought in funding from Wells Fargo Bank and other sources.)

Without the Alliance we could provide "basic education," as is our mandate from the state. With the Alliance, we are building a world-class, student-focused learning system.

THE VISUAL AND PERFORMING ARTS:
THE ARTS FOR EVERY CHILD

Our vision for the arts program grew out of a visit I made to Concord Elementary School in south Seattle. As I walked through the halls I was surprised to see pairs of students sitting or standing together, alternately talking and listening, while referring to papers in their hands. "What are you doing?" I asked a pair of young boys. "We're memorizing our lines," they told me, and then proudly recited them for me—a rather lengthy dialogue from *Treasure Island.*

When I went into their classroom, I noticed a group of boys and girls avidly discussing music. They were in charge of recording and playing the music for the show and were trying to come to an agreement about which pieces should accompany which scenes. In the corner, another group of children was writing a playbill that would be distributed to every class in the school before the performance, describing the play's characters, plot, and themes.

Upstairs on the school's soundstage, I saw the Concord News Team producing the news. Fourth- and fifth-grade reporters had called for interviews, written scripts, gone out on location, and shot the pieces with a camcorder. Now they were editing them for the final tape. The next day the anchors would take their seats at the news desk and tape the show.

All of these activities were part of Concord's whole-school emphasis on theater. Begun in 1995 at the initiative of the principal, Claudia Allan, the program involves every student in the school in learning a script, performing it before the school, and helping organize a full-scale production. Not surprisingly, the program has generated a huge amount of enthusiasm, along with significant opportunities to practice teamwork, problem-solving, and conflict resolution. It's also given children, especially those who are not strong academic performers, a tremendous shot of self-esteem.

Most of Concord's children do not come from homes where reading is part of the culture. Reading and rereading a challenging script, probing to understand the characters and the plot, are not activities that come easily. But the students are motivated to do them because they love the thrill of performing. So perhaps it is not surprising that the program has produced a remarkable improvement in reading scores. Some of the fourth- and fifth-grade students who had leading roles in plays increased their reading scores by two levels on the Macmillan Reading Inventory. Fourth-graders saw their standardized scores rise by twenty to twenty-five points.

Perhaps if these findings had been unique to Concord we would not have decided to make the arts one of our partnership areas. But they weren't. We were seeing similar results in other Seattle schools that had strong arts emphases, and data from studies around the nation were backing up our observations. In 1993 the College Entrance Examination Board found that among a sample of SAT test takers, students who had studied art and music scored significantly higher than the national average on both the verbal and math portions of the test; in 1996 business leaders quoted in *Business Week* magazine cited creativity, perseverance, problem-solving skills, and teamwork as among the attributes of employees who had been educated using the arts. For all these reasons we decided that we wanted *all* of our students to have the "Concord experience," the daily opportunity to express their creativity while learning basic skills.

However, we wanted it not just in theater, but in all the arts. We wanted every child to have a chance to draw and paint, act and dance, sing, and play an instrument. We wanted every child to have the experience of preparing work for presentation, in a gallery or on a stage. We wanted children whose greatest passion and success came from music or dance to have the chance to nurture their talent by working with professional artists. And we wanted our *teachers* to feel that the arts were integral to their students' development.

This was a far cry from the way the arts were currently viewed and taught in the district. Elementary art students were largely limited to paper, paint, and clay—no printmaking, no serious sculpture, no photography. Elementary music students were limited to singing and music appreciation—no orchestra, no chorus, no individual instrument instruction. Few schools offered dance or drama at all.

To help us find ways to give every child the "Concord experience," the Alliance convened the Arts Compact. Eighty-five organizations joined, from the Seattle Art Museum and Seattle Symphony to smaller organizations such as neighborhood arts centers and puppet theaters. They joined because despite the fact that working with us would mean extra work for their organizations, we would be advancing their own goals: We'd be teaching 47,500 children to appreciate their discipline, we'd be building future audiences and supporters for their programs, we'd be funneling students, and therefore dollars, to their centers.

While one group of district and community educators developed "curriculum frameworks," measurable objectives for what every child should know by the end of every grade, another group of teachers and compact members began planning new arts programs. Suppose, they mused, when the art museum planned its major new exhibit on Leonardo da Vinci, they worked with educators in the schools to develop learning opportunities that were tied to the schools' curricula? Leonardo was a mathematician, scientist, and inventor as well as an artist, and a leading figure of the Renaissance. Visiting the exhibit could lead to questions and explorations in science, math, social studies, and the arts. Working with curriculum specialists or teachers in the district, museum educators could develop educational activities and suggestions that were tied to the curriculum in various grades. These materials could be posted on a Web site where they would be available to every teacher. So no matter where a teacher taught, no matter where a student went to school, they would have equal access to the art museum's material.

As the working group explored the resources in the community, they developed a long list of possible programs, which our arts curriculum director then began to describe to principals and teachers in the schools. Each school would be required to meet the curriculum frameworks, but would be permitted to do it in its own way. By working with the curriculum director, they would find and implement a program that would meet their students' and teachers' needs.

Now, the schools are planning their offerings, and the Alliance is calculating the costs of implementing these programs district-wide. The costs will not be small. To raise the money, the Alliance is preparing a prospectus for corporate investors and foundations, a list of the specific items investors can buy. Indeed, the Alliance has raised $350,000 to cover arts field trips for students district-wide, and training for teachers in integrating the arts into their curricula. Similar investments over the next few years will enable us to roll out these programs district-wide.

SIGHTS AND SOUNDS OF EXCELLENCE

Imagine seeing your child perform on the stage of your city's finest professional theater. Imagine the thrill he or she would feel performing in such a prestigious hall to an audience of 3,000 people. Imagine the diligence with which she would work to polish her performance, and the personal excellence she would attain as she worked to be the best she could possibly be. That is the experience we give to our young actors, artists, dancers, and musicians once a year at an event called Sights and Sounds of Excellence.

The idea for Sights and Sounds occurred to me my first year in the district as I visited our schools and heard and saw how talented our students were. I was seeing artwork as good as some I'd seen in galleries. I was hearing jazz bands and orchestras that could have been playing on the stage. I thought, My gosh! We have to show the city how outstanding our students are in the arts! So I called Virginia Anderson, director of the Seattle Center, which manages the Opera House, Seattle's premier performing arts facility, and, thanks to Virginia, the city agreed to lend us the Opera House, complete with stage crews, lighting crews, janitors, and ushers, for one night, free of charge.

Over the next several months our arts teachers worked with students to prepare for the event, selecting students at all levels from across the district. The chosen students were elated and worked incredibly hard to prepare. By the night of the event, as they stood backstage in their costumes, or out in the lobby near their artworks, they felt (alongside their opening night jitters) an enormous sense of pride. That feeling was only enhanced the following day when one of the city's leading newspapers covered the event with a large color photo.

Since then, we have done Sights and Sounds of Excellence every year. In each of the last two years we have found corporate sponsors who underwrote our costs. As a result, the money we've earned from ticket sales has gone to fund other arts programs. We anticipate that Sights and Sounds of Excellence will remain our premier arts showcase for many years to come.

THE SCHOOL-TO-WORK COMPACT: PREPARING EVERY STUDENT FOR LIFE AFTER HIGH SCHOOL

"How did you decide to be a bus driver?" "Did you have to take a test?" "Do you have to be able to read?" The children called out their questions, shyly at first, then with more confidence. The second-graders from Sanislo Elementary School were exploring the world of work in downtown Seattle as part of their career awareness curriculum. So far they'd met a museum curator and docent; a hotel doorman, manager, and chef; and a farmer and a vendor at the public market. Now they were interviewing the driver of a city bus. The bus driver laughed at the barrage of questions and answered them as if he were on prime time television. Yes, he had to be able to read; yes, he'd had to take a test; no, he hadn't wanted to be a bus driver all his life.

Back at school the second-graders debated the pros and cons of all the jobs they'd seen, then mapped the class's preferences on a chart. Bus driver and chef topped the list, with hotel manager coming in a close third. For these mostly poor and minority children, the trip had been an awakening. Most had never been inside a hotel or museum before. For some it was their first visit to downtown Seattle. None had considered job possibilities beyond fireman, policeman, TV star, athlete, or astronaut. The sheer enthusiasm of their discussion was exhilarating.

While the second-graders were conducting their interviews, 150 high-school students were ten miles south of the city at a training center at the Boeing Corporation designing a home entertainment center for Bill Gates. They'd figured out how to get to the center by city bus and managed to show up on time for the 8:30 training, and now, spread out over eight classrooms, they were sitting in small groups at computer screens, working on their class assignment. Each group hoped to convince "Bill" that theirs was the package to buy. When they finished their presentations they would use HTML programming language to create their own Web pages.

These students are at a weeklong Boeing computer technology camp, part of a high-school internship program called Urban Scholars in which

Boeing employees are the trainers. Before they came to camp they had eleven sessions of basic job-skills training taught at the *Seattle Times*, the Bon Marché Department Store, and other Seattle-area businesses. When school ends for the year, they'll each have a mentored summer job for which they will have to apply formally. For these students, as for the second-graders, this introduction to work skills is an eye-opener. They were chosen for the program because they were "at-risk," full of potential but marginal at meeting goals. The program is designed to catch them before they slip through the cracks, to give them the skills and the attitude they'll need to make it in a job. Both these programs are part of our school-to-work program.

When we sat down to design a school-to-work program, the need for such a program was clear. Many of our high-school students' plans for the future were no more realistic than those of the Sanislo second-graders *before* they took their field trips. Students who were not on target to graduate were planning to be doctors! Many lacked the basic skills they needed to get and hold a job. Most had little idea of what they would do when the doors of high school closed behind them. We already had a vocational/technical program, as most districts do, with high-school "career labs" that taught woodshop and automotive skills. But these programs were far too narrow. They limited students to what they could learn in school when what we needed to be teaching was how to thrive *out there*. We needed to get students out of the classroom and into the offices and factories, laboratories and retail stores where they would one day be working.

With this vision in mind we asked the Alliance to convene a compact, or governing board, for our school-to-work program. The Alliance recruited executives from Boeing and Immunex, the president of the University of Washington and the chancellors of the community colleges, the mayor and the county executive, representatives from United Way and nonprofit agencies, and the head of the King County Labor Council. Each member pledged the resources of his organization to help us develop the system.

Within weeks, representatives from these organizations had been organized into subgroups to plan different aspects of the program. One group developed a grade-by-grade list of skills and experiences that every child should have in order to graduate ready to work. The list included school-based experiences, career awareness experiences, career planning activities, work site experiences, and career specialization experiences. In effect, the list formed a blueprint for career preparation that all students could follow regardless of their career aspirations.

Another subgroup of the compact worked with our staff to break the world of work into four "career pathways" into which most careers would fit. They selected health and human services; engineering, science, manufacturing, and technology; arts, media, and communications; and business and marketing. These pathways would be used to help us give students the broadest exposure to the world of work, while eventually enabling them to pick a career that was right for them.

With the four pathways set, we began to focus on the elementary schools. What kinds of experiences could we provide for children to make the grown-up world of work seem relevant? To test different models, we used local and federal grants to develop four "career awareness" curricula. For instance, third-graders visited the ballet and a museum, and attended a children's theater performance to study careers in the arts, and fourth- and fifth-graders visited the Seattle waterfront to study maritime careers and careers in marine biology. These field trips were integrated with each grade's main academic unit so that much of their reading, writing, math, science, and social studies also related to those careers.

Meanwhile, at B.F. Day Elementary, students piloted a second career-awareness curriculum. They created and operated a school "village," complete with its own money, its own bank, and its own medieval castle. Each class planned and operated a business with children filling all the roles. Some manufactured the merchandise, others wrote the ads, some worked the cash registers, while others helped customers and stocked the shelves. All students took part in their business's finances, computing costs, prices, and profit. By the end of the year students had used a tremendous amount of reading, writing, and math to operate the village, they had learned to work cooperatively in teams to make their businesses run, and they had developed firsthand knowledge about such basic business skills as profit and loss, inventory, marketing, and sales.

At the same time the elementary schools were working on their career awareness curricula, we began to think about the high schools. Developing programs for high-school students would be more complicated because the experiences they needed would be much more job-specific. What did we need to teach students who were preparing for a career in health? For a career in engineering? And how could we provide the enormous number of internships we would need to serve 13,000 high-school students? Again, we approached the Alliance, which is helping us create industry-specific links between school and the world of work. They are helping us shape our curricula so that we focus on skills industries will need in the coming years. They are helping us steer students toward fields in which they know jobs will be available. They are recruiting internship and job-shadow placements from the other businesses in their fields so that we can eventually have the 13,000 slots we need.

Because rolling out these kinds of programs district-wide is enormously complicated, we are doing it in phases. Last year, the first year of the program, we piloted the elementary curricula in four schools; this year thirty schools will use them. By next year we hope to have a curriculum in every school. Last year we provided a job-shadow opportunity for every junior at West Seattle High School; this year juniors at three high schools will do job shadows. Last year 150 students took part in Urban Scholars; by next year we hope to have 2,600 internship placements lined up. Last year we introduced middle-school and high-school students to the career pathways; this year we required all high-school students to choose a pathway and pick a related course from the existing high-school catalog. Eventually all high-school courses will be related to at least one pathway.

THE ENVIRONMENTAL EDUCATION COMPACT: GROWING 47,500 GREEN GUERRILLAS

Outside Whitman Middle School, a boy in a sweatshirt and jeans that look like they belong to his older (much, much older) brother is inspecting a bush covered with dark blue berries. "Huckleberry," he announces. "Salal," counters a girl standing near him. She points to a drawing in a guidebook to northwest plants. "See, it has bigger leaves." Nearby two other students are hunched near the ground. "There he goes, see him?" A dark-haired girl points toward a patch of tall grass where a frog has disappeared. "Okay," her partner agrees, and writes "frog" under a column labeled "Wildlife" on her clipboard. These students are creating a wildlife habitat in an open area next to their school.

The Whitman students are engaged in this project thanks to a grant from the National Wildlife Federation. The Whitman habitat is one of many projects now underway in our schools as a result of our curriculum emphasis on environmental education. I began thinking about environmental education when I first arrived in Seattle. As a newcomer to the Pacific Northwest I was struck not only by the beauty of the area, but by people's passion about it. The mountains, the evergreen forests, the inescapable presence of ocean, lakes, and rivers, all seemed to be integral to the area's identity and pride—and spurred passionate debate among the citizens as they wrestled with issues of how to preserve it.

To give our children the knowledge they would need to make wise decisions about the world they would inherit, we decided to make ecology one of our nine areas of academic focus. But how to turn that good intention into academic programs? I called Dennis Hayes, president of the Bullitt Foundation, a local foundation with a focus on the environment, and asked him to help us figure out a way to encourage our 47,500 students to become "green guerrillas." Dennis convened the leaders of numerous organizations with an interest in the environment (the City of Seattle Parks and Recreation Department, the Audubon Society, the Governor's Council on Environmental Education, the Trust for Public Lands, and others), and under the direction of the Alliance for Education, this group became our Environmental Education Compact. The Bullitt Foundation gave us a leadership grant of $50,000 to begin planning and developing projects, Jane Goodall came to kick off our initiative at a day-long event, and in May 1996, we officially launched the effort.

One of the first things we did was hold a planning retreat of the forty organizations in the compact. The goal of the retreat was to determine what critical gaps existed in the school district and where we needed to focus our efforts. We ended the retreat with a list of three primary goals:

- to link students with the many organizations in the community that could provide environmental education experiences;
- to develop environmental education projects that would also serve as "service learning" projects since "service learning," or volunteering, was another of our nine curriculum emphases; and
- to train teachers in all disciplines to use the environment as a theme, because we believed that environmental education projects could be used for teaching math and science, reading and writing, the arts and social studies.

The compact formed work teams to pursue each of these directions. As with the arts and school-to-work initiatives, their goal was to develop not a series of discrete programs that could be implemented in individual schools, but rather district-wide programs that would give every child in the district equal access to environmental experiences. We wanted to create a universe of experiences that tied directly to the curriculum and that could be made available to every teacher in every school.

The first project to get off the ground was a field-trip program for kindergarten through fifth-grade students. The district had just received a grant from the National Science Foundation to use a series of hands-on kits for the teaching of science in the elementary grades. (The kits employed the "inquiry based" approach to teaching science, in which students learn by posing questions and then devising experiments with which to answer them, rather than by doing preformulated experiments that have been laid out in a textbook.) Craig MacGowan, a retired marine biology teacher from Garfield High School, came up with the idea of

developing a set of elementary-school field trips that were tied directly to
the NSF curriculum. Craig knew how random district field trips were and
how hard it was for teachers to plan them, so he proposed acting as an
intermediary between the community organizations and the schools. He
offered to select the community organization whose mission best related
to each grade's environmental NSF kit, and then work with those organizations to develop hands-on field trips that tied directly to the kit. Did
the aquarium lend itself to the fourth-grade ecosystems kit because students could study the various ways sea creatures are adapted to their environment? Then he would work with the aquarium education staff to
develop a field trip in which sixty fourth-graders at a time could come and
work with aquarium staffers to see, touch, and learn about those adapta-
tions firsthand. In addition, he would schedule the field trips for every
school so that for each class the trip would happen automatically as part
of its NSF curriculum.

Craig's proposal perfectly fit our objectives for the environmental
education initiative, so Craig approached the twenty-five organizations whose programs best matched the science kits (the zoo, the aquarium, the Burke Museum at the University of Washington, the county
hazardous waste and wastewater departments, several parks and outdoor
education sites, several recycling centers, and the city's electric utility).
The organizations were happy to participate. They all served Seattle
schoolchildren already and were happy to have our use of their facilities
organized and planned in advance. They liked the idea of supporting
the schools in an environmental program since that meshed with their
own goals, and of course they appreciated the fact that admission fees from
our classes would bring them a sizable amount of money. So with funding
from two local foundations and the North American Association for
Environmental Education (NAAEE), we began to pilot the program.
In 1996–97 six schools participated; in 1997–98 the number grew to
twenty-three. In the 1998–99 school year thirty-one schools will participate, and the number will climb until all sixty elementary schools are on
board.

But we didn't want the field-trip resources to be available only to the
elementary schools. So to make them and other environmental resources
available to all teachers, we also created an environmental home page on
the World Wide Web. Developed in partnership with the Seattle Public
Library, the home page links students and teachers with field-trip opportunities, curriculum ideas, resources in environmental education, and
schools and students in the United States and abroad. We aimed to create
a kind of "one-stop shop" for teachers and students interested in pursuing
environmental education.

The Environmental Education Home Page: http://seeh.spl.org/>

While Craig was creating the field-trip program, the team working on linking environmental education with service learning was also hard at work. In partnerships with the city of Seattle, the National Wildlife Federation, the YMCA Earth Service Corps, Youth for Environmental Services, VISTA, and other organizations, they developed projects that took students in grades K through 12 out of their classrooms and into neighborhoods and wilderness areas to do projects that both contributed to the community and provided cross-disciplinary learning opportunities. Students worked to clean up streams, restore salmon runs, plant native plants along riverbanks to prevent erosion, help restore a wilderness forest, and analyze sources of water pollution. Back in their classrooms, they analyzed the chemical makeup of contaminated water; studied soils under a microscope; discussed the impact of humans on the environment; researched native plants on the Internet; prepared and conducted interviews with specialists in ecology, horticulture, and wildlife management; examined the impacts of logging on a community and on the environment; and studied the growth of a forest through its multiple stages. All of these activities, which took place in approximately thirty schools, were the result of pilot projects funded by the National Wildlife Federation, the NAAEE, and other environmental funding organizations. The Alliance is now looking for additional money to extend these pilots to every school in the district. In the meantime, each school that has done a project has documented what it has done, and its records are made available to other schools. In this way, even before we receive additional funding, other schools can begin to replicate the projects.

The area that is the slowest to get off the ground is teacher training. We have used grant money to provide scholarships to teachers to attend environmental-education workshops held by other organizations, and the National Wildlife Federation has trained teachers in ten schools to develop and use schoolyard habitats, as the teacher at Whitman has done, as an element in a cross-disciplinary curriculum. But we hope, over the next few years, to find enough money to do more comprehensive teacher training. We would like to be able to train teachers at every level and in every subject in how to incorporate environmental activities into their curriculum. Research has shown that hands-on environmental service projects, especially in middle and high school, can help students maintain or recapture an interest in science, and that if the environmental activities are used in other curriculum areas, the students' interest will spread to those as well. Environmental education can be one more way to reach those children who are not turned on—at least initially—by academics.

We have accomplished these projects with approximately $225,000 in grants, garnered over the last two years. The wide range of the projects has been made possible by the fact that our partners—especially the city of Seattle—have been extremely generous in donating time and services. We discovered, when we took our vision to the community, that there are many organizations that share our goal of raising a generation of environmental stewards.

SOMEDAY . . .

Three years ago I had a vision of what our schools could become, and now, just three years later, they are starting to achieve that vision; they are truly becoming hubs of community-wide learning. But watching that progress is sparking new visions. Why should we limit our partnerships to businesses and nonprofit organizations? Why not partner with the city and county too?

Why, for instance, must schools and county mental-health organizations be mutually exclusive? Where is the need for mental-health services greater than among the teenage population? Stress, peer pressure, and self-doubt are rampant; the risk of suicide is high. Yet most teens, seeking independence from their parents, have few, if any, stable sources of adult guidance. Why not place county mental-health facilities *in* our middle schools and high schools?

Why shouldn't schools be licensed by the county to administer nicotine patches? Most smoking starts during the teenage years. High schools already teach the dangers of smoking; some even offer cessation programs. Why not go a step farther and do something even more effective? And why not partner with the county to fight teenage crime? Why not use students' driver's licenses, one of their most prized possessions, as a crime deterrent? Get caught with a weapon, in school or anywhere; get caught associating with a gang; get caught riding in a car that contains a weapon, and you lose your driver's license (or your chance to get a learner's permit) for at least a year.

Such partnerships raise a fundamental question: *What is the role of school?* Is it just to teach our children the reading, writing, and 'rithmetic skills they'll need to get a job? Or is it something larger? If our role is to help children achieve, to help them be the best they can possibly be, shouldn't we be concerned with their mental and physical health, and with their ability to harm themselves and others? Some people complain that our public schools are trying to do too much, but I think just the opposite. I think schools can do much *more*. We just need to expand the way we define our role—and then form partnerships with our communities in order to accomplish it.

ALL YOU HAVE TO DO IS INSPIRE—THEN ASK!

When we initiated these programs, we did it because it was the only way we could comprehensively create and offer the programs our students needed. What we didn't realize was how invigorating the partnerships would be to the community as well as to the schools. We were surprised by the eagerness with which our prospective partners embraced it. Businesses and individuals who had never given money to the schools suddenly began to do so—because we were offering investment options that advanced their own interests. People who had never thought they might have something to offer to children found themselves leading field trips through their work sites, or hosting student interns, or advising us on what our graduates will need to know to get jobs in their field. People who had never thought about the schools' importance to Seattle's future began voting for school levies because they saw the relationship between their own lives and the schools. In every area, people who had no connection to the schools found themselves taking on roles to make these programs real—because they were as excited by our visions as we were. In effect, by broadening our curriculum and developing these partnerships, we've begun putting the public back into *public* education.

QUIZ:

WITH LIMITED BUDGETS, WHICH IS THE BEST INVESTMENT A SCHOOL DISTRICT CAN MAKE TO FACILITATE LEARNING?

All of the following: athletics, basic academics, foreign languages and cultures, technology, and visual and performing arts.

Children are motivated by different things and learn in different ways. School districts need to work with their communities to find resources in all of these areas and bring them into the schools.

Checklists for Change—How to Help the Public Schools in Your Community Achieve the Victory

- Love every child entrusted to your care. Believe that every child will learn. Don't write off any child based on past performance.

- Keep adult issues out of the classroom.

- When your school is considering changes, evaluate every change by asking, Is this in the best interest of the children?

- Participate in proposed changes. Make your views heard. Remember that while change is uncomfortable, it is often necessary. Give changes a chance. What seemed unacceptable at first may become positive after a period of adjustment.

- If there are changes you'd like to see in your school, take them to your principal and your school governing board. Build support for your ideas with other teachers. Look for successful examples of your ideas in other schools.

- Hold all your students accountable to the same standards, regardless of their ethnicity or socioeconomic status.

- Hold your students' parents accountable: Send home assignments for them to do with their children; call and ask how the homework is going. We cannot force parents to help us educate their children, but if we give them the tools and the encouragement, we can help them begin.

- Ask your principal to bring in community resources that support your work in the classroom: volunteers, money, equipment, materials, and opportunities for field trips and job shadowings.

- Develop a plan for using volunteers so that when they come, they feel like help to you rather than a burden, and so that they feel welcome rather than intrusive.

- Assess your students frequently, not just two or three times a semester, so that you have an objective sense of how well they are doing.

- Stop promoting children who can't do the work. They will only get farther and farther behind. Create individualized plans for children who are behind—and for those who are ahead.

- Communicate frequently with parents. Give them small, concrete assignments. Most parents have the same goals for their children that you do—but they need your help in knowing how to participate in their children's education.

IF YOU ARE A PRINCIPAL . . .

- Articulate a clear vision for your school.
- You are responsible for the climate in your school. Make sure the focus is on children.
- Recognize that your role is 75 percent business leader and 25 percent educator. If you are not comfortable in that role, get additional business training. Ask your superintendent and your local business community to help.
- Market your school to your local business community. Tell them all the exciting things you are doing. Encourage them to contribute money, resources, and expertise and to send their employees to volunteer.
- Communicate! When implementing a change, increase communications with everyone who will be affected. Explain over and over again in many different settings what you are doing and why.
- Articulate all the steps of the change: What will change? Who will be affected? What is the time line? What will it cost? When and how will the change be evaluated? What will happen as a result?
- Listen! Hold parent meetings, teacher meetings, and community meetings to gather input from constituents. Hold meetings in your neighborhood so that everyone who wants to participate can.
- Hold your teachers accountable. Set clear performance goals for students and base teachers' evaluations on how well their students have achieved the goals.
- Lobby your superintendent and go out to your community to get teachers the tools they need to do their jobs: supplies, a well-maintained classroom, respect from the community.
- Ask every teacher to give you a syllabus. Check the syllabi to make sure that they cover the district's curriculum frameworks. Send the syllabi home to parents.

- Ask your teachers to report to you regularly on their children's progress so that you can monitor the achievement of every child. Create individualized plans for children as soon as they begin to fall behind.
- Don't let teachers promote children who aren't ready. Inform parents as soon as you know their child is at risk of not being promoted. Make them part of the child's individualized plan.
- Find tutors in the community who can tutor children who are behind. Find money to pay them, if necessary, by getting grants or corporate donations.
- Call parents frequently. Bring them in for conferences, even in middle school and high school. If parents won't come in, do home visits.
- Call businesses, nonprofit organizations, and government agencies whose work is related to areas of your curriculum and ask what they can provide for your students and teachers: field trips, job shadowing and internship opportunities, classroom materials, in-service training for teachers, access to research documents, etc.
- Don't hide from the media. When a "bad" story occurs, open your doors and let the media in. Even bad stories disappear after a day—unless you try to cover up.
- Create your own good news. Send stories to the media. Ask parents to write stories and take photos. Make it a goal to send three stories a year from each school.
- Write editorials for the newspaper. Ask parents to write editorials on issues you feel need coverage. Use them to educate the public and build support on issues.

IF YOU ARE A SUPERINTENDENT . . .

- Establish the belief that every child will learn.
- Articulate a clear vision for your school or district, including the changes necessary to get there: How will the school or district look and operate when the change is complete? How will students' performance be increased? How will students be safer? What measurable benefits will this change bring, and to whom?
- Articulate all the steps of the change: What will change? Who will be

affected? What is the time line? What will it cost? When and how will the change be evaluated? What will happen as a result?

- Communicate! When implementing a change, increase communications with everyone who will be affected. Explain over and over again in many different settings what you are doing and why.

- Listen! Hold parent meetings, teacher meetings, and community meetings to gather input from constituents. Hold meetings in locations all over town and at different times of day so that everyone who wants to participate can.

- Weigh every budget decision against the following three questions: How will this expenditure help the children learn? How will this budget cut affect the children's learning? Are there places to make budget cuts that will have less impact on the classroom?

- Recognize that your job is a business job that happens to be in the field of education. You need to:

  - make sure your schools are serving their customers efficiently and effectively—market your business to your community. Most of your shareholders (taxpayers) are not currently using your business. Unless you tell them otherwise, all they know about your business is what they read in the paper or see on TV.

  - improve shareholders' return on investment by improving your students' test scores. They are the measure by which taxpayers judge the quality of their schools.

  - develop superior customer service.

  - listen to your customers and respond to their needs.

  - get leadership and business training for your principals so they can run their businesses effectively.

- Decentralize decision making in your district so that teachers have an authentic role in running their schools.

- Recognize that the world has changed: Schools have to compete for students' attention. If they are going to succeed, they have to be more exciting than the streets.

- Don't hide from the media. When a "bad" story occurs, open your doors and let the media in. Even bad stories disappear after a day—unless you try to cover up.

- Create your own good news. Send stories to the media. Ask parents to write stories and take photos. Make it a goal to send three stories a year from each school.

- Write editorials for the newspaper. Ask staff and principals to write editorials on issues you feel need coverage. Use them to educate the public and build support on issues.

- When you are planning a change (such as raising graduation requirements or establishing higher curriculum standards), go to the media and ask them to help you explain it to the public.

IF YOU ARE A PARENT . . .

AT HOME:

- Read to your child every night. Every single night. Work your way through the classics or through the newspaper, just read. The experience of reading together is integral to helping your child learn. If you choose to do just one thing, this should be it.

- As a parent, you are ground zero in your child's education. Everything you do influences how your child will learn. You may be surprised how much the little things can help. . . .

  - Read, read, read—not only should you read with your children, you should openly encourage them to read by themselves. Start a reading campaign right in your own home—reward your children for every book they read (a little bribery here isn't a bad thing, considering the results). Get creative. Do your children like adventure? Turn them on to the great books about Daniel Boone, Tom Sawyer, Annie Oakley, and anything by Jules Verne. Do they like animals? Show them books on dinosaurs, horses, dogs, and alligators. Are sports popular in your house? There are hundreds of great books about baseball players, the history of soccer, or figure skating.

  - Get a library card for each of your children. Show them how to use it and talk to them about the incumbent responsibilities. Make a plan for regular visits, particularly during the summer, when libraries have such wonderful reading programs for children.

- Oversee your children's homework. Set aside time each night, spread the books around the family dinner table, and get down to work. If they don't need help on a particular night, be on call.

- Welcome children into adult conversations. How will they ever spread their wings if they are not challenged to think at higher levels and develop their own opinions?

- Discover where your children's own intellectual curiosity lies by simply talking to them. Encourage them to ask questions. If you don't know the answer, work together to find it.

- If your children like to cook, welcome them into the kitchen. There are lots of great educational tools to be found in the kitchen— cookbooks to read, measuring to be done, directions to follow, fractions to be worked out.

- Make every effort to watch TV with your children. You *will* be surprised by what they are watching. Talk to them about the issues.

- The next time you plan a trip or family vacation, get out the map. Show your children where you'll be going. Tell them you're going to need a tour guide in each state—have your children read up on places you'll be visiting, so they'll be able to educate the entire family along the way.

- When you go to the grocery store, ask your child to help you make change.

- If you're looking for a cool spot on a summer Saturday afternoon, head for a museum or a library, or take them for a picnic in the park—and bring a book.

AT SCHOOL:
- If you want to know how your school is doing, and if you hope to influence its operation, you need to be visible at the school. You need to spend time there, get to know the principal, the people who work in the office, and some of the teachers. Parents who are visible are the ones who are asked to join committees and give their opinions when the

school is making decisions and setting policies. Here are some ways to do this:

- Call your child's teacher and ask how you can help. Does she need help in the classroom? Preparing materials? Chaperoning a field trip? Let her know you're available. If you don't hear from her for several months, call again to remind her.

- Form a teachers support committee. Organize a committee of parents from your child's classroom who are also interested in getting involved. Select a committee head and give that name and number to the teacher. Tell him that whenever he needs help to call the head of the committee, who will in turn recruit committee members for the job. What can you offer? Classroom and hallway decorators; field-trip chaperones; fund-raisers for books, materials, and special supplies; assistants for the school play? Working through a committee spreads the burden—you can raise money or solicit donations from local businesses much easier than a teacher can. And by taking the pressure off the teacher, you are allowing him to put all his energy into *teaching*.

- Call your child's teacher or principal. Offer to be a publicist for her classroom or school. What can you do? Contact local media— newspaper, radio, TV, magazines—with information about a great teacher, a super student, a school achievement (Have the school's math grades gone up? Have a record number of students made the honor roll? The science club's rocket actually works?), or with news about upcoming school events, like fund-raisers, plays, field trips. Get in touch with other parents and have them write letters to the editor. Inform your local media that you're willing to be a liaison to the schools. Even publicizing the projects and accomplishments of the school or classroom to other parents is worthwhile.

- Call your child's teachers and offer to write a biweekly newsletter about what the class is doing. This will take very little effort. Things to include: schedule of upcoming quizzes and tests, news about recent class trips, updates on the biology project (green things growing in egg cartons), fate of the class hamster, winner of the spelling contest, and, of course, a Student of the Week. There are terrific benefits to this; it gives the teacher a venue for speaking to the parents, it lets parents know what to expect in terms of tests, and it involves them in their child's classroom.

- Contact your child's teacher and volunteer to be class historian. Working in conjunction with her curriculum, and collaborating with students, lead a discussion on what is meant by primary source material. Archive the class's activities for that year. Ask the question, What is history? What makes history? At the end of the year, invite all the parents in for dinner and a show-and-tell of what their children consider to be their own contributions to history.

- Some teachers don't readily use parent volunteers. If your teacher doesn't, call the school office and ask which teachers do; then call those teachers and offer your help to them. You won't be helping your child directly, but by helping another teacher you will be making yourself visible at school—and perhaps encouraging your child's teacher to use volunteers.

- Join the PTA and become an active member.

- Read the school bulletin carefully. Volunteer help when the school asks for it. Most schools recruit volunteers for fund-raising events, science fairs, and other activities. If there hasn't been a formal call for helpers, call the volunteer coordinator (most schools have one). Ask what you can do for the school.

- If you work full-time and can't be at school during the day, call your teacher or the head of the PTA and ask what you can do on evenings and weekends. Can you prepare materials? Research curriculum topics? Purchase supplies? A lot of sports events are held in the evenings and on weekends—go show your school spirit!

- Establish a relationship with your principal over the phone. Call her after special events to tell her how much you enjoyed them. Call every once in a while to compliment her on something that has gone well at school. Let her get used to hearing from you and thinking of you as an involved parent.

- Meet with your child's teachers on a regular basis (no matter what grade your child is in). To arrange a meeting, call each teacher and simply request a meeting at her convenience. At the meeting, ask how your child is doing, tell the teacher how *you* think the child is doing, and ask how you can help support the child's education at home. If a teacher balks (most won't), call the school office and find out when that teacher's prep period is and where she is likely to be. Then show up. Apologize for taking up her planning time, but explain that you felt it was important to meet her and discuss your child.

- Join your school's governance committee. Most schools have a site council or a leadership committee made up of parents and teachers that makes policy recommendations to the principal.

  - When you attend meetings and weigh decisions, always raise the questions, Is this in the best interest of our children? Will this boost their academic achievement? Ask for specific answers: Which children will it help? How will it help them? Are there children who will suffer if we choose this course of action? Are the gains to the children significant, worth the disruption caused by change? Are there adults who will benefit from this decision? Whose interests are we serving with this action, the adults' or the children's?

IF YOU ARE IN A COMMUNITY SERVICE ORGANIZATION OR CIVIC GROUP . . .

- Make supporting the schools a priority for your club: Ask your school superintendent or your local school principal *what they need*, and ask how your organization can be a resource. What do you have to give? A network of committed individuals willing to get involved, a community space for meetings, a fund-raising apparatus?
- Adopt a school. Most districts have adopt-a-school programs, where organizations can work with a school to ensure that needs for outside volunteers, tutors, and mentors are met by offering the service of individual members, organizational support, and financial and material resources. (Simply call your district's headquarters; speak with the superintendent's office or the office of the volunteer coordinator.) Match each of your group's members with a teacher so that he or his business can help support the teacher in her classroom. If your district does not

have an adopt-a-school program, offer the resources of your group to the superintendent to organize one—compile a roster of community organizations, ethnic groups, and businesses willing to get involved and ask your superintendent to create a committee of teachers and principals and school board representatives with whom you can work to determine what needs there are and what the community can do to be of help.

- Develop a Get the Word Out campaign. Have your members publicly acknowledge the great accomplishments of neighborhood students and teachers in their advertising and promotion and community activities, whether it's through their individual businesses, their church groups, or citywide events, like a fall festival or the Third Avenue Street Fair.

- Sponsor a Community Day, where for a day volunteers gather to clean playgrounds, paint equipment, do simple maintenance. Coordinate this at either the district level or at a single school. Contact your superintendent or principal, offer to provide the organization and the materials—what you need from them is direction. Where is the most help needed? What schools had to sacrifice custodial work for books? Which schools are in the most need of a little elbow grease? Then get the word out; talk to the local newspaper and radio station about running free announcements about the time and the place. Ask your members to volunteer their time, money, and equipment. Most of all, ask them to spread the word—signs in their windows, flyers in coffee rooms and cafeterias, notices in church bulletins.

- Fund-raising—make public education one of your annual charities. Schools always need money for library books and textbooks, computers, playground equipment, field trips. Pick one goal (because people are more likely to give when they know exactly where their money is going) and have a fund-raiser. Community service organizations have the resources and expertise to mount larger and more sophisticated fund-raisers than the PTAs at the school level. Work with them.

  - At district level, contact the superintendent and offer your fund-raising resources (mailing lists, names and numbers, contacts with the chamber of commerce, telephones and computers, and, most of all, ideas). Determine what is most urgently needed and how much money it will take to address this need; the type of fund-raiser you have should be determined by how much money has to be raised.

- At the school level, call the principal, ask what special projects she would love to have but can't afford (sending her eighth graders to Washington D.C.? creating a relationship with a sister school in Ukraine? sending the whole school to the symphony? replacing all the playground equipment?). Again, determine what is needed and how much it will cost. Then, in tandem with the school and PTA, make a plan. Be creative. Remember, simply by offering your services—that of a community organization—you are bringing to the school a brand-new level of participation and excitement.

- Compile a list of members in your organization who are willing to come into the school and spend an hour a week reading to a student, or one afternoon a month working with a teacher to help decorate classrooms or hallways, and send that list to the principal. Your list should include names and phone numbers of everyone willing to donate their time, what they are willing to do, *and* the name of a member willing to be coordinator of each area: one to schedule reading companions, one to schedule classroom decorators, one to schedule tutors at Saturday Academies, etc. Saturday Academies that offer extra help to at-risk students? Offer to start them!)

IF YOU ARE IN BUSINESS . . .

- Call the superintendent of your district. Ask to see the district's strategic plan. If the district does not have such a plan (or if it does not make academic achievement its number-one priority) offer your expertise to compile one. Offer resources to help them get there: loaned executives, who can help develop plans and budgets; executives who can help attract money from the private sector to implement their plans and programs; support in the legislature to help win stabilized funding and education reform at the state and local levels.

- Call your local principal and offer your assistance and expertise with the business aspects of running a school. Does he need help with:

Budgeting?

Marketing?

Public relations?

Streamlining the systems within his building (e.g., transportation, food service, instruction, building management, human resources, parent communication)?

Developing or computerizing information systems to better manage student data?

Team building and leadership techniques?

- Offer to be a public school liaison to other businesses or to your city's chamber of commerce. Work with the district and the business community to create an alliance of businesses that can work with the school district to help it change.

- As a businessperson, you have enormous resources. Offer:

  - Summer internships for students. (Notify your superintendent's office that your company would be willing to provide a certain number of internships to high-school students interested in X, and ask if they have an internship coordinator to whom you could speak. If they don't, offer to work with the district and high-school principals to develop such a program. This would be a good time to involve the chamber of commerce or an alliance of businesses.

  - Job-shadowing opportunities for younger students. Again, simply call your local principal. Discuss what time commitment you are willing to make (one afternoon a week? one afternoon every other week? one week a semester?). Giving students any opportunity to see what a job is all about is an extraordinary gift. Offer to speak with other businesses in your field or in your neighborhood.

  - A site—farm, hotel, local supermarket, bank, etc.—for field trips. Offer to work with teachers to provide a knowledgeable docent (yourself or one of your employees) to explain how your business works and to answer questions.

  - Office personnel. Allow your employees to take an hour a week to work with at-risk children. Facilitate this by contacting your principal and explaining that you would like to offer your employees the opportunity to tutor at-risk children in her school. Ask her if there is an individual already within the system working with volunteers. (There probably is.) If there is a volunteer coordinator, put her in touch with one person at your company who is willing to be coordinator on that end. The school's volunteer coordinator will help integrate your business's efforts into her existing volunteer program. If there is no volunteer coordinator, offer to assist the school in developing one—by offering to contact other businesses for additional volunteers, and to provide materials and organizational assistance.

- Office equipment to enhance teachers' work in the classroom.
- Office facilities. Does your office have a conference room with a computer, fax machine, and telephone in which seniors can gather to write research papers, complete group projects, apply for jobs or internships, complete college applications? You will need to be able to provide individuals willing to donate their time (one Saturday a month?) to chaperone and troubleshoot with the computer. There are children who simply don't have these resources and for whom such an opportunity may be just the encouragement they have needed but never been offered.

- Invest in your local schools. Give money, but first ask to see a business plan. Ask what your return on investment will be. If your principal cannot supply these things, don't back off. Tell him what you are prepared to give (or simply that you are prepared to contribute financially) but that you and others are unwilling to commit resources blindly. Offer to assist him in preparing a business plan for the school and for specific projects. What do you look for in a business plan? A goal? A budget? A time line for implementation? Your assistance and expertise will be invaluable to him in securing other financial contributions as well. Schools must have outside money to survive, and by encouraging principals to run their schools like a business, all money—whether from the district's budget or from outside sources—will be more efficiently used.

- Use your lobbyists and influence to help local legislators understand that schools need stable funding in order to run like businesses. They can't run with constantly declining dollars.

- Tell your superintendent that you hold your employees accountable for meeting performance objectives and that you expect her to do the same. Ask: What objectives does she hold her principals, teachers, and students accountable for? How does she determine whether those objectives are being met? If the answers do not support academic achievement, use your influence in the community to make this a public discussion. Take it to the papers; build awareness by discussing the situation with business associates and in the business and professional groups you belong to. As a businessperson, you have the power to make people listen and influence change.

- Adopt a school. Most districts have adopt-a-school programs, where organizations can work with a school to ensure that needs for outside volunteers, tutors, and mentors are met by offering the service of individual members, organizational support, and financial and material resources. (Simply call your district's headquarters; speak with the superintendent's office or the office of the volunteer coordinator.) If your district does not have an adopt-a-school program, offer the resources of your business to the superintendent to organize one—compile a roster of other businesses and professional organizations willing to get involved and ask your superintendent to create a committee of teachers, principals, and school board representatives with whom you can work to determine what needs there are and what the community can do to be of help.

- Participate in school district job fairs and career days.

- If you advertise widely—whether it's via print ads or television—talk to your advertising agency about creating ads and commercials that are shot in schools and that feature students and teachers engaged in exciting activities.

IF YOU BELONG TO A RELIGIOUS ORGANIZATION . . .

- Across America, religious organizations have traditionally been staunch allies of their communities, providing guidance and support to families, a haven for children, and a center for neighborhood activities (in addition, of course, to being a source of spiritual guidance). As a participant in a religious organization, ask your church or your temple or your mosque to get involved in public education—and to make these services available to all children.

- Is your church affiliated with a school? If so, ask your clergy how you can work in tandem with the neighborhood public school. Can you share after-school activities such as reading groups, tutoring, even organized after-school play groups? (This may save both institutions money on necessary chaperones and materials as well.)

- Form a schools committee. Your religious organization can provide a pool of willing volunteers for all kinds of school activities. Ask your clergy to form a committee to act as a liaison with a local public elementary or middle school. Then elect one member to contact the principal. Offer her the services of your group. Does she need tutors? Does she need readers for those children who aren't being read to at home? Would she be interested in a book drive? A homework hotline? Is she having a difficult time rounding up chaperones for field trips? Simply offer your church as a source of volunteers and extra help. To facilitate this, compile a list of willing volunteers. Put a sign-up sheet in the common room/library/coffee room or a notice in the bulletin; ask for names, phone numbers, and availability.

- Religious organizations are great fund-raisers (bingo, raffles, bake sales, car washes). Go to your local public elementary-school or middle-school principal and ask what sort of projects she would love to have but can't afford—field trips, pet rats, a new microscope? Offer to host a fund-raiser on behalf of your church. You can offer the congregation as one source of funds, and ask members to use their businesses to get out the word. Not only does this generate funds for the school, it creates a wonderful sense of community and neighborhood support—and it gives the schools a partner in teaching our children!

- Does your church or temple or mosque have an extra meeting room or library? Use this room as a haven for latchkey kids. Call your local school principal or classroom teacher (she may even be a member of your congregation) and offer her the use of your facilities. Tell her you'll provide volunteer chaperones, extra books, and art supplies during that crucial three-thirty P.M. to six P.M. time period. Ask your clergy to announce this at services and put notices in the bulletin and flyers for sign-up. When you coordinate this with a school, be very specific about the number of volunteers you have—don't take in more children than you can care for. Ask the principal for guidelines—are there particular books the children should be reading? should kids simply do homework? or can they play games and do art projects? If you are overwhelmed by the response (too many participants), phone another church in the neighborhood. Explain your program—and your constraints—and ask it to get involved. To ease the burden, you can share days of the week or even weeks in the month. Ask your volunteers for a commitment of one afternoon (2½ hours) a month—that's all it takes to make an enormous difference in a child's life.

- Ask your clergy to develop a formal mentoring program where ten at-risk children are "adopted" by the congregation and mentored through their high-school graduation. Ask members of the congregation to make serious commitments to these children: attention, time, caring, expertise, an open home, and a willingness to do whatever it takes to see them through graduation.

- Ask your congregation to endow one scholarship a year to a state university. What a gift! If your religious organization is small, team up with another institution. Ask wealthy members of the congregation to match the funds you raise. Do this in conjunction with a mentoring program, and watch how hard a child will strive when she knows people care and are willing to take a chance on her.

IF YOU ARE IN THE CLERGY . . .

- Put positive education messages in your bulletin. Feature a teacher in your congregation every month: Tell what she is doing, what projects her class is working on, what field trips they are looking forward to. Feature a Student of the Week—and ask members of the congregation to award him with a treat like a book from the local bookstore, a free hamburger for the student and a friend, or maybe a gift certificate from the local sporting goods or music store. Send a message to our children that working hard in school and volunteering in the neighborhood make them valued members of not only the congregation but of the entire community.

- Preach about the importance of education, and about the values our teachers are working so hard to instill in our children. Reinforce the message that these same values are shared by the entire congregation and that the congregation stands behind each and every teacher and student.

IF YOU ARE IN AN ETHNIC ORGANIZATION . . .

- Begin a campaign to make education a value in your community. The ethnic communities that place education first are the communities that are doing best in our society.

- Offer to work with teachers to educate them about the mores in your culture that may have an impact on how children and families relate to school. In some cultures, men are not permitted to speak directly to women, which means fathers cannot talk to their children's female teachers. In other cultures, competition is frowned upon, making children appear "lazy" in school. Help your local school find ways around those cultural collisions so that the children of your community can excel.

- If your organization sponsors ESL (English as a second language) classes, open them up to families, or ensure that reading classes for children are scheduled at the same times as adult classes. (This will be an incentive to adults—they won't have to find child care and they will know that their children are getting extra tutoring.)

- If your culture's native language is taught at the local high school, develop a partnership with the language teacher. Offer to have members of your organization come in to speak about their own culture, and have the students work with your members as tutors.

- Open up your meeting room on Saturday mornings to children as a haven where they can read, do homework, and work on art projects. Recruit tutors and volunteers from your membership, and from the schools themselves. (Will the local university offer a credit for a semester's worth of Saturday tutoring?)

- Contact the elementary schools that children of your culture attend. Make the principal and teachers aware that you are there to help. Do the children's parents speak English? Can they read to their children? Are they wary of the school system? Do the parents need assistance with the subsidized lunch program? These are all things the school needs to know in order to educate the children. Your help will be invaluable.

- Find mentors for children among your community—and make your facilities available for after-school and Saturday tutoring programs. In particular, keep your eyes open for children who are falling behind or falling through the cracks. If you are unsure what needs to be done, contact the child's principal or teacher. They will appreciate your willingness to get involved; indeed, they may be aware of the problem but unable to speak to the parents, or the parents may be too wary of the school.

- Encourage high-school children in your community to consider becoming teachers. Public schools need more minority teachers.

- Poor minority parents who had bad school experiences themselves often see teachers as people who sit in judgment of them. Encourage parents in your community to see teachers as part of a support network for children instead.

IF YOU ARE IN THE MEDIA . . .

- As a member of the media, you are in the incredible position of being able to influence thousands of minds simply by broadcasting a few words—whether it is through the nightly news, the local newspaper or radio station, in an advertisement, or in the church bulletin. Use this power constructively to highlight public education. Praise a school or a teacher or a student—any coverage of the schools will make your community aware of its children.

- Provide regular coverage of the positive things that are happening in your district's schools. Uplifting and inspiring events happen in our schools every day. Focus on local education heroes—a teacher who is making a difference, a principal who's making things happen, a gifted student or a student who has finally learned to read.

- Be aware of what children are watching—and what your role in their viewing is. Ask yourself before you put a program on the air: Is there a way to tell this story that will have a positive impact on children and families?

- Whether you work at a radio or TV station or in print journalism, make it policy to investigate what is going on in your community's schools. One hard and fast way to effect change is to get the community involved.

  - Cover, in depth, all school board meetings. While only one hundred people may attend the actual meeting, use your resources to bring the issues and discussion to thousands.
  - Ask the community to weigh in—broadcast upcoming meetings.
  - If a school levy is on the election board, give the superintendent the opportunity to make his case—and don't hide it on page nineteen.
  - Follow the actions (or inaction) of your superintendent and school board. They're responsible for educating your children. There is no better way to effect change than by simply letting people know what is going on in their district.
  - Follow the actions of your state legislature. Property tax reform and the setting of statewide curriculum standards are among those pieces of legislation that will impact the way your school district operates.

- If you work on the local paper:
  - Call your superintendent and offer to create and run public service announcements supporting an initiative of the schools (a reading campaign, a homework campaign, a come-to-your-parent/teacher-conference campaign, etc.).
  - Make a schools feature a permanent component of your local coverage.
  - Develop a partnership with the student newspaper or yearbook staff. Invite students to contribute one article a month at the caliber of your professional reporters. In exchange, give them a byline and show them how a real newspaper or newsroom works. You'll be promoting fledgling journalists (and future employees!) as well as ratcheting up awareness of public education, and showing your community that you care about its children.

- If you work in a TV newsroom, make coverage of the school a top priority.

  - Run one positive segment a week on a school or teacher or student. There are thousands of heroes right in our own backyards.
  - Call your superintendent and offer to create and run public service announcements supporting an initiative of the schools (a reading campaign, a homework campaign, a come-to-your-parent/teacher-conference campaign, etc.).
  - Offer internships to interested high-school students.
  - Finish each night's segment with one student success story or run video clips of schools behind the credits of your news broadcasts.
  - Call the media department of your school district and offer to help them with their TV studio.
  - Run segments on where your community's schools stand in relation to other districts in the state. Many communities are surprisingly unaware of the state of their own schools. Informing citizens, constructively, of the reality of their own schools is a very effective way to bring about change.
  - Donate equipment you no longer use to the school district.

- Increase your positive children's programming: made-for-TV dramas with positive themes, cartoons that reinforce positive values, educational programming that teaches children about other countries, cultures, or times.
- Limit your adult-themed programming to after nine at night.

IF YOU ARE IN THE ARTS . . .

- Give extra tickets to your shows and performances to the schools.
- Run summer arts programs for children.
- Go to your local school or school district and say you'd like to help develop an arts curriculum drawing on resources in the community.
- Create an alliance of arts groups whose mission is to support the schools.
- Talk to school personnel about how studying the arts helps boost academic achievement, critical thinking, and cooperation.

- Donate instruments, sheet music, art equipment, stage lighting, video equipment, and other items that are still in good condition but you no longer need.
- Ask artists and performers you know or work with to volunteer in the schools.
- If you don't already have a school field-trip program, create one. Call the curriculum department at your school district for help.
- Get together with other arts organizations in your area to develop an awards program that recognizes teachers who integrate the arts into their curricula.

IF YOU ARE RETIRED . . .

- Volunteer once a week in your local school. There are a million ways you can get involved. Simply call the school and speak with the volunteer coordinator. Tell her who you are, what you believe you have to offer, and the amount of time you're willing to commit. Not sure what you have to offer? How about:

  - Reading once a week to a child (or group of children) whose parents work nights or are unable to read themselves, or who are not proficient enough in English.
  - Offering your services as a field trip chaperone—even making yourself available for one trip a semester will be a boon to a teacher. You'll see the zoo in a whole new light!
  - Visiting a classroom and talking to the class about . . . growing up on a farm? living through WWII? the Depression? seeing television for the first time? watching man walk on the moon? All of these are topics that come up for discussion in classrooms across the country— and you are much more interesting than a textbook.
  - Offering your services to a local church or community center's latchkey program.

- Phone the local elementary school and speak with the principal. Offer to put together a group of senior citizens for his school. Tell him you'd like to offer group support for: fund-raising, tutoring, reading, storytelling. Ask what she needs. Your connections to the rest of the community through friends, social and professional clubs, and as a consumer are invaluable.

- Call your local library. Ask if they have a need for storytellers. This is a great way to read with children.

- Get to know the children in your neighborhood—smile at them and ask their names. Ask them what book they are reading and what they're learning in school. Show them the community cares about their education.

- Support education levies: Your community (and your property value) will rise only if its children are educated.

- Donate a book to your local school library.

CHAPTER 6

WE CAN ACHIEVE THE VICTORY WHEN . . . WE EMPOWER OUR TEACHERS TO TEACH

QUIZ:
WHICH STATEMENT IS TRUE?

(a) Teachers' unions are right to fight so hard for their members. Teachers are the most important element in the education system and must be given maximum support.

(b) Teachers' unions put too many controls over who can teach in our schools. To achieve true reform we need to dismantle the unions.

Answer on page 150.

One Friday toward the end of October 1995, one of our second-grade teachers came to see me. It was late when she arrived—most of the staff had already gone home—and when I went to greet her in the reception area I found her sitting in a chair in the corner, looking rather forlorn. We shook hands, introduced ourselves, and as soon as she'd settled into a chair in my office she blurted out her reason for coming: She wanted to quit. The system, she felt, had ceased to be about teaching. She and I talked for an hour, and eventually she agreed to stay. But I knew that she was not alone in her frustration. As I traveled around the district I saw similar evidence everywhere. In teachers' lounges I heard teachers talk about how tired they were, how little planning time they had, how unrecognized they felt for their efforts. In private conversations in my home they told me how shut out they felt from decisions about how their students learned: decisions about textbooks and curriculum, about the types of teachers hired by their schools, about the kinds of training they could get. From the coordinators who supervised the schools I heard observations that principals played favorites among the staff, that they made decisions autocratically, that distrust between principals and teachers was poisoning the atmosphere and distracting teachers from the task of teaching.

Our district was full of excellent teachers; teachers who genuinely loved their children, who worked incredibly hard, who had tremendous creativity and initiative that they used to help the children learn. But they were being thwarted by a system that didn't recognize their expertise or give them the support they needed to do what they had come to do. We weren't even treating our teachers like competent professionals—and we needed to be treating them like heroes!

One day that fall I was walking past the auditorium in our central administration building when I heard a presentation going on. Curious, I poked my head inside and saw that a group of new teachers was being welcomed to the district. That's great, I thought, it's exactly what new teachers need—to know how much we appreciate them, what we expect from them, how we will support them. But as I watched for a few moments I realized that what I was seeing wasn't the presentation I'd expected. It wasn't our director of human resources doing the orientation. It wasn't our director of academic achievement. It was a representative from the union. The teachers were receiving no formal welcome, no orientation, from us, their new employer, but they were getting a hearty welcome from the union! This incident summed up for me the degree to which the district had abdicated its responsibility for teachers (and demonstrated why the union was so strong). Until we provided the support our teachers needed, we would never achieve our goals. Until we focused all of our efforts on the classroom, we would fail. The union was filling the leadership vacuum. The union was right. "It's the teachers, stupid!"

But if we were going to provide that kind of support, then our entire district would have to change. Somehow we would have to transform it from a district where distrust and disempowerment were the norm to one where all systems nurtured teachers' efforts, from a district where teachers were threatening to quit to one where teachers longed to work. We'd have to make Seattle a "teachers' district." How could we do that? How, in a time of dwindling resources, increasingly difficult students, and 3,000 teachers spread over 100 locations, could we make the major attitudinal and systemic changes that would be necessary? How could we change a culture that had been entrenched for decades? The task would not be simple. We'd have to change the way principals treated the teachers, the way decisions were made in each school, the way teachers were supported in the classroom. We'd have to change the way teachers were trained, the amount of time they were given to plan, and the way they were recognized for their efforts. And we'd have to change all these areas simultaneously. Our students didn't have time to wait for us to do them one at a time. We needed victory in the classroom immediately.

THE CAMPAIGN FOR VOLUNTEERS

The first thing to do, we decided, was to get help for teachers where they needed it most: in the classroom. We had an average of twenty-eight children in our classes—already too many—and now, with our new focus on academic achievement, we were asking teachers to improve every child's performance. We wanted every child monitored; we wanted no child left behind. We wanted every child encouraged. There was no way teachers could meet that standard without extra help.

So we launched a campaign for volunteers in the schools. I went to the business community and asked them to lend us their employees as tutors. We approached community colleges and universities to develop tutoring partnerships with their students. We asked all of our principals to recruit volunteers from their parent communities and from businesses and nonprofit organizations in their neighborhoods. As a result of these efforts, the number of volunteer hours in the schools rose from 427,000 a year to over 670,000. We headed for the million mark.

The volunteers were put to work in classrooms. They worked with individuals and small groups of children who needed extra help. They worked in after-school homework clubs and tutoring programs. They helped teachers prepare materials and joined teachers on field trips and in multidisciplinary projects that required the participation of more than one adult. Their presence meant that teachers who used the assistance, particularly in the elementary schools, had more time to work closely with students who needed extra attention, more flexibility in tailoring instruction to the diverse needs of their classes, and more opportunities for enhancing their curriculum with special activities. Volunteer assistance and the positive attitude about our schools were a first, tangible indication that the district was listening to teachers' needs and responding.

At the same time we were recruiting volunteers from all sectors of the city, we were also going to the business and nonprofit communities for donations of money and curriculum resources. Teachers told us they needed additional resources for teaching reading, so we were generously given a $100,000 grant from a local foundation to purchase books for our class-rooms and libraries. Teachers told us they wanted computer access and in-struction for their students, and research access to the Internet, so we got the University of Washington, IBM, Microsoft, and other companies to donate hardware and software that would help teachers use computers to enhance instruction.

We didn't have money to decrease class sizes across the district; it would have cost $3 million to decrease class size by one student. We didn't have money to buy large amounts of additional materials. But by working with the community we brought resources into the schools that responded to teachers' needs.

GIVING TEACHERS MORE TRAINING

But bringing volunteers and curriculum resources to the classroom was only a first step in giving teachers the kind of support they needed. If we really wanted to strengthen our support for teachers, we would have to change the relationship between teachers and their principals. Our prin-cipals had become principals because they were excellent teachers. But most teachers have never been trained in leadership or management, so our principals lacked the leadership skills they needed. If we wanted our principal/teacher relationship to change, if we wanted our teachers to feel inspired and supported, we would need to teach our principals these skills.

So, as I've mentioned before, we created a leadership training program for principals. (See box on pages 65–67.) We taught them how to develop a vision and measurable goals for their schools and how to keep everyone focused on them. We taught them how to get extraneous issues out of the way so teachers could focus on academic achievement. We taught them how to evaluate teachers, and how to encourage teamwork. And we es-tablished a set of expectations about how teachers were to be treated and valued in our district: Teachers were the professionals on whom the achievement of our vision depended; principals were there to *serve* them so they could accomplish our goals.

We began the leadership workshops in the fall of 1996 and made it clear that we expected principals to begin using the material immediately. Our school coordinators, who supervise the schools directly and report back to me, reinforced the leadership messages, and I, too, reinforced them whenever I met with principals and visited schools. By the 1996–97 school year we were seeing some marked changes in principal/teacher relation-ships. Teachers were reporting less divisiveness in schools; coordinators were bringing me fewer problems between principals and staffs; the number of times I had to go to a school to talk to a principal because of tension with his or her teachers declined. One parent who was very active in her school's PTA remarked to me, "You know, I've been involved in this school for five years and it's always been like a hornet's nest. This is the first year I don't feel that. It's December already and nobody has taken me aside to complain about somebody else or tried to get me to take sides on some issue."

GIVING TEACHERS MORE CONTROL

But improving the leadership skills of the principals would not be enough. Teachers didn't simply need bosses who were collaborative and responsive. They needed genuine input into the decisions that affected their lives. We weren't uniformly letting them choose their own curriculum materials. We weren't letting them make decisions about the types of specialists their schools would hire to meet their students' needs. We weren't giving them a voice in choosing new members of their teaching teams.

The district had already decided to decentralize its operations—to give principals the authority to go along with their increased responsibilities by giving each school control over its budget, its curricular emphases, and its staffing. Now, we needed to make sure that teachers were given a significant role in crafting those decisions. To do so we asked each school to create five teacher-staffed committees. These committees would make recommendations to the principal in the areas of budgeting, academic achievement (making decisions that affected curriculum, assessment, goal setting, and student evaluation), teacher training, hiring new teachers, and school climate. A sixth committee, the school's Leadership Team, which included parents and the principal as well as teachers, would work on overall planning for the school. This committee structure meant that instead of being considered hourly workers whose jobs were to implement policies set by others, teachers would be empowered to use their professional expertise to shape the environment in which they worked. For the first time, they would have a powerful voice in developing the policies and procedures that affected their students' education. What all of this meant for the district was exciting! We were becoming a district where teachers would be charting the course toward academic achievement, where principals were becoming bona fide leaders, a district that truly believed that the victory was in the classroom.

GIVING TEACHERS RECOGNITION

At the same time we instituted measures to improve working conditions for our teachers, I also wanted to increase the amount of respect they commanded in the community. Our teachers worked incredibly hard! They worked a million miracles a day! We needed our community to know that—and we needed our teachers to feel the community's appreciation. So we made a point of recognizing teachers in all of our speeches. As I spoke to groups around the city—to business groups and church groups, to school personnel and parents, to radio audiences and newspaper reporters—I praised the work of our teachers for doing society's most important job. The speeches reminded the community about the uncountable acts of love and dedication our teachers performed every day, of the difference they were making in individual students' lives, of the staggering importance of what the teachers were doing. The reminders built *excitement* about the schools in the community, and as a result more people volunteered, more businesses contributed, more parents reached out to say thank you. The excitement circled around and found its way back to the schools, where it fueled our teachers' fire.

I didn't want our recognition of teachers to be solely verbal, however. Praise is wonderful, but you can't take it to the bank. So I also sought ways we could provide tangible tokens of appreciation. What could we give to teachers—short of more money, which we didn't have—that would make them feel appreciated? After casting about for possibilities, I came up with two: a gold card offered through a local bank that would entitle them to discounts at selected stores, and a special teachers' license plate that would enable them to park for free at selected private lots around town. Immediately several of our administrators grumbled: It wasn't fair to give these perks to teachers only; everyone in the district should get them. They missed the point! The point was to recognize teachers, to single them out, to declare them our heroes whose efforts would win the war. Despite the grumblings, we pursued the perks with a bank and a parking lot company and we hope to have them available soon.

By the end of my first year in the district, most of these efforts were under way. Interestingly, at the same time we were making them, we were pushing our teachers to work harder and smarter than they had ever worked before. We were asking them to change their curricula to conform to the district's new curriculum frameworks, to adopt new methods of assessing student learning, to file quarterly reports on their students' progress, to create syllabi that outlined what they would teach on a week-by-week basis, to develop individualized teaching plans for their at-risk students. We had made it clear that academic achievement was the centerline of our operation and that teachers were required to do whatever it took to raise their students' performance. Certainly there were some who complained about the added responsibilities, but the majority of teachers felt excited. They liked the emphasis on achievement; they were motivated by having concrete targets; they felt as though they were being treated like professionals—as though they were being given both the *responsibility and the authority* to do what they had gone into teaching to do: help every child learn.

A NEW APPROACH TO THE UNION

My first year in the district was also the *last* year of our teachers' union contract. Customarily, we should have been using that year to negotiate a new contract. But I didn't want to do that. Our existing contract was terrible. It encouraged teachers to behave like hourly workers rather than professionals by stipulating the number of hours they could work rather than the goals they were working to achieve. It prevented principals from asking for teachers' lesson plans, thereby stripping them of the ability to monitor what was taught. It made it virtually impossible to fire a teacher who was incompetent. And it gave teachers twenty-seven days out of the classroom each year, effectively turning 15 percent of the school year into nonproductive time. Essentially, the contract protected teachers at the children's expense. There was no way I wanted to renegotiate that contract. I wanted to burn it and start all over! We needed a wholly new contract in order to create the child-focused district we were envisioning. Without one, our progress would be seriously impeded.

Fortunately—remarkably!—my views were shared by our union's executive director, Roger Erskine. We were blessed, in Roger, with one of the most progressive and foresightful leaders of any union in America. He favored a more collaborative, less adversarial, role between the union and the district, and he envisioned a new role for the union, one in which the union was not simply an advocate for better working conditions and pay, but rather a professional development organization working to make its members the best teachers they could possibly be.

Unlike more traditional union representatives, who make teachers' interests their sole focus, Roger believed that the union's real job was to promote children's academic achievement. He felt that an environment that promoted student achievement would automatically promote teachers' interests. Roger also held a revolutionary point of view on teachers who were ineffective. Unlike traditional union representatives, who tend to protect teachers at all costs, Roger believed that unqualified teachers did a disservice to the profession and had to be removed. Under his leadership, the union had initiated the STAR program, a "peer review" program in which the union assigns a mentor to new and/or struggling teachers to help them develop their skills. The program was one of only a handful of peer review programs in the country, and its emphasis on support and training made it loved by teachers, as well as a national model. But an even more surprising element of the program, by traditional union standards, was its policy on teachers who continued to perform below expectations after the mentoring period had ended: These teachers were asked to leave. Roger believed, as we did, that both children *and teachers* gained when they were held to a high standard.

In essence, Roger shared the district's philosophy and goals. We couldn't have asked for a better partner in carrying out the reforms we needed in order to achieve our vision.

SEEING EYE TO EYE

In the fall of 1995 Roger and I sat down to discuss a new union contract. There were five things Roger felt teachers needed if they were to function as high-performing teams:

- input into hiring decisions for their school and the ability to fill school vacancies with the people best suited to their teams;
- input into their school's strategic achievement plan (the document that set goals for student achievement and strategies for achieving those goals);
- input into their school's budget;
- the ability to choose their own training; and
- to be held accountable for student performance.

My administrators and I agreed. In fact, with our committee structure we had already given teachers 3½ elements out of the five: input into their school's budget and strategic achievement plan, the ability to choose their own training, and input into hiring decisions for their schools. We strongly supported the idea of letting teachers fill vacancies with the people best suited to their teams, but the seniority clause of the existing contract, which required us to fill vacancies with the most *senior* qualified teacher, prevented us from giving them that authority. We also supported the idea of holding teachers accountable for student performance and had taken steps to do so (see Chapter 4). So as we began our discussions about a new union contract, we were in the rare position of seeing eye to eye.

Roger and I saw eye to eye on something else as well. We both hoped that we could change the adversarial nature of the contract. The existing contract was a 300-page legal document that discussed every conceivable breach of trust and responsibility that could occur between teachers and the district. What Roger and I envisioned was a document that would recognize that teachers and the district were *partners* in the education of children, a document that instead of focusing on harms to adults would focus on goals for children, that instead of detailing lengthy legal procedures for resolving disputes would state that disagreements would be resolved through simple discussions that focused on our shared goals.

Despite our agreement, however, we knew there would be major obstacles to getting such a contract written and approved. For one thing, teachers would be wary about voting to hold themselves accountable, and those who favored the protections of seniority in hiring would resist dismantling that system. But an even bigger obstacle would be the climate of distrust that existed in the district. There was no way teachers would approve a contract that relied on "shared goals" and "partnership" to settle disputes rather than on carefully crafted protective clauses. How, then, could we get the contract we needed to achieve the district's goals?

Roger had recently returned from Detroit, where he had been working with General Motors and the employees of its Saturn division to help draft a revolutionary "trust agreement" that replaced their former 400-page United Auto Workers contract. The agreement did away with the intricate detailing of harms and repercussions, and in a mere thirty pages established that because management and employees were working toward the same end, the manufacture of a high-quality car, they could work together in a climate of trust; grievances could be talked out in light of their common goals. Well, if a trust agreement worked for Saturn, we wondered, why wouldn't it work for the schools? So Roger and I began to talk about fashioning a similar agreement for us. The idea was not to create a binding contract replacement—that could come later. Rather, we wanted to craft a document that would establish a climate of trust in which a new contract could be negotiated.

Roger wrote the agreement, which stated that within each school, staff and administration would jointly craft a vision and that teachers would have "an authentic role" in making the decisions that brought that vision to life. Disputes were to be resolved as quickly as possible through discussions. Ongoing disputes would be resolved by a panel consisting of Roger and myself, and if necessary, two other individuals.

In the spring of 1996 the union took the trust agreement and contract extension to a general membership meeting for a vote. Of the 400 or so people at the meeting, perhaps fifty were skeptical. But the majority of teachers were encouraged. They felt it was a positive step forward, a chance to improve the climate in their schools.

The trust agreement went into effect at the beginning of the 1996–97 school year, and throughout that year it was seriously tested. Teachers complained that principals were still acting unilaterally, principals complained that teachers were still banding together to defeat their actions. Several times Roger brought me cases of principals having acted as if the trust agreement had never been signed: A principal was bullying her staff, threatening their jobs if they didn't comply with her wishes; another was making budgetary decisions without consulting the teachers; another yelled repeatedly at her staff in the hallways, demoralizing the teachers and embarrassing them in front of students. In every case I went to the principals to discuss the incidents and told them their behavior had to change. By spring, we began to notice a difference. The number of problems employees were reporting hadn't changed, but the issues they were bringing had. Instead of reporting primarily problems with fellow teachers and principals, teachers were now seeking help with problems related to promoting students' academic achievement. The fact that complaints had shifted to achievement and *away* from interpersonal issues we felt was a marked sign of progress. It meant that the trust agreement was working. Overall, the district had taken a large step forward. We had raised to the conscious level that respect and collaboration and trust between principals and teachers was pivotal to our efforts, and we had acted on that belief by intervening in cases where trust was lacking. We now had a climate in which we could begin negotiating a new union contract.

NEGOTIATING IN A SPIRIT OF TRUST

But even with Roger's agreement, negotiating a new contract would not be easy. Many of the union's members wanted to preserve the protections of the old contract and were opposed to instituting teacher accountability or eliminating seniority in hiring. If we were going to move the teachers to our way of thinking—to focusing on children instead of benefits and protections—we'd somehow have to move the discussion past the old contract and into a realm of shared problem-solving.

To achieve this kind of bargaining climate, however, we would need to have the right people on our team. Fortunately, we were able to convince the city of Seattle to loan us their chief labor negotiator, Lizanne Lyons, who was experienced at "interest-based bargaining." Her approach to negotiation—"Let's see where we have common interests and how we can work together"—made her the ideal person to act in the spirit of the trust agreement. She was joined on the team by a researcher and by a number of former principals who had a good feel for the problems and potentials in the district. The union team was made up of Roger, the union's vice president Nicky Amadeo, three teachers, a paraprofessional, and a school secretary. Neither side did any formal training of their teams, deliberately. Training would have encouraged the old-style adversarial mode of negotiation; we wanted collegial *discussions* about how we could best work together.

On the very first day of discussions, the two teams set ground rules for what they were about to do: We're not here to talk about what you get and we get; we're here to decide how we can work together to create the best learning environment for children. For the team members on the union side this was not a wholly comfortable or natural way of thinking. Three or four of them had been in the district for many years, had had run-ins with principals or with the district, and were not convinced that the kind of trusting relationship we were trying to build was possible. But the rest of the negotiators talked repeatedly about where they hoped to end up, about how this would be a process of putting all concerns on the table and working together to solve them, and the union negotiators agreed to try to put their doubts aside in order to comply. In the spirit of joint problem-solving, the negotiators agreed that when they came to serious disagreements they would not caucus—withdraw from the table for a team huddle, as is traditionally done in contract negotiations—but rather they would continue to try to work things through together. And they agreed that if someone became "positional," rigidly defending a single point of view, anyone could call a time-out and the group would stop the discussion, refocus on what it was trying to achieve, and look for another way to solve the problem. To keep themselves focused on the outcome, the teams made a giant banner that said IT'S FOR THE KIDS, which they hung in the negotiating room along with pictures drawn by children. As the process unfolded and Lizanne went to the school board to brief them on their progress, she would take the banner and pictures with her to help them get into the spirit of the negotiations.

The negotiators began the bargaining process by looking at the wide range of issues that were viewed as problems by each side and then, after talking to the respective members, they narrowed the list to three major issues that were seen as significant problems by both sides:

1. *Giving teachers a decision-making role in their schools:* Teachers had long wanted to be involved in crafting the decisions that affected their professional lives, particularly decisions regarding their school's strategic achievement plan. But they were often thwarted by principals who made decisions unilaterally. So the question the teams started with was: What is the ideal way to make sure that the people who are involved in implementing decisions are also involved in making them? Ultimately, they decided to place key decisions in the hands of staff committees.

WE EMPOWER OUR TEACHERS TO TEACH   143

- Each school was required to create a leadership team whose members would be selected by staff.
- The team would have an "authentic" role in developing the school's strategic plan and budget.
- The team would have to sign off on the plan and budget before they were approved by central administration.

But the negotiators didn't want teachers' input limited to the strategic plan and budget. So they recommended that schools create additional staff committees in areas such as curriculum, professional development, and parent and community relations. They tried to codify as much as possible the kind of collaborative decision-making they felt was needed in the schools, thereby requiring all schools to decentralize their decision-making process.

2. *Hiring:* The negotiators began their discussions by asking, What is the best way to staff our schools? How can we make the best match between children and teachers? Everyone agreed that teachers needed a voice in choosing their colleagues. But in the past, hiring had been done almost entirely through central administration. Schools would post openings and teachers would apply; the most senior applicant would automatically be assigned the slot.

Principals, understandably, disliked having staff forced on them, so they worked around the system by hiding vacancies until the spring hiring period was over, at which point they were free to go outside the district and hire whomever they wanted. There were many teachers who liked the protection of seniority because they knew it assured them a job. However, there were also many who felt that because of the principals' manipulations, seniority actually hurt them.

There was another problem with the seniority system as well: It didn't create the best match between teachers and schools. Most schools adhered to a specific educational program or philosophy. A teacher placed in a school by the district may not necessarily be familiar with, or even in agreement with, the school's educational methods. He or she was left to learn and apply them as best he or she could.

Now, as the negotiators considered all of these issues, they found they had a clear vision of what they wanted: They wanted teachers to be able to apply for any jobs in the district, and they wanted teams at the school to make the hiring selections so schools could pick the best teachers for their building.

Yet, there was no way to create the kind of hiring flexibility they wanted as long as seniority remained a factor. It simply got in the way.

Regardless of who made the hiring decisions, as long as schools were required to take the most senior applicants, better-qualified teachers would have to be turned away and schools would continue to manipulate the system in order to make the best matches they could.

But seniority in hiring was a sacred cow. There were teachers who had stayed in the district specifically to get seniority so they could have their pick of jobs, and now the negotiators were proposing to strip that away! The team members returned again and again to the table, searching for other ways to create the flexibility they wanted. But each time they came to the same conclusion: Seniority would have to go.

All right, the union negotiators finally agreed, we can eliminate seniority as a hiring criteria, but in its place we want some safeguards. We want assurances that hiring decisions will be made fairly, with teachers having major input. So the team drew up language that stipulated how the hiring would have to be done.

- Hiring would be done by a team that included staff. (The actual composition of the team would be left to the individual schools, which would be free to include the principal, parents, and even students if they wished.)

- If the principal was not on the team, the team would give him or her the names of up to three qualified candidates. The principal would be required to pick one of the three.

Once the negotiators settled on the hiring policy, they took a look at a related issue that also affected the quality of the match between a school's teachers and its students: the issue of teacher transfers. Under the old system, principals had used transfers to move teachers out of their schools. They had given the teacher a "satisfactory" evaluation, then sent him or her to the "substitute on contract" pool, from which the teacher would be placed in a new job by seniority. Teachers were unhappy with this system for two reasons. The first was that if their performance was truly unsatisfactory, they wanted help making their teaching better; they didn't want to become someone else's problem. The second was that they questioned principals' motives; they felt that principals sometimes used transfers to remove teachers with whom they had personality conflicts or disagreements, rather than teachers whose performances were truly unsatisfactory. The district was also unhappy with the transfer system. We saw it as a system that promoted mediocrity. Instead of identifying teachers who needed help and getting them the help they needed, it moved nonperforming teachers from school to school. So on both sides, the teams wanted change.

The new hiring system made that easy to achieve. The negotiators agreed that teachers could initiate a transfer any time they wanted: As soon as a job was posted, any teacher could apply. Principals, however, were limited in making transfers. They could transfer only teachers who had satisfactory evaluations, and only those with whom they had "irreconcilable differences." And in order to effect a transfer, they had to find a job for the teacher at another school. That meant they would have to negotiate with another school to set aside its interview process and take the transferring teacher before all others. In effect, the provision required principals to keep teachers whose performances they were displeased with and find ways to help them improve.

3. *Evaluating teachers*: Evaluation was the toughest of the three issues because teachers felt it had the most potential for harm. In the past, teachers had felt that principals were sometimes less than fair when it came to doing evaluations. They felt that some principals used the evaluation process to "get back at" teachers with whom they had personality conflicts or disagreements. They deeply wanted to design an evaluation system that would get teachers the help they needed to strengthen their performance.

So the teams began by asking the question, What is the best way to ensure the quality teaching of children? What kind of evaluation system will encourage principals to help, rather than denigrate, teachers who are having trouble? To find an answer, they did a lot of research. But all of their discussions brought them back to the same place: In order to create an evaluation system that was in the best interest of children, they would need to factor in student achievement, which seemed impossibly complex. How would they factor into a teacher's evaluation the achievement of a child who had already been in six different schools? What about the achievement of a child whose last teacher had been given an unsatisfactory evaluation? What about the progress of a child who had been sick for a large part of the year? How could they design an evaluation system that took all those elements into account?

After an enormous amount of data gathering and deliberation, they finally decided that they couldn't. But they didn't want to let go of the idea; if their goal was to design a system that benefited children, student achievement had to be a component. So they agreed to write an interim solution into the proposal. They agreed that:

- Teachers' evaluations would be tied to student achievement.

- The way student achievement would be measured would be determined jointly by each teacher and his or her principal.

- Measures could include (but would not be limited to) classroom evidence, test scores, and other assessments consistent with the school's strategic plan.

- A teacher could not be evaluated as unsatisfactory in the first two years of the contract based on student achievement alone.

- By the third year of the contract, the district and the union would establish universal criteria for using student achievement as a factor in teacher evaluations.

The negotiators wrote this part of the proposal knowing that some union members would find it difficult to accept. But as had happened with the seniority piece, the negotiators came back again and again to the same conclusion: If they were developing an evaluation system that truly worked in children's best interests, they had no choice but to tie it to student achievement.

"IF WE'RE GOING TO HAVE EVERYBODY PULL ON THE OARS FOR STU-DENTS HERE, THEN WE HAVE TO GET PAST THE ADULT BATTLES. WE HAVE TO GET PAST WHAT YOU WANT AND WHAT WE WANT AND FOCUS ON WHAT'S BEST FOR CHILDREN."

—ROGER ERSKINE, EXECUTIVE DIRECTOR, SEATTLE EDUCATION ASSOCIATION

TIME TO VOTE

With all three pieces in place, the teams had done what they'd set out to do: draft a contract proposal that addressed the district's toughest issues in a way that focused on children *and* modeled trust between the district and the union. The negotiators had achieved something truly revolutionary. Any one of the provisions would have strengthened the district, but the three of them together took the district light-years ahead in its quest to become a truly student-focused, world-class learning system.

The negotiators took the proposal to the school board and to the union's board of directors. Then it was time to put our proposal to a vote of all the union's members. The meeting was held on a Friday after the last day of school, and as often happens at such meetings, turnout was low. Of the 4,600 union members, only 1,201 showed up. When the vote was tallied, the negotiators were surprised: The proposal had lost by a vote of 675 to 526. Not a whopping defeat, but certainly not a success. Both si... agreed to revisit the proposal over the summer and resubmit it to a vote in September.

Over the summer the union queried teachers about their objections. Many had rejected the proposal because they disapproved of eliminating seniority in hiring and of tying evaluations to student performance. But they also uncovered other concerns. And so, over the summer, the negotiators met six or eight more times, refining the language to ease the teachers' concerns.

In mid-August the union held another information meeting, at which they explained the proposal again, along with its few new caveats. They also sent an explanatory mailing to members laying out the problems the proposal had been designed to solve, the ways they felt it solved them, and the vision of a more collaborative relationship with the district in which teachers would be more respected and empowered.

The second vote on the proposal was held just before the first week of school. This time, instead of holding the vote at a membership meeting, the union did a mail-in ballot. They believed that doing so would increase the number of voters, and it did. Almost 2,000 members voted—their highest return ever on a mail-in ballot—and this time the percentages in favor and opposed were reversed. Whereas in June the proposal had lost by a vote of 675–526, this time it won by a vote of 1,038–636. A landslide.

Both the district and the union were elated. We were excited about what the new contract meant for teachers—that they would be treated as professionals who can make wise judgments for their students. We were excited about what it meant for students—that they would benefit from management, hiring, and evaluation practices that had been designed in their best interest. And we were excited about what it meant for the country—that such collaborative agreements were possible. We knew that other districts had moved to "site-based management," the practice in which schools become self-governing to varying extents. But few districts had given teachers as much budget input as we'd now done; none had tied teacher accountability to student achievement; and, as far as we knew, none had eliminated seniority in hiring and permitted teachers to be hired solely on merit. The fact that a union and a district had agreed together to make these choices was revolutionary—and, we thought, tremendously hopeful for the future of public education.

MAKING IT WORK

It is now April 1998, seven months since the contract was approved. This year, in every school, a committee of teachers was involved in writing the strategic plan and the budget. In most schools the process went smoothly; the collaboration was good. In about a quarter, the decision-making was still somewhat autocratic. We are working with those principals to help them change their leadership style. This spring, as we enter the hiring season, hiring teams in every school are being trained in the legalities and mechanics of hiring; principals are preparing to post *every* job so that they can have their staffs complete before the start of school. Also this spring, teachers will sit down with their principals for a formal evaluation. Back in the fall, just after the contract was signed, each teacher met with his or her principal to decide jointly the student-measurement criteria they would use to evaluate the teacher's performance. The criteria varied from teacher to teacher: Some chose to be evaluated based on the performance of all the students in the class, others based on a random sample, still others based on a target group of students. Some chose to use portfolios of students' work showing progress from fall to spring; others chose to be evaluated on the basis of test scores and class assignments. During the first three years of the contract, schools will experiment with numerous ways of holding teachers accountable as we work our way toward our ultimate accountability measure.

Some teachers are extremely nervous about these measures; they still fear that principals will use them unfairly. But we have promised to monitor each process—decision-making, hiring, and evaluation—and to work with schools to help them build a truly respectful, collaborative climate.

We feel there is no question that this contract has taken us a giant leap toward where we want to go. But we're not all the way there. The contract is 192 pages long; we're still hoping to replace the pages of fine print with the belief that we can iron out differences through simple discussion of our mutual goals. We'll try for that in our next round of negotiations. But we are tremendously proud of the work we've done—and of the model we've created for how teachers' unions and school districts can work together.

KEY PROVISIONS OF THE CONTRACT

1. *Site-based management:* Teachers will have an authentic decision-making role in their schools.

- Each school will have a leadership team whose members will be selected by staff consensus. (The team may include the principal, parents, and students, as well as teachers, paraprofessionals, secretaries, and other staff.)

- The leadership team, in cooperation with the principal, will develop the school's strategic achievement plan and budget. The leadership team must sign off on both before they are submitted to central administration.
- The school is encouraged to develop committees in such areas as budgeting, curriculum, professional development, and parent and community relations. Committee members are to be chosen by staff consensus. The work of all committees must support the school's strategic plan.

2. *Hiring:* Hiring decisions will be made by teams at the schools in order to best match applicants with student needs.

- Hiring teams will interview and decide among applicants.
- If the principal is not a member of the hiring team, the team will supply the names of three qualified candidates and he or she must pick one of the three.
- Seniority will not be a factor in hiring; any teacher may apply for any job. (Seniority will be retained as a factor in layoffs, rehiring after layoffs, and salary levels.)

3. *Evaluation:* Teachers' evaluations will be tied to student achievement.

- Each principal will meet with teachers by November 15 in order to establish goals and expectations for the teacher.
- For the purposes of evaluation, the way student achievement will be measured will be determined jointly by each teacher and his or her principal.
- Student performance measures may include (but are not limited to) classroom evidence, test scores, and other assessments consistent with the school's strategic plan.
- Teachers may not be evaluated as unsatisfactory in the first two years of the contract based on student achievement alone.
- By the third year of the contract, the district and union will specify criteria for measuring student achievement for use in teacher evaluations.

QUIZ:

WHICH STATEMENT IS TRUE?

(a) The unions are right: Teachers are the most critical element in the education system and must be given maximum support.

However, that support need not come at the expense of children. When unions and school districts become allies rather than adversaries, the kinds of regulations that place teachers' interests over children's can be negotiated away.

CHAPTER 7

WE CAN ACHIEVE THE VICTORY WHEN ... WE RUN OUR SCHOOLS LIKE BUSINESSES

> ### QUIZ:
> #### A PRINCIPAL'S PRIMARY JOB IS:
>
> *(a) to be a liaison with parents*
> *(b) to be a "master" teacher*
> *(c) to be a chief executive officer*
>
> Answer on page 166.

I was sitting in my office one day, shortly after I arrived in Seattle, when I heard an angry voice coming from the reception area just outside my door.

"Look," the woman was saying, "I've been to the school, I've been to the Parent Information Center, I've talked to you people on the phone at least five different times. What is your problem? I just want to enroll my child in school. I don't understand why this has to be so difficult!"

The woman was right: There was no reason for our enrollment procedures to be so complex. But she'd pointed out something even more disturbing. Our student assignment system was the Achilles' heel of our district. It turned a lot of people off from coming to our schools. But it was also symptomatic of the entire district. Our whole district was operating in a way that didn't mesh with our customers' interests. We made it hard for families to enroll. We didn't let them pick the school their children would go to. At many of our schools we didn't offer the programs and services they wanted. And when they came to us for help, we didn't have good customer service. This was no way to run a business!

Of course, the schools had never thought of themselves as a business. They thought of themselves as educators, a profession that required a very different set of skills. But as the former CEO of several multibillion-dollar businesses that operated within the U.S. military, I naturally looked at the school system in business terms, and doing so gave me clarity about our problems. I had to evaluate the product we were to produce, that is, our graduate. I could see that our production systems had serious flaws, and that we were experiencing major customer dissatisfaction. I could see that our customers were leaving us for the competition—in the suburbs and in private schools—and that there was discussion about takeovers from charter schools and vouchers. We were a business in trouble!

As the CEO of this ailing business, I had high aspirations. I wanted to be in the Fortune 500 of educational institutions. But the only way I could get us to the very top was by using the same kind of *market-based* thinking the real Fortune 500 companies used and by backing it up with solid business systems. We'd have to act as if every one of our customers had a choice about whether or not to use us, and we'd have to do everything we could to become every customer's first choice. We'd have to listen to our customers and give them what they wanted, we'd have to align and enhance our production systems so they produced the best possible product, we'd have to find investors to capitalize our enhanced production, we'd have to market ourselves so that customers would know what we had to offer, and we'd have to provide excellent customer service. We'd have to think and act like a business if we wanted to rise to the top of our market.

This was another philosophical shift in public education. The schools were accustomed to operating as if they were part of a command economy, like the one in the former Soviet Union: Money and students were allotted by central administration; the survival of individual schools was guaranteed, regardless of customer satisfaction; and customers had to accept the product whether they liked it or not. Nothing in the system required schools to excel. What I was proposing was radically different. I was imagining a district in which the schools had to *compete* for students in order to stay open, in which the quality of their product and their ability to offer parents what they wanted would be the determining factors in whether or not they survived. Of course, there was a significant difference between our schools and a commercial business. We weren't producing a product or service; we were producing people, the most complex organism on earth.

And that not only made our job harder and more complicated, it changed the nature of the systems we used to do it. Businesses are essentially rational operations; they are governed by systems and procedures that can be standardized and controlled. Boeing, for instance, when it manufactures airplanes, controls its operation virtually 100 percent of the time. It sets specifications for its raw materials and can refuse any that don't meet its criteria. Once the materials enter its factory, it controls their storage and their handling to protect them from contamination. Once the materials are in production, Boeing can stop and start the assembly line whenever necessary to weed out defects and control the manufacturing process. These and other controls make it relatively easy to control the final product.

The schools, I had noticed, were quite different. They were a *nonrational* business. We couldn't turn away children, for example, if we thought they'd be hard to educate, and we could protect them from "contaminating" influences for only about a third of every day. The rest of the time they were out in the community picking up messages that were often counter to our goals. Unlike airplanes, which are uniform and can be assembled in only one way, each of our products was unique and had to be individually built. Unlike steel, which doesn't need to be motivated to become part of the final product, our students needed constant motivation to become the achievers we wanted. And unlike Boeing, which needs machinery and electricity to keep its assembly line in motion, our system depended on *love* to produce each individual final product. For all of these reasons I'd found the schools to be a decidedly nonrational business.

But that didn't mean schools were an impossible business. These non-rational elements were things I thought we could work with. We could find ways to teach each child, regardless of his or her educational challenges. We could work with our parents and our community to counter the harmful external influences. We could find a way to harness each of these nonrational elements to our advantage in order to produce world-class schools. What was more troubling, I felt, was that in addition to the nonrational elements in the system, there were so many irrational elements. It was irrational, for example, that we couldn't easily fire teachers who weren't doing their jobs. It was irrational to bus children far from home when busing hindered rather than promoted achievement. It was irrational to graduate children who couldn't do the work. Public education had a lot of nonrational elements: those we could work with. But the irrational elements would need to be stripped out if we were going to produce Fortune 500 schools.

LISTENING TO OUR CUSTOMERS

But how could I get the entire district to change? How could I get it to think and behave in a way that was so different from what it was used to? I'd have to start by creating a market-based mind-set, and I began to do that by calling myself CEO. I didn't formally change my title; my business card and my colleagues still referred to me as "the superintendent." But in both formal and casual conversations with my staff and in speeches and meetings with outsiders I referred to myself as the CEO of Destiny, Inc. CEO because we were running a market-based school system; Destiny, Inc. because our children were our future. I called our principals CEOs too. They didn't fully understand why yet: We'd have to train them in the business skills they'd need to be chief executives of their corporations. But just giving them the title began to get them thinking. It began to suggest that we were operating under different expectations and different rules.

The next thing we needed to do was to begin listening to our customers. If we were going to behave as if our customers had a choice about whether or not to use us, we needed to know what those customers wanted. So we began to solicit community input systematically: We held community forums at schools throughout the district; we sent surveys home to parents; we sent questionnaires out to businesses, service organizations, and civic leaders. And I talked to everyone I met—on street corners, in restaurants, at gas stations, at my speeches—asking them what they wanted from their public schools.

The feedback was very specific: People wanted schools that opened at eight and closed at five and that offered a wide range of programs; they wanted more sports programs; they wanted increased exposure to the arts and summer programs with enrichment opportunities that lasted all summer. They wanted schools that went from kindergarten through sixth grade, and kindergarten through eighth grade, in addition to K through 5. They wanted schools that were close to home, rather than at the end of a forty-five-minute bus ride. They wanted schools that were safe. But, above all, they wanted schools that challenged their children to their highest potential—that enabled each child to learn at his or her own pace, that pushed children to do the work, that didn't move them on to middle school when they were still reading at the fourth-grade level, that graduated them with the skills and the attitudes they needed to go on to higher education or get a satisfying job.

Over the next two years, as I've explained in other chapters, we made massive changes in order to respond to these customer concerns. We

broadened our curriculum, eliminated mandatory busing, trained principals in leadership, instituted anti-violence programs, focused *everything* on
student achievement. And as we made these changes, we reduced the ir-
rationality in our system and drew closer and closer to our vision.

Soliciting customer feedback didn't stop after that initial set of forums
and questionnaires, however. If we were going to be a market-based system and give our customers what they wanted, we'd have to solicit community feedback on a regular basis. So once a year we send a questionnaire
to parents asking for comments. The questions ask parents about the
school climate, the academic program, the safety of the building and the
buses, the leadership of the principal, and the communication provided by
the school. Once a year we survey and hold forums for middle-school and
high-school students, asking similar questions. We also solicit feedback
from the community before we make any major decisions. When we were
thinking of ending busing, for instance, and introducing the weighted student formula; when we implemented standards for exiting each grade;
when we raised our graduation requirements; and when we decided to offer
the option of all-day kindergarten for a fee, we took our plans to the community. We held community forums in schools across the district so that
parents and other interested citizens could help us shape the plan. We hold
thirty to forty such forums each year, often returning to a neighborhood a
second or third time to gather additional feedback. We have to do this; if
we're going to run our schools like a business, if we're going to make it to
the Fortune 500, then we have to listen to our customers. After all, they
want what we want: world-class schools.

BRINGING IN INVESTORS

But responding to community concerns takes money—and money was the
one thing we didn't have. As I've said before, a combination of issues had
reduced our budget by $35 million just as I arrived. Yet each year we were
taking in more children with expensive educational needs, we had to raise
our teachers' salaries as they earned additional training credits and seniority, and our aging buildings were becoming more expensive to maintain. We barely had money to continue what we were already doing, never
mind add expensive new programs. So how could we respond to the community's concerns? We did what any business does when it needs to grow:
We looked for private investors.

I'd never been in the situation of having to ask for donations before.
In the army and in Fulton County I'd crafted budgets for my departments,
and had often argued for my requested level of funding. I'd prepared material for Secretary of Defense Weinberger when he lobbied Congress to

increase defense spending back in the early 1980s. But I had never asked people to donate money to a cause. I thought about how I would want to be approached if I were a potential investor, or if a business were asking me for venture capital. I'd want to know why the requested program was important, how it fit into the business's comprehensive plan, how the business planned to spend my money, what benefit the business would see once the program was enacted, and what return I would see from having funded the effort. What I'd want, in essence, was a solid business prospectus. So that's what I felt we'd have to give our donors. This approach was confirmed for me when I talked to a philanthropist who had invested millions of dollars in our nation's schools. "The hardest thing about making those donations," he said, "has been watching them go down a black hole."

So working with the Alliance for Education, our fund-raising and project development partner, we began to approach our potential investors in very concrete terms. Instead of asking for money for the general fund, we asked them to underwrite specific, visible programs. Instead of giving them "feel good" data about why our program was important, we gave them a business plan that detailed what we planned to do, how the money would be spent, and what measurable results we expected to see. Instead of talking strictly about the benefits to us, we discussed the investor's return on investment in light of his or her corporate objectives: more computer literacy in a pitch to Microsoft, more appreciation of sports in a pitch to the Supersonics, recognition for the company when we put their name on banners and thanked them in speeches at public events. To relieve donors' concerns further, we structured our fund-raising so that most donations go through the Alliance, rather than directly to the school district. The Alliance provides reporting and stewardship of their donations, just as any independent charitable foundation does, and thereby gives donors reassurance that their money will be carefully managed and targeted directly to the project they are funding.

We also showed our funders the results of their investments. When Boeing, Washington Mutual, Cole & Weber, the Seattle Supersonics, and other companies became sponsors of our annual reading campaign, we invited them to walk through schools during the twenty minutes each day that the schools shut down to read, and showed them how standardized test scores rose at the end of that academic year. When Windermere Real Estate and Safeco Insurance underwrote arts programs for our students, we invited them to our end-of-the-year Sights and Sounds of Excellence concert in the Seattle Opera House so they could hear those students perform. When the Seattle Foundation gave us $100,000 to buy books for our libraries, we held special programs for them in our libraries and at literacy programs so they could hear our children read. We made the results of our donors' investments visible so they knew where their dollars were going. We showed them, as any business needs to do, that it was profitable for them to give.

As a result of this approach, we've attracted millions of dollars in private donations that are enabling us to implement the range of programs we promised our customers we would provide. We received $100,000 from SAFE, a consortium of individuals who have come together to raise money to support sports programs in the schools; $200,000 from a foundation to create programming in the arts; $200,000 from a local foundation to create an environmental education curriculum; and $500,000 to bring technology into the schools. We received $200,000 from Wells Fargo to create a leadership training program for principals. We received $7 million in grants from businesses to create career labs and curricula for our school-to-work program so we can graduate students with the attitudes and skills they need to pursue a career. We received $1 million from telecommunications pioneer Craig McCaw to develop a reading program that will help at-risk elementary students develop the reading skills they need to exit third grade. And we received a $4 million commitment from business executive Stuart Sloan to turn an inner-city elementary school into a model school for helping low-income children achieve. Our businesslike approach to solicitations, combined with our programs' demonstrable results, has convinced these investors that we can use their money to get results. They see that we are doing what we say we will do: helping every child learn.

BEYOND BAKE SALES: ENCOURAGING PEOPLE TO GIVE MONEY TO THE PUBLIC SCHOOLS

But we didn't want just big donors to give to the schools; there weren't enough of them! We needed to find ways ordinary people could contribute as well. We needed to create a "pyramid of giving," much as universities do, in which our relatively small number of major donations from corporations, foundations, and wealthy patrons would be anchored by a large number of smaller donations from families and individuals. The schools, of course, were already doing small-scale fund-raising: Our combined PTAs and site councils raised hundreds of thousands of dollars every year. But those efforts were targeted at individual schools. Now, in addition, we wanted to create a way to encourage individuals to contribute to the district. We wanted to create a system that would help people make donations on a regular basis—just as they did to their university alma mater—in order to create world-class programming district-wide.

The university model, in fact, seemed like an apt comparison. People understand that while state universities can provide a *basic* education with the money they get from the government, the additional resources necessary to provide an *excellent* education must come from private sources. We faced the same situation. We could provide a basic education with the money we got from the state and city, but in order to reach our vision, in order to create world-class schools, we needed additional dollars.

So, through the Alliance for Education, we have embarked on a campaign to create a giving pyramid for the schools. In 1997 we held our first annual Friends of Seattle Public Schools fund-raising campaign. Using telemarketing and direct mail, we solicited donations from tens of thousands of Seattle area families and individuals. Each solicitation explained our vision for the district and why private donations were critical to its success. In the first month of the campaign we raised $70,000. We hope that as the campaign becomes an annual event people will anticipate it and plan for it, just as they now plan their gift to their college or United Way. And we hope that as the habit of giving becomes established, the size of people's checks will grow.

Meanwhile, the Alliance for Education has begun training our individual schools to do fund-raising. Our goal, again, is to replicate the university model: While the university development office seeks funding for major campus-wide projects, each school on the campus has its own alumni base and fund-raising mechanism. By creating a similar system in the district, we hope to help each school supplement its district-supplied budget. To spur the effort, the Alliance fund-raiser visits the schools, meets with their principal and leadership team, and gives them a crash course in writing proposals. She helps them target corporations and foundations that are likely sources of money for the projects they are seeking to fund, and helps them wordsmith their proposals to make them maximally effective.

SELLING THE SCHOOLS THE WAY NORDSTROM SELLS NORDSTROM

It didn't take long to figure out that we'd need well-constructed business plans to convince businesses and individuals to contribute. But I knew that wouldn't be enough. The only way we'd generate the gargantuan amount of support we needed would be to *market* the schools constantly and deliberately. We'd need to communicate to the community over and over and over again the excitement we were feeling, the amount of change that was taking place, and the quality of what we were doing. We would need to sell the schools the way Nordstrom sells Nordstrom if we wanted to get investors excited enough to give.

We'd also need to market that way if we wanted to achieve all our other goals. We needed thousands of businesses and community organizations to partner with us in our nine focal areas. We needed thousands of volunteers to come to our schools and tutor our at-risk students. We needed 100,000 parents to feel the excitement of the schools so they would read to their children and check their homework. And we needed the half-million citizens of Seattle to feel a sense of excitement about the schools because that excitement would find its way back to our buildings and set our teachers and students on fire. To achieve all those goals, we would need to market—on television, on radio, in the newspapers, in speeches—and make the public schools a thrilling, positive story that everyone was telling. That, I believed, was the job of every school-board member and every principal, and particularly of the superintendent, who needed to be the district's "chief marketeer."

So we began to market. We accepted every speaking opportunity we were offered—at every church, every neighborhood group, every business luncheon, and every conference—because everyone gave us a platform to market the schools. We appeared on every radio show that would have us—from national public radio to conservative talk shows— to discuss the changes we were making and to respond to listeners' concerns. We went to the editorial boards of the newspapers to explain why the changes we were making were necessary and how they would boost student achievement.

We were so aggressive in marketing the schools that businesses began offering us advertising opportunities: Ackerley Outdoor Advertising gave us free billboards. KIRO News Fax, a business publication faxed daily to 80,000 businesspeople in the Seattle area, offered us free space in each edition to run a message about the schools. One of the local television stations created a series of public-service announcements that emphasized reading. I knew we were beginning to have the "saturation" effect we wanted when taxi drivers, waitresses, parking attendants, and business executives began stopping me to say how excited they were about what our school system was doing for their children.

We *had* to accept and pursue these marketing opportunities because otherwise, how could we communicate our excitement? How would people know about our thirty-one National Merit Scholars, about our Washington Middle Schoolers who had won the statewide Math Olympiad two years in a row, about the fifteen-point gain our students averaged on the SAT? We had to go out into the community to tell these stories because otherwise the community would manage us by anecdote. They would believe bad stories they'd heard about the schools years before and not realize that for every bad story there were a million good ones. We needed to communicate those stories because we needed to get people *excited* about what we are doing. Their excitement would fuel success in every class-room. And there was another reason why I needed to market the schools aggressively. I needed to challenge the community. The influence of parents, of neighborhoods, of the media, all had an indelible impact on our students. If we wanted those forces to help us in our job, we needed to challenge them to do so.

IMPROVING OUR CUSTOMER SERVICE

All the marketing in the world, though, wouldn't make families happy with our schools if we continued to have poor customer service. So we created a Customer Service Department. All phone calls, letters, and visitors who were expressing a problem with the schools would now be delegated to them. That meant people like the irate mother trying to register her child, or parents who were protesting the fact that their child had not been assigned to her first-choice school, or parents who were angry over our refusal to transport their child to an alternative school across town, would now have a single trained, capable, and friendly place to go to get their complaints handled.

The Customer Service Department would *not* be charged with resolving the complaints, however—and this was critical. We were going to great lengths at that time to systematize all of our operations so that every system in the district would promote student achievement. If we let the Customer Service Department resolve the issue every time a parent called to complain, we would undermine our own systematizing efforts. So instead, we made the Customer Service Department the *broker* between the angry customer and the department that was in charge of that particular issue. The Department's job was to ensure that the parents received *prompt, accurate, and courteous* responses—but the solutions to the problems were left to the relevant departments.

To achieve the highest level of service possible, I sent Susan Byers, our new director of customer service, to Nordstrom, the upscale department store known for its superior customer service. (This must be one of the few occasions when an employee was actually *sent* to Nordstrom on work time!) Susan spent time with the customer service manager at one of the stores, and then came back and trained every member of her staff in "the Nordstrom way."

Because the Customer Service Department would be handling enormous numbers of inquiries and complaints, we also devised a computer system that would track every customer input and every district response. The way it worked was simple. Whoever received a customer's input—whether it was a customer service representative, a secretary in a school, or someone else in the district—would log the concern on the computer along with her promised date of response. She would then refer the problem to a customer service representative. The customer service representative would get back to the customer to learn more about the problem, and after promising a fuller response within a reasonable period of time, would contact the department that was needed to help resolve the problem.

We also asked everyone, from my office to the offices in our schools, to anticipate issues that would generate customer concern, and to log those issues on the computer so that immediate responses could be given. In the case of large, district-wide issues (such as our decision to close schools for four days a year in order to accommodate teacher training), or issues that had appeared in the press (such as my statement that I thought it would be a good idea to give nicotine patches to students), my office prepared a briefing explaining the issue and the reasons for our action. This way, all across the district, people were armed to handle customers' concerns.

We installed the computer system, trained our customer service representatives in how to use it, and they, in turn, trained people across the district. Within a week we knew the system was working. The mother of a high-school student called central administration to complain that her son's football game had been canceled. *While* the woman was on the phone, a customer service representative typed the name of the school on her computer and saw an entry, logged the day before, explaining that the game had been canceled because the students had repeatedly misbehaved. She explained that to the mother, who disagreed with the school's decision but felt no need for further action. What previously would have taken numerous phone calls between our office and the school, and at least a day's delay in getting back to the mother, was accomplished courteously and accurately in under five minutes.

Poor customer service does not cause people to leave the public schools. They leave for more fundamental reasons. But poor customer service causes people to lose faith in public schools. It is symptomatic of larger, underlying problems. Creating excellent customer service—and treating all of our customers the same way, regardless of which school they attend or which part of town they live in—is a basic courtesy we extend to the people who use us, and a symbol of the changes we have made to enable all students to achieve.

MAKING THE PRINCIPALS CEOS

At the same time we were creating the customer service system, developing new programs in response to customer feedback, and recruiting investors to fund our new offerings, I was talking, talking, talking about market-based schools. And I talked about it nowhere more strenuously than with our principals—because they were the ones on whom the impact would be the greatest. We were creating a system in which individual schools would survive or fail based on their ability to provide what the market wanted—and principals needed to understand that if they were going to be able to lead. As they heard me talk about serving our customers, about focusing our production systems on building the best possible product, about marketing our schools to attract customers and investors, they began to understand what it meant to be CEO of a school.

Key to my concept of creating market-based schools was decentralizing control and truly making principals executives. That meant we would be giving our schools far greater responsibilities than they currently had. For starters, each school would be given total control over its budget and staffing. In the past, central administration had made all funding decisions for the schools. The district had determined the number and type of teachers each school would receive—an expense that accounted for 88 percent of the school's budget—and then gave the principal discretion over the remaining 12 percent. The 12 percent went primarily for supplies. Under the new plan, schools would receive 100 percent of their budgets, and the freedom to determine their own staffing plans. A school could decide, for example, that it wanted to become an arts magnet school and rearrange its budget to make that happen. A school that wanted to create an emphasis on technology could choose to eliminate its specialist positions and spend less money on books in order to buy computers.

We also gave schools control over their custodial and security services. Previously, custodians and security guards reported to administrators downtown. But if we were going to hold principals accountable for the cleanliness and safety of their buildings, we needed to give them not just responsibility, but also control.

But probably the biggest change we required of our principals was that they cease to be *managers* and instead become *leaders*. Most of them were spending their time dealing with bus schedules, making sure their buildings were operational, disciplining students who had misbehaved. Those were not leadership functions. What principals needed to be doing was setting a vision for their school communities, and then inspiring their teachers, students, and parents to achieve it. They needed to be setting goals for their teachers, helping the teachers set goals for students, and working with the teachers daily to make sure the students reached them. They needed to be observing their teachers, making sure they had the skills to do the job, and seeing that they got the support and training they needed. They needed to be meeting with parents, talking with them about their children and about the parents' role in education. They needed to build teamwork among the teachers, keep them focused on achievement, and rid their schools of the hundreds of other issues that got in the way. They needed to be "working" their communities, recruiting volunteers and resources for their teachers, getting the community excited about what was happening in their schools. Principals needed to stop being the chief disciplinarians of their schools and become their *chief education officers*.

When I explained this to the principals, most of them agreed, but they said they didn't have time; their current duties kept them far too busy. I said: You're right! So you need to delegate your management functions to someone else. Here, in central administration, I don't get involved in day-to-day management issues. I leave those functions to others. You have a custodian: Raise his pay and make him the building manager; let him deal with all the building-related issues. You have several secretaries in your office: Pick one, raise her pay, and have her deal with the bus schedules. Give all of your management functions away so you have time to lead!

COMPETITION

By giving our schools this much operating freedom, we would be bringing yet another business element into the district: competition. Suddenly schools had the capacity to control the nature and quality of their operations individually. Thanks to our new union contract, they could hire the best teachers for their teams, and they could hold their teachers responsible for student achievement. They could also juggle their budgets to strengthen their academic program. They had all the tools they needed to make themselves maximally attractive to parents. And given our new system for assigning students to schools, in which families had the pick of any school in the district, this ability was critical. As a result, schools began to change their programs in order to make themselves more competitive. At Coe Elementary School, for example, the principal and teachers felt that classes were too large. So they gave regular classes to their four specialists (who had previously pulled students out of classes for tutoring in math and reading), and supplemented those classes with aides to help the children who were behind. By essentially adding four new classroom teachers to their staff, they reduced class size at Coe from twenty-eight to twenty-three. The staff at Lawton Elementary took the opposite route. Because their school had a high concentration of gifted students, they decided to strengthen their program in that area. They replaced a regular classroom teacher with a half-time drama teacher and a half-time "gifted" teacher, and the two developed a gifted curriculum using drama as the basis for enrichment activities. As a result, average class size at Lawton rose from twenty-five to twenty-eight children, but the staff felt this was the best way to meet their students' and their community's needs.

Schools are also beginning to market themselves. At Rogers Elementary, which is in an upper-middle-class neighborhood, the principal is actively marketing to families whose children attend private school. She realized that every student lost to private school meant $3,000 less for her budget. So with the help of a parent who was active in the neighborhood, she began calling the families of prospective kindergartners, as well as families whose children were already in private school, and inviting them to the school for an introduction. Her sessions, at which she talks up the school's strengths and its customer-service focus, are bringing some of those households into the Rogers family. Martin Luther King Elementary sent brochures to parents of all school-age children in their neighborhood, and families held evening coffees at their homes so prospective parents could meet the principal. Chief Sealth High School has always had strong music and performing arts programs, and is now using them as a "selling point" to attract students. To call attention to itself, the school books its choir and marching band at events in downtown Seattle during the Christmas holidays, and invited (and got) Al Gore, the Vice-President of the United States, to visit their school.

In effect, by creating competition among our schools, we have created "charter schools" within our district: We have enabled them to function independently in response to the needs and demands of their communities, and we have required them to succeed in the marketplace in order to stay in business.

Turning principals into CEOs and reversing the way an entire school district thinks about its ways of doing business is not an overnight phenomenon. But as one principal said, "There's a lot of pressure—creating this new vision for our schools, nurturing it along, and feeling accountable for making it happen. But we have the controls to realize it. And that's very exciting."

By bringing the forces of the market to bear on our schools, we've given them the tools and the responsibility to succeed. We've focused everything that happens in our ninety-seven "retail outlets" on the only thing that matters—our educational bottom line.

SHOULD WE HAVE VOUCHERS AND CHARTER SCHOOLS?

Should states adopt vouchers and charter schools? For me, the answer is an unequivocal no. Both alternatives rob money from the public schools. In Washington State, there are 70,000 children attending private school and another 20,000 who are home-schooled. Under both the voucher and charter systems, each of those 90,000 children would take approximately $5,000 from the public education budget. That's $450 million. We can't afford that!

The argument for charter schools is essentially an argument over deregulation and class size. Charter schools would be exempt from many of the regulations that govern traditional public schools, including regulations about curriculum and, in some states, learning standards for students. But the real regulations people want to avoid when they support charter schools are regulations imposed by teachers' unions. Charter school supporters want to be able to hire the teachers they want, regardless of their seniority or teaching credentials, and they want to be able to remove teachers easily if they feel that those teachers are no longer performing. They don't want teachers' unions dictating who they can hire. In the traditional public schools, we would like those freedoms too! That's why in Seattle we have worked with our union to eliminate seniority as a factor in hiring, why we're looking for ways to get temporary credentials for professional biologists and software designers and automotive mechanics so they can teach our students based on their real-world experience, and why we've said principals must give "unsatisfactory" evaluations to teachers who are not performing and either help those teachers improve or encourage them to leave the system. If union regulations are a problem, then they need to be fixed—not left in place for the majority of children while being circumvented by the few.

Charter school proponents also tout as a selling point the fact that their schools and classes are small. (The typical charter school has 150 students, compared to 250 to 700 in traditional public schools.) They're right: Small schools and classes are desirable. But if small is right for some children, why isn't it right for all? The answer, of course, is affordability. If we were to have 150-student schools in the Seattle School District, we would need three times as many schools. The state can't afford that. But is it right for the state to "afford it" for some children while denying it to others?

The reality of charter schools and vouchers is that sophisticated parents will learn to "work the system" (as they do now) and will get these "elite" services for their children. Meanwhile, the majority of children will remain in the traditional public schools, which will have even less money than they have now to pay for basic education.

Over the last several years, charter-school bills and initiatives have appeared before our state legislature and the voters, and each time they have been voted down. But it is entirely possible that one day soon charter legislation will pass. If that happens, I know what I will do. I will say to the legislature, "I believe you are right. Charter schools *are* in the best interest of children. They are in the best interest of *all* children. Therefore, I want you to charter every school in the Seattle Public Schools!"

Interestingly, while people are debating charter schools and vouchers, I believe they are missing the point. The real challenge to public schools is not those two alternatives; it is technology. We can already transmit massive amounts of data over the Internet, and, using interactive video technology, we can bring the world's best teachers into homes and classrooms all over the world. *This* is what will change the face of public education, and it is here that educators and policy-makers should be looking. Hockey player Wayne Gretzky once said, "Never skate to where the puck is; skate to where it's going to be," and that's what we need to do in public education. The puck may seem, for the moment, to be in the arena of charter schools and vouchers, but it's skidding quickly toward the technological opportunities of the future. That's where we need to be heading.

QUIZ:

A PRINCIPAL'S PRIMARY JOB IS:

(c) to be a chief executive officer

Effective principals run their schools the way CEOs run their businesses. They lead the employees, manage the budget, serve the customers, market to the public. They do all the same things corporate CEOs do. Their goals, of course, are to educate children, not to make money, but the methods they use for achieving those goals are the same as those used in business.

CHAPTER 8

WE CAN ACHIEVE THE VICTORY WHEN . . . WE MAKE THE MEDIA OUR PARTNERS

QUIZ:

THE SCHOOLS' RELATIONSHIP WITH THE MEDIA SHOULD BE:

(a) invite them in: the media perform an important function

(b) keep them at arm's length: the media should cover big stories but otherwise stay out of the schools

(c) keep them as far away as possible: media coverage hurts the children

Answer on page 180.

On a bright August day in 1995, just two weeks before I would officially take over as superintendent, I was sitting in my temporary office when the telephone rang. It was the communications director of the district. "I thought you should know. A part-time worker in one of our summer schools was just accused of molesting a fourteen-year-old student."

Over the next few hours, the first details of the story came out. The worker was a convicted felon who had served time for manslaughter, been paroled for good behavior, and then several years later been hired by one of our schools. He'd been our employee for close to fifteen years. Now the girl was reporting that he had raped her in a school office during the summer-school session.

Our very first action was to apologize to the girl and her family, and to send representatives to offer them assistance. Our first priority was to take care of the student! Then, because the media were already aware of the case, we made our apologies public and publicly condemned the incident. We vowed to find out everything we could about the incident and to make sure that such an event never happened again.

Not surprisingly, the story became front-page news. The school community was shocked; how could this have happened? How could we have hired someone with that background? The public was far more outraged; we had violated their trust in the most egregious way. Feeling the wrath of the community, the media hammered us. They pointed their fingers at everyone and clamored for a head.

Over the next two weeks I immersed myself in the school district's hiring practices and emergency procedures. I hadn't even taken over as superintendent yet and would have much preferred to work on my vision and strategic plan, academic achievement, and the budget, but those things would have to wait. For the moment, the print and broadcast media were driving our agenda.

Many on the staff believed that the way to handle the incident would be to say as little as possible. They were embarrassed about it and felt that the more we said, the longer it would stick around. Be quiet, they felt, and it will go away. But my feelings were exactly the opposite. Bad news doesn't improve with age. The *last* thing we wanted to do was to pretend the incident hadn't happened. Our city had entrusted us to run their schools. They'd entrusted us to spend their money, make decisions, manage programs wisely. Now their trust was shaken. How we responded to the crisis would rebuild that trust or sever it, and once it was severed it would be hard to regain.

On September 1, I took over as superintendent. Immediately, I brought in the communications director and we mapped out a plan. I would be the spokesperson on the incident. Our policy would be that good news could go out through anybody, but bad news would go out only through me. We agreed that we wouldn't lie, we wouldn't protect people who had done wrong, nor would we be put on the defensive by the media. We would collect as much information as we could and we would tell the story to the public the way we wanted it told, explaining our four-part plan:

1. *We are doing everything we can to find out exactly what happened.* We are cooperating with the police in their criminal investigation

and, in addition, have launched our own internal investigation to find out what transpired on that day.

2. *We are doing everything we can to find out why the event occurred.* We are doing an investigation of all the events that pertain to the hiring and employment of this man.

3. *We are doing everything we can to make sure this never happens again.* We are reviewing our hiring and employee-review procedures, we are looking for loopholes in the system that would allow an undesirable employee to be hired and retained, we are reviewing all of our employees to make sure that no one else in our employ poses a threat to the safety of students. We will not permit *anything* to jeopardize our children's safety.

4. *We will speak with the media daily and will keep the public informed about the results of our investigations and about what we are doing to ensure the safety of the children.*

After that I did talk to reporters daily about what we were learning. I called them and made myself readily available whenever they called me because I needed them to know we would be straight with them. I needed to establish trust. I also needed their information! Our own investigation was constrained by the limits of our time and money, but the media had assigned numerous investigative reporters. They had more time than we did to dig to the bottom of the case. As the pieces came together, we held press conferences to share our findings with the public.

When we felt we had a solid understanding of how the event had happened (problem in our hiring and evaluation systems), I held another press conference and said to the public frankly, "Let me tell you what is wrong with our system." I then laid out all the decision points where we should have made sure the man was not on our payroll. And I told the public exactly what we were doing to ensure that this never happened again:

• We had reconfirmed that we would not hire felons or anyone who had any history of violence, or sexual misconduct around children.

• We had asked all employees to file new employment applications and were in the process of reviewing every single one. If we saw anything that looked unsuitable for an employee of the public schools, that person would be investigated. Anyone who lied on their application would be released.

• We were having every employee refingerprinted and the fingerprints were being checked against criminal records.

- I had issued a "standards of conduct" letter explaining the standards we expected all employees to uphold while working around our children.

- We had appointed a special task force within the human resources department to monitor these actions until they were completed.

After that press conference, the public scrutiny abated. Our district had rallied to find the root of the problem, and as a result, I believed, our students would be safer in the future. I also felt strongly that the media had played a crucial role in helping us resolve the problem. It was their relentless questioning that had ultimately enabled us to make the repairs to the system that would improve security in the future.

They had also been a vehicle for taking our story to the public. Without them we would have had to go school by school, calling multiple parent meetings to inform our families about what we had learned and how we were solving the problem. But instead, they took our messages out in a citywide blitz, reaching not only parents but citizens as well, far more effectively than we ever could have done on our own.

I was pleased as I reviewed our actions in this case. We had permitted an outrageous incident to occur and had endured the intensity of the media spotlight—but we had come out of the episode stronger. We had a heightened awareness of potential dangers, we had a strengthened hiring and security system, and we had reestablished our trust with the public as a result of having been open and honest with them. This was the first time, but certainly not the last time, we worked with the media as partners.

LEARNING FROM A MASTER

From 1981 to 1984 I worked in the Pentagon as executive secretary to Secretary of Defense Caspar Weinberger. Weinberger was a superb strategist; he was a master at getting the support he needed to turn his ideas into action. And central to any Weinberger strategy was the media. Reaching millions of people instantaneously, with a power that exceeded reason, they had the ability to turn the public—and therefore Congress—toward or against any program. He believed that a large part of his job, therefore, was to encourage the media to report fairly and favorably on his agenda. And his agenda was a big one. In the years I worked for him, my staff and I prepared four budgets for Congress, each one the largest defense budget to date. Winning approval of those budgets was necessary to achieving his goals. Therefore, working with the media became a primary activity in our department.

Weinberger's strategy with the media was to be constantly available.

He met with reporters daily (not referring them to press aides, as many Cabinet members did); he encouraged them to call him to make sure they had their facts correct; and he stayed late after press conferences to answer questions. Unlike many in Washington who feared the media, or held them in disdain, Weinberger treated the media with the utmost respect— and they returned the favor. Ten years later, as I took the helm of the school district, I knew I would need to follow his example. I would need the media to help me build support for the schools.

HELP US RAISE THE CHILDREN

Just as Weinberger couldn't achieve his goals for the Defense Department without popular support, we couldn't achieve our goals for the school system without the support of our community. We needed taxpayers to approve our levies. We needed businesses to invest in our programs. We needed clergy and ethnic groups, service clubs and retirees to come in and tutor our children to ensure that every child would learn.

I wanted the media to acknowledge the unparalleled power they had to shape our community's attitudes, and to agree to work with us to shape those attitudes in a positive, pro-education way. That might mean featuring one-minute pieces on the evening news about students who had performed exceptionally. It might mean running articles that showed the impact of tax levies on individual schools in order to put human faces on the levy issue. It might mean hosting school-district representatives on call-in shows when we were weighing policy changes so that families could give us feedback. It meant that we wanted the media to ask themselves repeatedly as they chose their news stories and designed their programs: What can we do to promote education? How can we help the schools?

How could we encourage the media to work with us this way? What strategy could we use to get them to think about our mission while also fulfilling their own? I believed we could appeal to their sense of moral responsibility. We could simply ask them to do what society needed them to do: We could ask them to *help us raise the children.*

WE MADE A MAJOR PHILOSOPHICAL SHIFT: WE BEGAN TO WORK WITH THE MEDIA TO *BUILD* THE PUBLIC WE NEEDED!

ADOPTING A MEDIA STRATEGY

Of course, if we were going to ask the media to play this role for us, we would need to be proactive. We couldn't sit around and wait for reporters to come to us; we'd have to seek out the reporters. We couldn't wait for news to unfold; we'd have to go to the media with our stories. We would have to work with the media in a way that would encourage them to *want* to be our partners. To do that we have pursued a five-pronged strategy:

- *Build trust with the media.* Be open and honest with the media. In response, you'll get balanced coverage of your schools.

- *Tell your good news!* There are millions of great things happening in your school district every day. Publicize them!

- *Go on the offensive.* Be clear and consistent in what you communicate. Help the public see your actions in light of your big guiding principles.

- *Build an ongoing relationship with the media.* Don't wait for an event to talk to the media. Talk to reporters frequently. Help them understand where you are going, what you are doing, and why. Give them a context to understand events that happen in your district.

- *Ask the media to help you take issues to the public.* The media is an excellent conduit to and from the public. Ask them to take your ideas and proposals to their audience so that you can engage in a constructive public dialogue.

BUILDING TRUST WITH THE MEDIA

From the day I'd first talked to the media during the summer-school incident, I knew that establishing a trusting relationship would be the only way we would get our messages reported quickly and accurately, and the only way to get reporters the information they needed.

To promote a trusting relationship with the media, I went, within weeks of my arrival in the district, to all of the media outlets. I went to the editorial boards of the two major newspapers, the *Seattle Times* and the *Seattle Post-Intelligencer*, and I met with the management and news directors of each of the local television and radio stations, KOMO, KIRO, and KING-TV. In all of these outlets I introduced myself and shared my vision for the schools. Then I told them we couldn't achieve that vision without them. I said, "We need you to help us raise the children; we need you to help us build the public we need."

The individuals I met with made no promises, of course, but I sensed that they appreciated the fact that I had come to see them. Since then, I have continued to reach out to them. And I have always made myself immediately available anytime a reporter calls. I have a tremendous respect for the power and the importance of the media. So I do everything I can to build and keep their trust.

TELL YOUR GOOD NEWS!

The second tenet of our media strategy was *Tell your good news*. And we had plenty of it to tell. We had a new vision and a plan for getting there. We had 3,000 wonderful teachers who were working miracles every day. We had tens of thousands of children who were working very hard to learn. If we were going to get the public excited about working with us, we needed to be aggressive about broadcasting this news. So we sought out opportunities to tell our story to the media. Our communications director, Dorothy Dubia, kept lists of every media outlet; now we knocked on the doors of all of them. From the conservative talk radio station KVI to the public radio station KUOW, from the major TV news shows to the local cable access station, from the major daily newspapers to the little weeklies that served neighborhoods and families with children, we did as many interviews as we could line up. We had to get our message out! In every venue we described our vision and how we were carrying it out. By the end of my first year, we had tangible successes we could report. Standardized test scores were up by one to four points across the district. Our Washington Middle School math team had won the state's Math Olympiad. Bands and orchestras from Garfield and Roosevelt High Schools and Washington Middle School had won national competitions, Garfield two years in a row. We took each of these successes to the media—proudly, aggressively—to make sure the public knew we had achieved them. And each one confirmed the earlier messages in the public mind: The schools are really improving!

Doing this kind of communication was not just the job of the superintendent and communications staff, however. I wanted all of our administrators and principals to understand that communication was their job too. To this end, we encouraged our principals to solicit media attention proactively. We asked each school to send three articles with photographs to the newspapers every year, describing exciting events their students and teachers were involved in. We asked them to write three letters to the editor, or three guest editorials, and to send those to the papers as well. With three articles, letters, or editorials from each of our ninety-seven schools, we could have our schools in the newspaper every day for a year! To help them with this task, our communications department did briefings. They went out and talked to the schools about how to file news stories that the media would find interesting and gave them names of people to contact. Our principals are becoming increasingly aware of how the media can help them. In the coming years, as our schools become savvier about marketing themselves to customers, they will turn to the media more and more as a partner in helping them realize their goals.

GO ON THE OFFENSIVE

The third tenet of our media strategy was *Go on the offensive*. By that we meant we had to be clear and consistent in what we communicated. Everything in the district was focused on two things: building academic achievement and keeping our schools safe. Therefore, as we talked with the public we needed to help them understand how those two overriding objectives drove virtually all of our actions. There was no doubt that in the months and years ahead we would make decisions with which some people would not agree. But we also knew that if we made all decisions based on what was best for the children—and communicated just that— the majority of the public would support us.

In the spring of 1997 we encountered tenacious opposition to a move we wanted to make and our opponents took their grievance to the press. We felt strongly that their position was counter to the interests of Seattle's schoolchildren. It was only by going on the offensive and reminding the community about our deepest principles that we prevented a potentially damaging loss of public support.

For over a year we had been looking for a temporary home for the students at Ballard High School while the old high school was being completely rebuilt. The district had studied many options as a temporary home for Ballard, but all the sites had serious and costly problems. However, there was a building at Sand Point, a former navy base that was being transferred to the city, that seemed perfect. It, too, would need extensive renovation, but it would cost $6 million less to prepare than any school-district building, and once Ballard was completed, could be used to house students from another soon-to-be-renovated high school. So we approached the city and they agreed to look into the matter.

Enter the Sand Point Neighborhood Association. The neighborhood association opposed the idea of a high school in their midst. They claimed it would destroy their property values and that the district wanted the building not just for two short-term construction projects, but for our long-term use.

The neighborhood association took their views to the media as soon as they heard we were pursuing Sand Point. They explained their reasons for wanting to deny us the site; in return, we explained the reasons we wanted it. Now, this is the kind of situation in which a school district can come out looking ugly—like a big bureaucratic behemoth waging war on a small group of neighbors. So we went on the offensive; that is, we talked about the situation in the context of our biggest issues. We had promised the community that we would give them a new high school in which their students could learn and that we would do it on time and within budget. Sand Point was the means of keeping that promise.

Over the next several weeks, the issue appeared in one paper or the other almost daily. The front-page news coverage was balanced; both sides' arguments were covered. But in almost every letter and editorial on the editorial pages, the Sand Point neighbors were taken to task for painting an unflattering and inaccurate portrait of high-school students and for putting their own interests above those of the city. The school district was generally commended for seeking a sound, money-saving solution to a problem. By asking the media to see the conflict within the bigger context, we effectively elevated the discussion from a story about David and Goliath to a referendum concerning what kind of schools we want our children to have.

As the story played itself out in the media, the city deliberated over its decision. Unfortunately, timing became our nemesis. To get Ballard students into Sand Point in time for the start of classes in the fall, we needed to start renovations by early March. But as time passed without a decision it became increasingly clear that that was unlikely to happen. So quietly we gave up our bid for the project and arranged to move the Ballard students into a building of our own. But I consider it a high point for us, nonetheless. The public perception of the schools could have become tarnished so easily, and we couldn't afford to have that happen; we needed the community's support in order to accomplish our goals. But instead, by reminding the community via the media what we were working so hard to do, we built up even stronger support for our vision.

BUILDING AN ONGOING RELATIONSHIP
WITH THE MEDIA
The fourth tenet of our media strategy was *Build an ongoing relationship with the media.* We didn't want to wait for an event to spark media coverage; we wanted to talk to the media constantly about what we were doing and why. That way the media would understand our decisions, would know the thinking behind them, would be informed when major stories came up, and would be able to report those stories in their full educational context.

To create this kind of reciprocal relationship, our communications department kept up a steady flow of information to the media outlets. They knew that the media always have column inches to write, airtime to fill, and intractable deadlines by which to do that. So our communications staff would send reporters stories that could be filed AOT ("any old time") and offered themselves as a "go to" source, meaning that reporters could call them for background information on other education stories they were doing. If a reporter was doing a piece on an all-girls school in California, for example, she could call the district for information on gender-specific education, despite the fact that we didn't have any gender-specific schools. Offering information in that context was helpful to the reporter; it also gave our communications people a chance to pitch a related story (say a story about our African-American Academy, which served not a single gender but primarily a single ethnic group).

There was another benefit to having this kind of relationship with the media as well: Whenever a potentially damaging story hit, reporters were less inclined to jump on its sensational or negative elements and better able to see the story in the larger context of what we were trying to achieve. Perhaps the best example of this occurred when the school district was hit with a rash of bomb threats.

In April 1997 I was visiting McClure Middle School when a secretary found me in a hallway and handed me a note: *Bomb threat at Franklin*. I immediately raced to Franklin High School. By the time I arrived, the students were huddled outside, coatless and freezing in the chilly April air. The bomb squad was inside the building. When the officers emerged thirty minutes later, we could see that they were empty-handed. The entire episode took about forty-five minutes, but the school day had been severely impacted.

Back at district offices I talked with Dan Graczyk, our director of logistics, about our vulnerability to bombs. We agreed that our monitors did an excellent job of keeping unauthorized people from entering our buildings, but that short of having airport-style screening devices at every door of every school, there was no way to keep explosives out. We could, however, make sure we were prepared, so we asked every school to be ready for evacuation drills.

The drills turned out to be fortuitous: In the next eighteen days, four more schools received bomb threats. The threats were made over the telephone by adolescent-sounding voices, and when the calls were traced, most came from convenience stores near the targeted schools. It became clear that we were the target of student pranks.

Well, you can't receive a bomb threat and evacuate a school and not make the evening news. So four times in eighteen days, viewers saw film clips of students huddled on the sidewalk and heard me repeat that we would find the perpetrators and expel them. But unexpectedly, after the fourth story had aired, I got a call from Joe Barnes, the news director at KOMO-TV, our ABC affiliate. Joe was concerned about his station's coverage. Were they merely prolonging the crisis by encouraging copycats? he wondered. Did we want the coverage to stop?

Can you imagine such a call? I was elated. "No! I *need* you to cover these stories! I *need* you to put me on the news so that I can say to people, 'These "pranks" are actually felonies,' or to say, 'We're paying one-thousand-dollar rewards for information that leads to the arrest and conviction of a perpetrator.' Without you I couldn't get those messages out. Please don't stop the coverage. We need your help."

So the TV coverage continued. That station changed its reporting to emphasize the consequences of making a bomb threat. Within the schools, conversations about the bomb threats took on a far more serious tone, and gradually students came forward with the names of classmates who had been involved. Over the next month the incidents continued, but the callers were caught, the rewards flowed, and finally the incidents stopped.

I know that some of my principals disagreed with me when I asked the news director to continue the coverage, but I knew we had to keep our constituents informed; we had to enlist the community's help; we had to go to the media.

I was amazed—and infinitely pleased—when Joe Barnes came to me and asked if we wanted KOMO to stop its coverage. The media doesn't usually do things like that! Why did they make that offer? I believe it was because Joe had heard our message and understood that there was more to the issue than just the story. He understood that the way the media treated the story would have an impact on our children. Would he have made that decision if we had not developed a relationship with KOMO over the previous eighteen months? Perhaps. But I believe that our efforts to develop a mutually beneficial, ongoing relationship with the media spurred him to do precisely what we had asked the media to do: help us raise the children.

ASKING THE MEDIA TO HELP US WITH ISSUES

The fifth tenet of our media strategy was *Ask the media to help us take issues to the public.* If we wanted to make and communicate decisions in a way that was in sync with our community, then we needed to take that issue to the media so they could help us communicate it to the public and gather community feedback.

One of the very first issues we did this with was the issue of disproportionality, the gap between white students' and minority students' test scores. The district had been trying for years to tackle the issue, but despite their efforts, the gap had edged steadily upward. I believed, if we had any hope of improving the situation, we'd have to get the minority communities involved. Many on my staff disagreed. As with the summer school incident, they felt the gap was embarrassing for the district and that the less we said about it the better. "No," I countered. "We can't solve this problem if our citizens can't see it. We *have* to talk about it, because how else can we fix it?" So we began to talk frankly with reporters about our minority children's performance. So we went to the big daily newspapers to reach the widest audience, but we focused on the minority media outlets—the radio stations that served black audiences, the weekly newspapers that served our ethnic communities. At each one we discussed the lagging test scores and explained why we needed the communities' help in turning them around. We are only half of the equation, we said. If you don't send your children to school ready to learn, we can't work miracles. We need you to read to your children at night. We need you to see that their homework is done. We also exhorted the communities to "adopt" their own students, to set up tutoring programs after school, to assign mentors to monitor children's progress, to provide role models for children who lacked them at home. There were some in the minority communities who felt that by publicizing the achievement gap we were reinforcing racial stereotypes, airing dirty laundry, contributing to rather than helping solve the problem. But our response was straightforward: If the public doesn't understand this problem, how can they help us fix it? Do you want to lament your children's performance or do you want to take action to address it?

This media attention did not produce an overt change in minority community activity. Tutoring and mentoring programs did not spring up as we'd hoped. But the attention created an awareness. It made the issue of minority achievement a *community* issue as well as a schools issue, and it sparked meetings and discussions about how to proceed. Talking about the gap in performance also created awareness outside the minority communities. Several foundations, corporations, and individuals approached us wanting to know what they could do to help. As a result, Stuart Sloan, the owner of a chain of supermarkets, committed up to $5 million of his personal money to turn an inner-city elementary school into a model school. Several other individual donors committed several hundred thousand dollars more to strengthen several other schools in low-income neighborhoods. The Coca-Cola Foundation donated $300,000 to fund the Pipeline Project, which sends University of Washington students into the schools to tutor our children. Might these donations have happened had we not publicized our gap in test scores? Perhaps; the multiple measures we were taking to transform the schools reassured potential donors that we would use their money wisely. But awareness of the performance gap showed them a glaring area where they could make a difference, and that chance to have an impact spurred them into action.

Another useful and appealing function afforded by the media is the opportunity to put an idea out there and almost instantaneously get feedback. It allows us to engage in a dynamic public dialogue on where the school district ought to go. So I began to use the platform of the media to test out new ideas. When I was considering requiring students to wear uniforms, I mentioned it first to a reporter. "Schoolchildren may be wearing uniforms," announced the TV news that night—and, sure enough, the public quickly told us how they felt. The uniform policy was a board decision, and the board decided to leave it up to individual schools. Seven schools decided to adopt uniforms. (Had it been my choice, we would have gone to uniforms the next year.) When we were considering giving teachers a full day out of the classroom each week for teacher training, I discussed the idea with a reporter. TEACHERS IN CLASSROOM 4 DAYS A WEEK? asked the *Seattle Times* headline the next day—and immediately we heard from parents and teachers that they were intrigued by the idea as long as it didn't shortchange academics. Because of the favorable response, we secured a grant that will allow us to study the idea.

People have criticized me for floating these trial balloons, as if I were teasing the public with fantasies we had no intention of fulfilling. What they don't realize is that this interactive decision-making process is a deliberate part of my leadership style. I cannot lead people where they do not want to go. But if I open a dialogue in the media, we can craft our vision jointly.

I know that our approach to the media is unusual. Most people in education are afraid of the media, afraid to invite them into their schools for fear that their secrets will be revealed. But there should be no secrets; we should go on the offensive and tell everything we know. Of course when reporters go into schools they're bound to find things that are broken; you can't run an enterprise as complex as a public-school district and not have problems. But those reporters will see many *more* things that are *right*. They'll see the millions of miracles teachers perform daily as they connect with students and help them learn. When school districts keep the media out, they suppress those stories too, and those are stories our communities need to hear.

One Sunday morning, just after I'd arrived in Seattle, my wife, Pat, and I were strolling in the public market when we passed a newsstand. I glanced at the Sunday paper and the headline caught my eye. In big letters it announced STANFORD ERA BEGINS. One of our sons graduated from Stanford University, and reflexively I picked up the paper, expecting to see a story about the college. To my surprise, my picture was beneath the headline alongside a lengthy story about the schools. "Look at this," I called to Pat, and handed her the paper. She looked it over, then gave it back to me. "Don't get excited," she said, "it's a slow news day." "No," I told her, "it's not going to stop. This city cares about its children. That's our name in the paper, but the story is really about children."

In my first days in Seattle we were on the defensive with the media. Since then, we've been the subject of an unprecedented amount of positive coverage. That's because we have fed the voracious public and media appetite for information about education. We are not the only ones to benefit, however: We've seen an increase in coverage about schools all over Puget Sound! We need this kind of coverage from the media. None of us can transform our schools without it.

QUIZ:
THE SCHOOLS' RELATIONSHIP WITH
THE MEDIA SHOULD BE:

(a) invite them in

Schools tend to see media as the enemy, when in fact the media can be their partner. They can help schools show their communities their countless successes, and help them engage in constructive dialogue with the community about how best to meet their children's needs.

CHAPTER 9

WE CAN ACHIEVE THE VICTORY WHEN . . . WE STOP BEING AFRAID OF CHANGE

QUIZ:
EDUCATION SHOULD BE:

(a) a safe environment where we do only things that we know will work. These are our kids!

(b) an environment where we are willing to try new things, but attempt to minimize risk

(c) a laboratory of change

Answer on page 194.

Not too long ago I went to an education conference at which the facilitator asked us to play a game. She had set up a ring toss peg at one end of the room and marked the floor at one-foot intervals, from one foot to sixteen feet, leading away from it. Then she handed us each three rings and asked us to pick a spot from which to toss. Most of the people in the room went to the one-, two-, or three-foot markers; a few people went to the eight-foot line. But I thought it would be more of a victory to get one ring on from the 16-foot mark than three rings on from the one-foot mark, so I (and a few others) went all the way back to 16 feet. The facilitator smiled at us. "Don't you think you're taking too much risk?" "Too much risk!" we all objected. "That's how we live our lives!" When my turn came to toss, I didn't get a single ring on. Later, however, after a chance to practice, I got two of my rings on. What a victory!

Afterward I thought about that exercise. I had taken away an important message: *Risk!* Don't build an organization that throws from the one-foot line. Our children don't have time for that. They need us to go for the big victories *now*. The facilitator's question, however, struck me as illustrative of the education culture. That culture as a whole is averse to taking risks. It's a culture of consensus, of reviewing every theory, idea, and bit of research before a decision is made and then deferring the decision until almost every stakeholder agrees. It becomes all too easy to analyze the problems and the answers endlessly, rather than take a risk and act. In the process, however, we shortchange our children.

One of my earliest encounters with this reluctance to change came less than a month after my arrival in the district. I was working in my office one evening when three of my board members came in and raised the issue of busing. They said they felt it was inherently unfair to bus children out of their neighborhoods. Could I find a way to end it? In response to their request, I began to study the issue.

The first person I talked to was Jamal. Jamal was ten years old and in the fourth grade. He was energetic and eager; when I stopped him in the hall of one of our elementary schools and introduced myself, he raised both his hands in an enormous salute, grinned at me broadly, and cried, "You're that superintendent dude!" When I asked him, among many other things, how he felt about having to travel so far to school, however, he grew sober. "I hate it," he said. "I hate getting up that early. Man, I get up at six-thirty! Do you know how early that is? I should be asleep!" He went on to describe how his mother woke him up and then expected him to help get his three younger siblings ready. By the time the girls had dressed and eaten, it was time to run for the bus. "Do you get breakfast?" I asked. He shook his head. "No. Most days I eat at school." "Does your mother ever come to school?" He looked as if I'd asked the impossible. "No," he answered. "It's too far away, and we don't have a car."

Jamal's teacher confirmed his story. She added that several times during quiet reading periods Jamal had fallen asleep, and she'd actually called his mother to suggest he go to bed earlier. Was Jamal's experience universal? Did other children who were bused fall asleep in school, depend on the school for breakfast, and sacrifice parent involvement? Over the next few weeks I talked to a lot more people. It didn't take long to see that the decades-old experiment was not producing the results it had been designed to achieve. Children of color were being bused in disproportionate numbers: Because white families fled the district rather than have their children bused, 95 percent of the children on buses were minorities. These children were spending an hour and a half a day in transit—the equivalent of thirty eight-hour days!—time they could have spent sleeping, doing homework, or sitting in a parent's lap. Their families were not participating in their school life despite the fact that family involvement is one of the key determinants of a child's success in school. And their academic performance was not improving! The gap between white and minority test scores hadn't changed since the program's inception.

Why had the district allowed busing to continue for so long? Because ending busing is a very difficult thing to do. School districts are under federal mandate not to segregate their schools. State money is often connected to desegregation plans. Communities of color understandably protest any move that might segregate the schools, and organizations such as the ACLU, the NAACP, and the Urban League fight to protect their constituencies from an education that would be separate and unequal. All of these organizations are doing what they have to do: protecting the interests of minority children.

So now we were faced with a dilemma. Busing seemed to be detrimental to the very children it was designed to serve, yet groups that wanted to see a better education for minority children would oppose an effort to eliminate it. What could we do? I believed we had no choice. We had made the academic achievement of *all* children our centerline. We had to do what was in the best interest of all children.

THE 80 PERCENT SOLUTION

One of the most important things I learned during my years in the army was to be prepared for change. Many people think of the Department of Defense and its component services as inflexible and unable to change. But the truth is actually quite different. The Department of Defense *embraces* change because it is preparing for threats that are constantly changing. The Department of Defense is in a constant state of adaptation.

What has made the military services so effective has been their ability to gather information, synthesize it, and then act upon the best information available. We knew that we would never have 100 percent of the information—no organization or business has the time or resources to spend on absolute certainty. We often had only 80 percent of the answer at the outset, but we made adjustments constantly on the way to the solution.

Well, that was the same kind of thinking we would need to apply to the schools. We couldn't wait until we had a solution that we knew with certainty was the 100 percent perfect way to go, or until we had one that would be pleasing to 100 percent of our stakeholders. We had to fix what was a serious problem *now*. And that meant getting our children of color off the buses and into the schools that were close to their homes, close to their families, and close to community support.

Changing student assignment would not be easy, however. As we phased in our new assignment plan, children of color would return to their neighborhood schools in the south end of the city, and they would bring with them a host of challenges. Many of these children were poor, many were bilingual or came from homes in which the parents had limited schooling. Many were performing far below their grade level. And because our south-end schools served denser neighborhoods, classes in those schools would be full. We would be bringing large numbers of children with significant educational challenges together in classes of twenty-eight or more with only one adult. Meanwhile, the schools in the north would be left with mostly white, middle-class children, and their classes would shrink as the bused students left. We wanted to end busing to boost the achievement of minority students as well as to provide fairness, but given those facts, how could we ensure that the achievement of children of color would rise proportionally with that of whites? *That* would be the challenge. Once we found an answer to that, we believed we could convince the community that our plan to end busing was in our students' best interest.

The answer, we felt, lay in what we were already doing. Reducing disproportionality, or the gap between white and minority test scores, was our second-highest priority, second only to raising academic achievement for all students, and we'd already introduced numerous measures to make that happen. We had also received several million dollars in private gifts specifically targeted for schools with large numbers of students of color. But we needed to do one more thing.

Quality schools close to home start with a key ingredient, the principal. The principal's job is difficult, and traditionally, successful principals of long standing have been permitted to select their schools. Most, as they approached retirement age, chose less-challenging schools. But that left us with brand-new principals in the most challenging schools when those schools needed seasoned academic leaders. So I asked five principals who had already demonstrated academic leadership if they would be willing to accept the challenge of leading more difficult schools. Every one agreed. These exceptional leaders saw my request as an honor; they liked the challenge of turning a troubled school around.

We still needed to address the concern about segregation. There was no question that the schools would become more racially homogeneous. Was there some way to dampen this effect? Yes. Instead of assigning students to their neighborhood schools, why not give them their choice of any school in the district? That way they could choose a school that was close to home—and most students had several in their geographic area—or they could choose a school across the city if they felt that was a better match with their needs. We couldn't afford to transport children to any school in the district, however; the number of bus routes would have been prohibitive. So we decided to create a "cluster plan" with schools grouped into clusters of four to six according to geographic area. Families could have the choice of any school in the district. We would provide free transportation, however, only to schools in their cluster.

Once we had our new cluster/choice plan ready and our new principal assignments made, we prepared to go to the community. We would need to show them that busing had not brought about achievement for their children to the degree expected, that the decision to end busing was not a racial issue but an educational one, and that our goals were the same as theirs: raising their children's achievement. We would also need to get their feedback. We knew we had an 80 percent solution; now we needed the community to help us make it better.

THE PEOPLE WHO COULD HAVE
DERAILED THE PLAN

We held community meetings at schools across the district; we met with the ACLU, the Urban League, and the NAACP; we made presentations to the state Human Rights Commission, the state Board of Education, and the state superintendent of public instruction. We met with groups of African-American parents, groups of Latino parents, groups of Asian and Native American parents. We came to these meetings prepared to explain to the community why busing jeopardized the achievement of minority students. We explained that children of color bore 95 percent of the burden; that the long bus ride required early wake-ups and walks to bus stops; that their parents, who needed desperately to be involved in their children's education, felt cut off from schools that were in unfamiliar neighborhoods miles across town. We explained all the measures we were taking to get minority achievement up.

Helping us explain the plan to the community was the school board. The board had been extremely supportive throughout the planning process. They had watched the busing program in action for fifteen or twenty years and had seen enrollment in the district drop from 100,000 to 41,000 during that time, in part because of middle-class flight. Now they played an active role in introducing the plan to the community.

Reaction to the plan was fairly consistent. A few individuals, concerned that we would implement the plan as presented without listening to their feedback, grew strident at the forums, wrote angry letters to the newspapers, and attacked the plan at school-board meetings. Most of the groups and individuals, however, agreed that the plan had merit and liked the idea of quality schools close to home, but they were skeptical of our ability to produce them. "You're concentrating children with tremendous problems," they said, "social problems, family problems, language problems, motivation problems. You're not giving them extra resources. How can you realistically expect their achievement to rise?"

They were right! We *would* be grouping students with significant educational challenges in fewer schools. Could we find money to give these children extra resources? At that time, our schools were funded the way all public schools were funded, with the district allotting dollars to each school based on the number of students it served. All students got the same allotment regardless of each student's needs. But now that formula began to seem suspect. If we really wanted every child to achieve, we'd have to create a funding mechanism that would permit us to give extra money to children with greater academic needs.

But how to do that? We had heard that Mike Strembinsky, the superintendent of schools in Edmonton, Alberta, Canada, had developed a "weighted student formula" that assigned money to different programs based on student needs. Joseph Olchefske, our chief financial officer, and I went to Alberta. We came away convinced that some version of Strembinsky's plan would work for us. Joseph, a former finance corporation executive was key. He set to work trying to figure out how to apply the weighted student concept to our district. Which "needs" were deserving of extra money—the need to overcome the disadvantages of poverty? Of living in a single-parent household? Of having parents who didn't speak English? How much extra money would it cost to compensate for each need? Working with his staff, Joseph determined that extra money should be allotted to students in three groups: students who qualified for free and reduced-price lunches (that is, students who fell within federal poverty guidelines); students for whom English was a second language; and students in special education. The money would follow children to the school of their choice. That meant that since schools in the south would have a disproportionate number of students with higher-level needs, those schools would receive larger amounts of money than the predominantly white schools in the north. Students in the north, who were closer to grade level, could be taught effectively, we believed, with the smaller amounts of money that would follow them.

Joseph presented his formula to our leadership team and we got incredibly excited. In a climate of bone-baring budget cuts, it felt as if we had minted new money. We knew of no other district that had tried such a maneuver (even Edmonton had not implemented anything on the scale we were planning), but it seemed like we could succeed.

Over the next year, as Joseph and his department worked out the details of the plan, the leadership committee went out to the community to describe the weighted student concept. Reaction was mixed and the overall message was You're getting closer—but keep working.

But now we faced a new challenge in acceptance of the plan. Parents of "nonweighted" students were concerned about their children getting less. We answered with a straightforward explanation: "You can tell what an organization believes in by how it spends its money. We believe in academic achievement for every child, and we are allocating money accordingly. Students from advantaged families are at or above academic standards, so the cost of closing the gap will be small; students with more challenging academic needs are farther from the bar, so raising them to the standard will cost more." Most parents seemed to accept this explanation. A few voiced their discontent to the school board, wrote letters to the newspapers, and tried to increase opposition to the plan, but large-scale protest never materialized.

Since our first set of community meetings, we had also changed the transportation plan. Some school-board members believed that while we had told parents they could choose any school in the district, the choice was a false one if we provided transportation only to schools in their cluster. That, they felt, was akin to segregation. So we changed the plan to provide transportation out of the assigned cluster if parents felt that attending a school in their cluster would not be the best situation for their child.

It was now May 1997. We had begun studying busing in August 1995, had made the decision to end it in November 1995, and had held our first round of community meetings between January and June 1996. We had hoped to have the community-feedback process completed and the plan approved by the school board by the spring of '97 so we could implement the plan for the '97–'98 school year, but with the community saying "Keep working on it," we clearly wouldn't meet that timetable. The start of the new program would have to wait until the '98–'99 school year.

HOW TEACHERS AND PRINCIPALS
MADE THE PLAN BETTER

At the same time we took the plan to the public, we also began talking about it inside the district. Here, too, reaction was mixed. Many teachers were initially unhappy. They believed strongly in multicultural education—one of the strengths of our district was that we had students from so many nationalities and cultures—and they were concerned that by concentrating so many children of color in south-end schools we would lose that diversification. They were also concerned that concentrating students of need would create impossible challenges in the schools. How can we adequately meet their needs? they wondered, raising the same concern as the community groups. The only way to teach them effectively would be to have smaller classes, more aides, and additional instructional materials. When we went back to the teachers the second time with the weighted student formula, their concerns were largely allayed. The added money would enable them to buy the extra resources they needed.

Principals had additional concerns, however. First, they disagreed with the groups we'd created for allotting dollars to students of need. Since we were now holding them accountable for student achievement, they wanted to make sure that *every* group of children that was significantly below grade level was given extra money. To this end, they lobbied us to add students who scored in the thirtieth percentile and below on standardized tests. We agreed with them that raising these students to grade level would require extra effort and attention and added children with low test scores to the groups that qualified for an additional "weight." Second, the principals were concerned that small schools would lose out to big schools as the money was apportioned. In the past, librarians, assistant principals, and secretaries had been supplied to every school, regardless of size. But under the new system money would be apportioned strictly on a per-student basis. Small schools worried that they wouldn't have enough to purchase those amenities. So we amended the plan again, giving every school a base package that included a principal, a secretary, and a half-time librarian in the elementary schools, and those positions plus two assistant principals, an attendance person, and an assistant secretary in the middle and high schools. The student allotments would come on top of that base package. The principals' third concern was that under the new system, schools with few students with "weighted" needs would see their budgets decline. They were right, and we answered them just as we had answered the parents: "The students in those schools are closer to grade level, so the cost of bringing them up to grade level is smaller. We have to give the money to schools where the gap between performance and grade level is wider." Principals of the "losing" schools grumbled, but it was a hard explanation to argue with strenuously since it advanced our most basic goal, academic achievement for all children. What's more, it was fair; unlike the old system in which some schools had been able to argue successfully for extra dollars, under the new formula the rules were the same for every school. They were about children. So that portion of the plan remained the same.

In the spring of 1997 the school board approved the weighted student formula. The board had been hearing about the formula for a year, and had been supportive all that time. They knew that the success of the new student assignment plan (the plan by which we assigned students to schools) hinged on configuring the schools' budgets in this way. So by the time the details were worked out and the package went to them for approval, their yes vote was assured.

In October 1997, the plan went to the school board. It had been a year and a half in development; we'd stayed close to our constituents with over thirty community meetings. And while not everyone was happy with the final product, the firestorm of opposition that could have derailed it had never materialized. The school board approved the plan in November 1997 and it went into effect for the 1998–99 school year.

We have created a two-year phase-in process. Children and families have strong ties to their schools; few want to leave once they're settled. So we've told families that we will continue to provide transportation to their current school for two years after the cluster plan goes into effect. It won't be until those two transition years are over, in the 2000–2001 school year, that we will have a full end to mandatory busing. However, the trend is showing that parents of color are choosing schools closer to home rather than bus rides for their children.

In the meantime, however, we *have* implemented the weighted student formula. (The school board had already approved that portion of the plan.) Schools with large numbers of "weighted" students have seen their budgets grow. They have used the extra money to hire additional teachers and teacher's aides in order to reduce the adult/student ratio. Bailey-Gatzert Elementary School, for example, where 88 percent of the students qualify for free or reduced-price lunches, 25 percent of the students are in bilingual programs, 28 percent are homeless, and 12 percent are in special education, has been able to bring class sizes down from 1:28 to 1:22. At Cooper Elementary, where 80 percent of the students qualify for free or reduced-price lunches and 25 percent are bilingual, the principal and staff used weighted student money to purchase a school-wide reading curricu-

lum called Success for All, a highly structured approach to teaching reading that the staff felt was well suited to the students' needs. They also hired
an additional PE teacher, eliminated a recess period, and added an extra
gym period each day. The second gross-motor period provides an important outlet for students' energy and enables them to concentrate better in
class; it also builds students' skills in cooperation and self-discipline, two
emphases at Cooper, where, until recently, rowdiness and uncooperative-
ness were the norm.

Few schools lost significant amounts of money, since all schools
still have weighted students. But for those that have, the experience has
been a challenge. Most have become creative in finding ways to make up
some of the loss. Eckstein Middle School, for example, lost $100,000. To
replace that money, the parent community held a fund drive using
phone and mail solicitations. They raised $30,000, enough to keep the
supplies budget intact. But the remaining $70,000 loss required cutting
back teacher time that was used to give remedial help to students and to
teach one class of German, and cutting the library assistant to half-time.
The school could have made its cuts elsewhere; the staff weighed cutting
back the school nurse or school counselor and cutting administrative staff.
But when they looked at the needs of the children, they felt the need for
those services was greater. Kimball Elementary lost even more money
because in addition to getting less money from the district, they lost two
teaching positions that had been funded by a city levy that ended. As they
prepared their strategic plan and budget for the coming year, they had several programs they strongly wanted to fund—all-day kindergarten for
all their students, a school counselor, an additional nurse, a Spanish-
speaking instructional assistant—but they knew there was no way they
could fund them all. So the staff and the parent community prioritized
their needs and decided that the most pressing concern was funding all-
day kindergarten. They have done that, but as a result have had to
increase class size slightly. Most class sizes will now be at the maximum
allowed in the teachers' contract: twenty-eight for kindergarten through
third grade; thirty-two for fourth and fifth grades. As at Eckstein, the
school became resourceful at finding new money. The volunteer coordinator (who is a parent) worked with the principal to write a funding proposal to a foundation; the proposal was funded and the school received
enough money to pay for a half-time counselor, one of their other top
priorities.

It is still too early to tell what impact the end of busing and the
weighted student formula will have on student achievement. But we know
what we would like to see. At the end of the first year we hope to see standardized test scores for minority students that are two to five percentile

points higher than they were the year before, and an increase in participation by those children's parents. Over the long term, we hope to close the achievement gap between minority students and whites. We also hope that ending busing will bring large numbers of middle-class students into our district as they realize that they *can* attend their neighborhood schools, and that those schools are as strong, as challenging, and as achievement-oriented as their private and suburban counterparts.

At one time, ending busing had seemed unthinkable. But once we made the philosophical shift that said children and their academic achievement were our centerline, we had no choice. That shift required us to put strategies in place that would make achievement possible for all students, district-wide. Those strategies—including the cluster plan and weighted student formula—have now empowered us to provide high-quality instruction to even the most challenging children at the tactical, or building, level. Because we made shaping that environment a collaborative process—because we asked for parents', students', and educators' input from the beginning and then responded to their concerns—the plan passed ultimately with little resistance. And most importantly, when a school district can demonstrate that it is making a decision that is truly in its children's best interests, who can fundamentally disagree?

"IF CHANGE IS SO EASY, WHY DON'T YOU GO FIRST?"
—SCOTT ADAMS, *THE DILBERT PRINCIPLE*

THE TOUGHEST CHANGE OF ALL

Change is never easy. In fact it might surprise people who have watched the number of changes we have instigated in our district to know that for our school board, teachers, principals, parents, staff, and me, there have been many sleepless nights as we've searched for solutions that will improve education for all children. It is especially hard when we have to look parents in the eyes and tell them that we can't give them what they want, what they believe is best for their child.

The most difficult change I've had to make since becoming superintendent was just such a situation. Shortly after arriving in the district, I visited Madrona Elementary School. Madrona was a beautiful old building on a quiet, tree-lined street, but the peacefulness of the exterior belied the state of confrontation inside. The school was home to two very different programs, a regular K–5 program in one half of the building, the district's elementary Accelerated Progress Program (APP) in the other, and the two programs were highly incompatible.

The K–5 program served 255 students, most of whom were minorities; the APP program served 450 students, most of whom were white. And as you walked through Madrona, it was hard not to feel the division between students, parents, teachers, and programs. The APP side of the building sported decorative bulletin boards and artwork created by parent volunteers, small clusters of children working in hallways and classrooms with more parent volunteers, and an assortment of gerbils, computers, books, and supplies that parents and children had brought from home. If you stopped to read the children's art and writing on the walls you'd read about field trips they had gone on, about special visitors to their classrooms, about the wealth of programs that had been made possible by parent contributions. The K–5 side of the building, on the other hand, despite the fact that it received a great deal of support from the APP parents, was considerably more spare. Hall displays were limited to what the hardworking teachers were able to do after the children had gone home. Classrooms were stocked with just the district-supplied essentials. Specialists worked with small groups of children in such basic areas as math and reading, but the parents of the K–5 children did not or could not provide the same level of exciting supplemental experiences. Throughout the building was a palpable sense of haves and have-nots, and this inequality did not escape the children. For the self-esteem and the confidence of the K–5 students, the situation at Madrona had to change.

In fact, the district had been trying to do something about Madrona for years. It had examined several sites as replacement homes for APP and had settled on Lowell School as the best alternative. Lowell, which was centrally located, had a capacity of 450 students but was serving only 250: 220 in a K–5 program and 30 in a program for children with profound disabilities. Of the 220 children in the K–5 program, 164 were bused in from other neighborhoods. Of that number, 26 were fifth-graders who would be moving on to middle school at the end of the year. That meant that if we converted Lowell to APP, we would disrupt 138 K–5 students who could be bused to other schools of their choice, and only thirty children from the Lowell neighborhood who could be given their choice of two other high-achieving schools less than a mile away. It is never a desirable or easy thing to ask families to leave a school, but this was the least disruptive way we could create a new home for APP.

Unfortunately, what made sense to the district didn't make sense to the families of the thirty children. They loved their school and were determined to stay, and, because the district had wanted to make this move in the past, they had organized their entire neighborhood—neighbors, businesses, community organizations—to fight the "closure" of their school. They accused the district of making a decision based on class, of relocating the Lowell children because they were poor and catering to the APP families who were middle class. And in the past, the district, concerned about appearing to bow to elite interests, had stopped short of moving the program. Administrators had studied option after option, hoping to find a less contentious solution.

After visiting Madrona many times, however, and after attending two large parent meetings at which the divisiveness between the K–5 and the APP parents was strident, I decided that the move could wait no longer. So we studied the alternatives once again, and after several months decided that the best place for APP would indeed be Lowell. We then held several community meetings to discuss the plan with parents and get public feedback.

We were expecting opposition, and we got it. From the moment the news of our plan surfaced, the parents began a coordinated campaign to change our minds. They called our offices daily, they flooded the newspapers with letters and editorials, they held a letter-writing campaign. But in the end, there was simply no place else to move APP.

More than at any time since I'd taken the job as superintendent, I wished I didn't have to act. But I had to. I wasn't making a decision about the 450 students in APP, or about the 255 K–5 children at Madrona, or even about the 30 families at Lowell. I was making a decision for *all* of them—and for the thousands of children who would be attending those programs in years to come.

I've thought back on the Lowell situation many times since then, not only because it was such a difficult decision but also because it exemplified a truism about making change: Change is rarely simple. No wonder we sometimes look ahead, anticipate the chain of events that a difficult action will trigger, and then, out of fear, or self-protection, or concern that we won't have a 100 percent solution, decline to take that first essential step. But we can't afford to do that! We are the stewards of our children's futures. They depend on us to do what is right so that they will have the skills and knowledge to build successful lives. We can't let our own fear of change and opposition derail us from our mission. Our children need us. We must put our own fears and egos aside and do what is right for them.

WE ARE A DOING ORGANIZATION, NOT A TALKING ORGANIZATION.

QUIZ:
EDUCATION SHOULD BE:

(c) a laboratory of change

We live in a world that is constantly changing—yet we use educational practices that were developed a century ago! If we want to have maximum impact on our children, if we want to prepare them for the world they will inherit, we have to adapt to our changing world. We have to experiment, take risks, even be willing to make mistakes—as long as every decision we make is made in the best interest of our children.

CHAPTER 10

WE CAN ACHIEVE THE VICTORY WHEN ... WE USE LOVE TO LEAD OUR CHILDREN

QUIZ:

WHAT IS THE KEY TO EFFECTIVE LEADERSHIP?

(a) providing clear direction

(b) getting all stakeholders involved in decision-making

(c) holding people accountable

(d) having a plan

(e) love

Answer on page 214.

By 7:40 every morning, Tom Bailey, principal of Chief Sealth High School, is out in the hallways greeting students by name. He gets most of them right, despite the fact that there are 900 students from 80 cultures in the school. The ones he doesn't know he promises to give a quarter to if he forgets their name the next time. Outside, Mike Silva, the school's security guard, wearing a magenta shirt and Hawaiian shorts that are visible a block away, is chatting with students about the local rock band, Soundgarden, and giving out high-fives. He, too, knows almost every student by name—and not because they've gotten into trouble. Both of these men have made it their business to learn the students' names because for many of the noble Sealth children, who come from some of Seattle's most difficult circumstances, Sealth is the most stable "home" they know. Unless their school staff knows them as individuals, their problems will be magnified. And so it is throughout our school district. Children and students will not learn from people who do not love them.

> Children will not learn from adults who don't love them.

Most people don't expect a general to talk about love. But we talk about love all the time, because love is a key leadership principle. Love is what the most famous military commanders use to inspire their troops to risk their lives in battle; it's what the most effective CEOs use to elicit maximum performance from their employees; it's what the best parents use to encourage their children to learn and grow. It's certainly what teachers and principals must use to get academic performance from their students. And it's what superintendents must use to lead their districts to achieve their visions.

I learned about love from my family. My parents, who were not formally educated and had few material goods to give, nonetheless had an unending supply of love, and they used that love to make us feel richly endowed. My sisters and I believed we could do anything: Our parents' love gave us that foundation. Once, when I was ten years old, the doorknob on the front door of our house broke. My parents were concerned because there was no way to lock the door and it would be at least a day before my father, who was working two jobs, would have time to fix it. So I decided to help. After school I got out some tools and set to work, and by the time my parents came home I had the inner workings of the doorknob strewn across the living room floor. I knew from the look on my parents' faces that I hadn't done them any favors. There was no way my father could put the lock back together, and the thirty dollars we'd have to pay a locksmith was a precious amount of money. My sisters had teased, "You're going to get it. Wait until mom gets home, and worse, wait until dad gets home." But to my surprise, neither my mother nor my father yelled. Instead they *praised* my attempt to fix it. And the feeling of that moment—the love, the respect, the belief they felt in me—made me feel absolutely powerful.

I felt a similar kind of love and respect from my sisters and my neighbors. They didn't all have the tolerance my parents had—the ability to overlook my antics of the moment and see the larger picture—but I felt from them that same kind of encouragement and caring. When I got a B for the first time in my seventh-grade French class, I think my entire neighborhood rejoiced. As adults they knew that I had triumphed over my sixth-grade setbacks. It was this foundation of support and caring that made me feel I could succeed.

I felt this kind of success-building love again when I joined the army. As I was coming up through the ranks—as a lieutenant, a captain, a major, a colonel—I was constantly aware of the love my officers felt: love for me, for their jobs, for my peers. It was in the passion and pride they felt for the army; it was in the way they looked us in the eye, deeply and respectfully, with genuine concern for how we were doing; it was in the way they worked hard to solve our problems. I realized that leadership was not a matter of dictating orders and commanding people to obey them. I realized that the very essence of leadership was love.

"JOHN, I DON'T LIKE YOU"

I had already been in the army for nine years, however, before I realized that I, too, had adopted that leadership style. It was 1970 and I was commanding an aircraft-maintenance company in Vietnam. We were in Long Thanh North, an isolated area in central Vietnam, and our job was to repair our unit's 450 helicopters and fixed-wing aircraft. I would work all day and often into the night, caring for the people in my command. At the end of the day I'd find myself thinking: Here I am, leading 450 men whose lives are in my hands. Do I have the tools to be able to do this?

I had led numerous units before—in Germany, in Korea, on an earlier tour in Vietnam. How, I wondered, had I done it then? Clearly I had been successful. My companies had achieved their missions. Their morale was high. The soldiers had worked hard and been enthusiastic. Was it something I had done that made them feel that way? Morale was high in this company too, despite the fact that conditions were not easy. What was I doing, what had I learned, that enabled me to bring out strong performances? I finally realized I was doing for my people what my officers had done for me. I was leading them with love. I was caring for them as people, not just as cogs in the military machine, and by being passionate about my own job, I was spreading my passion to them.

By 1976 I was back in the States as the commander of an aviation-support squadron at Fort Hood, Texas. I was attending an impromptu Friday evening happy hour on the base when Lisa Atwood, the wife of one of my best officers, came up to me. "John," she said, "I want you to know that I don't like you." I mustered the courage to ask her a sheepish "Why? What did I do?" With her hands on her hips she said, "You've made my husband love his job more than he loves me!" I couldn't respond. I knew the army has a way of gobbling up every millimeter of a person's attention, and her husband was one of the best leaders I'd ever had; he'd turned a gargoyle unit into the Venus de Milo. Apparently the love that I had received from my commanders and in turn passed on to my soldiers had been so contagious that he had caught it too. Lisa's comment was made partly in jest, partly in genuine vexation (and told me that I would now have to turn more of my own leadership toward our 1,000 families). What she could not have known, though, in saying what she did, was that she'd paid me the highest compliment.

LOVE AT T. T. MINOR

The kind of loving leadership that inspires people to perform is the kind school districts need—and it is nowhere more apparent than at T. T. Minor Elementary School in Seattle's inner-city Central District. Stand at the front door of Minor any morning at 8:45 and watch the buses unload and you will see children who are loved. Waiting at the bus doors will be Luevennie Bridges, Minor's principal, waiting to usher her children into a new day. As the bus doors open and the children cascade out, she greets each one of them by name, looks them warmly in the eye, and asks about a project they are doing. Walk through the halls of T. T. Minor and you'll hear Luevennie talking to her teachers. "I noticed Darryl looks down again today. What's going on for him at home?" "I noticed that Janine and Abdul have been absent a lot recently. Have you talked to their parents?" Even in these casual hallway conversations she lets her teachers know that nothing in their students' lives can go unnoticed, that responsibility for the children's achievement extends beyond the building's walls.

Every month she meets with every teacher to discuss their students' progress. She wants to hear immediately when a student is having trouble so she can find him or her a volunteer tutor. She wants to know why a student hasn't passed a unit test twice in a row—has the teacher tried teaching the material a different way? She discusses the individualized learning plan for every student, making her own high expectations clear. "If these children can't learn here, then they can't learn," she says defiantly, daring anyone to believe, even for a second, that her students are incapable of learning.

For Luevennie Bridges, helping the students learn means bringing in the parents—and that isn't easy in a school where the poverty rate is 80 percent. Most of these parents had poor school experiences themselves, so Luevennie goes out of her way to make them comfortable. She calls them on the phone just to share good news. "We're so proud of Cassandra! The way she read out loud today. I wish you could have been here!" "Thank you, Mrs. Johnson, for reading so much with Trevor. His reading is so much better!" She organizes sit-down dinners for her families with white table-cloths and flowers and a program by the children. And when she needs to urge a recalcitrant parent into doing more with her child, her words are firm, but her voice is kind. There's no mistaking that she is asking out of love for the child.

It's impossible to spend time at T. T. Minor and not feel that Luevennie Bridges believes in every student, so it was no surprise that when she handed out diplomas at the fifth-grade graduation (to which the children came wearing tuxedos the school had rented and gowns made by the grad-uates' parents) she didn't just hug the students as she handed them their papers, she engulfed them. The entire auditorium could feel her love. And it was also no surprise that in June 1997, after Luevennie's first year in the school, standardized test scores for these students, who are 98 percent African-American and live in one of Seattle's most impoverished and crime-ridden neighborhoods, rose by fourteen and fifteen points. That's what loving and leading can do.

One of my principals said to me, "Thanks for giving me the freedom to love my staff."

"I, JOHN STANFORD, SOLEMNLY AFFIRM . . ."

So how do we get all of our principals, all of our teachers, to love and lead like Luevennie Bridges? By talking about it, by making it one of our core values, by modeling it at every level of our system. It starts on the very first day of school.

Each year on the first day of school we hold an opening-day rally at a large stadium near downtown Seattle. Student bands play, cheerleaders lead cheers, teachers and principals deliver pep-rally-style speeches as we try to get everyone fired up about going back to school. Thousands of par-ents, teachers, and students attend. This year, as I thought about the cer-emony, I decided to add an extra element. I wrote an oath, which I asked Superior Court Judge Bobbie Bridge to administer. It went like this:

"I, John Stanford, do solemnly affirm that I will love, cherish, and pro-tect every child who is entrusted to my care. . . ."

OATH ON BEHALF OF CHILDREN

- I, John Stanford, do solemnly affirm that I will love, cherish, and protect every child entrusted to my care.

- I affirm that I will endeavor to prepare all students to meet the highest standards of achievement, conduct, and citizenship possible, knowing that this will help to maintain the health of our city both now and in the future.

- I affirm that I will work cooperatively with parents and members of the community to produce a world-class, student-focused learning system for our precious children and students.

September 1997

On the day of the ceremony, after all the other guest speakers had finished and before the All-City Band played their closing medley of stirring songs, it was my turn at the podium. I stood up and told the crowd that I would be taking an oath that affirmed my love for our children. I invited the judge to the stage, and as she began to read the words, I repeated them after her. At first I couldn't make out the noise that seemed to be accompanying me in the background, but after a moment I realized what I was hearing: It was the entire stadium full of people taking the oath with me.

I wrote the oath and took it at the rally because I wanted to make visible the importance of love in our district. When a teacher loves her students, she gives them the belief that they can succeed. When a principal loves her teachers, she gives them the energy they need to work with their students every day. When I love my principals and teachers, I let them know they are doing the most important job in the world. When a community loves its schools, it gives them the strength and resources to do their job.

The truth is that people want to succeed. Every person has a little ember burning inside, a spark that can flare up into achievement. Our job—as parents, as teachers, as principals, as superintendents and school boards—is to fan those embers. And the way to fan those embers is with love.

We have a family support worker in our district. Her name is Leah Wilson, but everybody calls her "Mom." She's the spiritual leader of every school she goes to. She meets with the families of our disadvantaged students and gives them clothes, or money to turn on the electricity, or food to keep them going. But mostly she gives everyone love. She wraps her arms around every child she sees and hugs as if the child were a long-lost cousin. "How are you doing in school today?" she'll ask, "I know you got an A!" And for as long as the children are in her arms, they know they *can* get A's because Leah believes they can do it. Every child needs a Leah. So does every teacher, every principal, and every superintendent.

THE PRINCIPLES OF LOVING AND LEADING

You've been in love. You know how you felt when someone believed in you. You felt you could do anything! That's how we make people feel when we love and lead them. If we follow the principles of loving and leading, we can make our students, our teachers, and our principals feel that way too. We can produce school districts where everyone achieves.

LOVING AND LEADING MEANS CREATING VICTORIES EVERY DAY

I walked into the lobby of one of our middle schools the day before school was scheduled to start. I was making visits to ensure that school would open successfully. I saw a parent sitting at a table behind a mountain of two-by-six-inch pieces of paper. "What are you doing?" I asked, wondering what the school was planning to do with all those pieces of paper. "Making sure tomorrow is a success," she answered. She was carefully copying a child's name onto every paper. She was making heart name tags so that every teacher would know every student's name. The school wanted to make sure that every child's first day was personal and loving—a success.

I build small successes with my "walking around fund." I have a checking account with $100,000 in it, money that was donated by businesses for discretionary spending. As superintendent, I have no school-district discretionary fund. It was cut to help make up our $35 million shortfall. I carry that checkbook with me wherever I go so that I can turn promising efforts into success. I wrote a $500 check to a group of high-school students who had completed an ambitious roller-blade trip across America to call attention to young people's perseverance. I wrote a $300 check to a group of students who were painting a mural. They had run out of paint, and I bankrolled their effort so they could complete their ambitious project. I wrote a $500 check to a principal at one of our middle schools to help finance a trip, and a $900 check to a secretary at an alternative school so that she could buy the first ever yearbook for their school. I asked them to leverage the money to raise the rest and they did! It thrills me to be able to write these checks and to know that the impact of the money goes well beyond the immediate project. It resonates long afterward in the confidence each person feels from having experienced that success. We must produce opportunities for victory every day. It isn't hard to do, and everyone needs one!

LOVING AND LEADING MEANS RECOGNIZING PEOPLE'S EFFORTS

Perhaps you've been in love and the person who loved you brought you a rose, or a note, to let you know how special you were. Do you remember how that made you feel? We need to make the people we lead feel every bit that special. We need to send them little tokens of appreciation, little notices that we see and recognize their efforts—because that will motivate them to keep trying.

> I carry a small bundle of three-by-five cards with me everywhere I go. They say "IOU a day off for your contributions to the values of our organization. Please see your supervisor to arrange the appropriate time." I hand them out when I see a person doing something wonderful. Recently I gave one to a teacher who was attending a meeting at her school where we were explaining our new exit decision policy to parents. Many parents had brought children to the meeting and as the meeting wound on, the children grew restless and began distracting their parents from the speaker. This teacher, despite the fact that she had come on her free time to hear the speaker herself, sat down on the floor, took out some paper, and organized quiet activities for the children. What love and heroism she displayed!

There is a middle-school teacher in our district who sends me a card every week praising an individual on her staff. She knows that when I come I'll say something to the people she's mentioned. The cards take her only a couple of minutes to write, but the people she's honored glow from her recognition for days. There are teachers in our district who send notes home to parents every afternoon, telling them about something special their child did in school. The notes take only ten minutes or so to write—time I'm sure the teachers would rather spend at home—but they color the entire evening, maybe the entire week, for the children and their parents.

RECOGNIZING THE HEROISM OF TEACHERS

The military is famous for its system of recognizing people's efforts. My army uniform, regardless of my rank, advertised my achievements: There was a Distinguished Flying Cross, Bronze Stars, Air Medals, Legions of Merit. These medals were my "hero's kit." We were never paid for the risks we took, so the army used the medals to recognize past service and to inspire us to do more.

We have heroes in our schools whose contributions are just as significant to the democracy as anything I did in the military. So we plan to create a medal of heroism in education. It will be an elegant award, which I will present to those in our district who have turned in a heroic performance: students who have significantly raised their grades, teachers who have strengthened the performance of an entire class, principals who have led their schools to a sustained increase in achievement. We will have dozens of categories, and hundreds of winners. It will be one more way to recognize our people's efforts and a way of inspiring them to do more.

LOVING AND LEADING MEANS CHALLENGING PEOPLE TO EXCEL

Before we announced our decision to require a C grade-point-average for high-school graduation, I asked students in almost every school I visited what they thought of the idea. In one of the high schools a group of students gathered around me in the hall. "Don't do it," one of them counseled. "I wouldn't make the cut!" A few others nodded. But the majority disagreed. "I think you should do it," one of the girls advised me. "If we knew those were the requirements, then we'd have to do it." "Yeah," another girl added, "we might not like it, but we'd have to do it." Another one weighed in, "It would make us work harder—and that's probably good." These students wanted us to push them to achieve.

That's what we have to do for everybody in public education because people rise to the level of expectation we hold for them. We must challenge our students to take the hardest courses, to turn every assignment in on time, to raise the quality of their work consistently. We must challenge our teachers to raise every student up to grade level, to find alternative ways of teaching the children who are failing, to raise every student's performance, even those who are ahead, by 10 percent each year. We must challenge our principals to set lofty visions for their schools—standardized test scores averaging in the sixtieth percentile, a dropout rate below 5 percent, zero incidents of violence.

We must challenge parents to send us their children ready to learn, having eaten and slept soundly, having done their homework, having acquired the belief that school is all important. And we must challenge our communities to help us in this job of public education; we must challenge them to give us their support, to volunteer in schools, to come in and share their expertise, to ask a teacher or a principal, "How can I help?"

Robert Browning said, "Let your reach exceed your grasp, or what is Heaven for?" and he was right. We must set high goals for the people we lead. We must make sure they have the tools to reach them. Then we must love them all the way there.

LOVING AND LEADING MEANS MODELING THE BEHAVIOR WE WANT

As a leader your behavior is contagious. Leaders have that effect on the people. If I come into my office grumped up, the people around me will be grumped up. If a teacher comes to school excited, the students will be excited. So if we want the people in our school system to behave a certain way, we need to model that behavior for them.

The modeling must start at the top. If we want to create an environment of achievement and hard work, then we must hold ourselves to the highest standards. If we want an environment of courtesy and respect, then we must never speak disparagingly of others publicly, even if we disapprove of their actions. If we want a reputation of hospitality and openness to parents, then we must be gracious to all the parents who come to see us, even those who criticize us roundly for decisions with which they disagree. We must not only talk these values, we must live them every day. If I as superintendent live these values, then I will model them for my principals, my principals will model them for their teachers, the teachers will model them for their students. Modeling is one of the most important things we can do in public education because our students will learn much more from what we *do* than they will from what we *say*.

LOVING AND LEADING MEANS MAKING IT FUN

We need to make school fun! One of the ways to do that is to bring the excitement and relevance of the world into our students' lives. That's why we've developed partnerships with the community to make our entire city a classroom. That's why at Garfield High School, which produced twenty-five merit finalists last year, students do math and science outside their regular math and science classrooms: They use "autocad" software and a wind tunnel to design a sport-utility vehicle, and work with architects and engineers to design and do blueprints for a construction lab at the school. That's why at West Seattle High School students aren't studying China only in the classroom; they're visiting the Port of Seattle, where they're meeting with Chinese trade delegations. That's why at B. F. Day Elementary School students aren't learning about math only during math time; they're calculating prices and profits in a student-run "village."

School is hard work! And everyone needs fun as fuel for their effort. That's why the principal at Sanislo Elementary School took her whole school to the top of Seattle's Space Needle to celebrate 50,000 nights of independent reading. That's why the entire faculty at South Shore Middle School jumped into a lake to celebrate the fact that overall student performance had climbed for the year. That's why Van Asselt Elementary School begins every Monday with a "victory assembly" where the entire school gets fired up to start the week. We need regular opportunities to celebrate.

School is *hard* for students, teachers, and administrators. So if we want to keep them going, we better make sure they're having fun!

LOVING AND LEADING MEANS KEEPING HOPE ALIVE

Here in public education we are in the business of hope. We have so many children who come to our schools from circumstances that are hopeless—from families who have lost their jobs, or lost their homes, or lost the belief that they can succeed. When these children get to school, we must be their hope. We must say in a hundred different ways, a hundred times a day, We love you! We believe in you! We know you can succeed! We have to say it so often and so loudly that we drown the voices from outside the schools that give the opposite message.

But at the same time, outside our walls, our communities must keep hope alive for *us*. Without their love and support we will get depleted—financially, emotionally, spiritually—and we will have no hope left to pass on to our children. Most of America's public schools are good, yet right now communities in America are dashing our hopes. Communities don't mean to be so negative, but the constant drone that schools are broken, that teachers are broken, that students are broken, is sapping energy from every classroom. If we listen long enough to that drone, we will fulfill the prophecy. So we have to plead with our communities: *Build up* our schools, don't berate them. Turn your concerns about public education into constructive action. We are your hope for the twenty-first century. Join us. Volunteer. Help us be the haven for children that you want us to be. Work with us to keep their hope alive.

LOVE ISN'T EASY

Loving and leading doesn't mean going easy on people no matter what they do; it means coaching people to do their best, it means pushing them farther than they may want to go, it means letting them know when you think they can be doing more. Loving and leading can mean giving *tough love*.

We often assume, when people disappoint us, that they can do no better. But that's rarely true. More often, they're having a problem that interferes with their performance. If we can find the source of the problem, we can help them overcome it.

Often, their problem is really *our* problem; the person isn't performing because we weren't clear in our directions. Marcelle, a senior at one of our high schools, told me she was sorry that she hadn't worked harder during her school career because now she wished she was going to college. She hadn't realized that her mediocre grades would eventually limit her ability to land a satisfying job. Was that Marcelle's fault? I don't think so. I think we failed to explain to her how important her education was. We failed to paint the picture for her of how everything she did in school would help her climb a ladder toward the future.

One of our kindergarten teachers, a thirty-year veteran, told me that she had been planning to quit before the district established its vision and academic plan. She'd lost her "juice," she said. She still loved working with the children, but as the problems of her low-income students had grown, she'd felt that the district's support had dwindled. In subtle ways their expectations of her and her students had declined. The result was daunting demoralization. It was the establishment of the vision—and the expectation that every child's performance would rise by 10 percent—that got her juices flowing again. The quarterly reports, her school's academic achievement plan, the knowledge that teachers and principals were being respected and supported and held accountable for student performance, all got her reinvigorated about her job. This teacher is one of our best kindergarten teachers; it would have been a tragedy to lose her. But our low expectations had caused her morale and performance to suffer.

For both these people, we had failed to do the loving thing: We had failed to set clear, high expectations for what we needed them to do. If we don't care enough about our people to give them strong direction, how can we realistically expect them to succeed?

LOVE 'EM AND LEAD 'EM

1. *Produce opportunities for victory every day.* Everybody needs a victory every single day. That's what keeps people going. That's why each month at our administrators' meeting (where all the principals and key department heads gather), I ask people to give me the name of someone who works with them or for them who deserves a note of thanks from me. I then write a note to everyone: "Dear Jim, I asked 150 supervisors for the names of people who are making massive contributions to our organization and they said you. I just wanted to send you my thanks and appreciation for what you do for our children."

2. *Make it happen.* Don't just talk about change, or about helping people, or even about loving people. Make it happen.

3. *Find a way not to be an obstructionist.* Anytime you create change, you run into people who liked things better the old way. That's only natural. But in the schools, people who stand in the way of change are standing in the way of making things better for our children. So when you encounter those people, talk about your vision; remind them about where you're going. And ask yourself every once in a while: Am I sometimes an obstructionist to changes that could make our schools better for children?

4. *Love the one you're with.* I've said this to my principals many times. One day a principal told me that she heard herself saying it to her staff. According to our new teachers' union contract, a senior teacher who is being displaced (because her school has eliminated her position, for example) has the right to take the position of a more junior teacher in her school (assuming that she is authorized to teach that position). A senior teacher in this principal's school had just exercised her right to do that—and the rest of the staff was devastated. The displaced junior teacher had been an excellent teacher and a very strong member of their team. To help her teachers accept the loss and move forward, this insightful and caring principal told her staff, "Whoever is on our team is on our team. We have to welcome her and work with her. We have to love the one we're with." The staff was buoyed by her words. They did welcome the senior teacher

and over the next few months they rebuilt the sense of teamwork they had had with the junior teacher.

5. *Don't do dumb things*.

LOVE IS A ONE-WAY STREET

It takes a lot of courage to love—because love isn't always returned. The
people we lead may give us back ten measures of love for every one we give
them—or they may give us nothing at all. But our job is to love them regardless, to remain constant, consistent, and caring even when we're feeling slighted. The payoff is not that they will love us in return. It is in
watching our people grow.

For school districts to be successful, this one-way street of love must
run, top down, through every level of the system. Teachers must love their
students; principals must love their students and teachers; superintendents
and school boards must love their students, teachers, and principals—all
without needing to have their love returned. We will know the measure
of our love by the performance of our children.

TEACHERS HAVE TO LOVE THEIR STUDENTS

I was at an event one day where I met a teacher from another district. It
was shortly after our opening-day ceremony, and I told her about the oath
that our entire stadium had taken. Her reaction was immediate. "Take out
the word 'love,'" she said. "I don't love all my children. I like them and I
want to help them. But I don't *love* them."

I thought of a boy I'd met named Julio who, in seventh grade, reads at
the fourth-grade level. Julio lives with his grandparents, who cannot read
at all. So who will help him sound out the words he doesn't recognize, if
not his teacher? Who will find him books that hold his interest while using
fourth-grade words, if not his teacher? Who will share with him the worlds
that open between the pages of a book, if not his teacher? Of course you
can do these things if you just *like* Julio, I thought. But how will you look
beyond his acting out, beyond his disrupting the class because he is scared
and embarrassed by his inability to read? How will you look beyond those
behaviors every day if you don't love him?

I thought of the words a principal said to me, describing her predominantly low-income school. "A lot of our kids don't have parents at home,
or only one parent. For many kids, the most meaningful adults in their lives
are the teachers. If a teacher loves a child, if she says 'You can do this; I
will help you,' that's the major factor in whether that child will learn."

But teachers can't love their students unless their principals love *them*. It's just too hard, too stressful, facing students every day. Teachers need their principals to love them just the way my army commanders loved me: by looking them in the eye, by seeing their concerns, by helping them solve problems, by fighting to get them what they need to succeed.

Eric Benson at Nathan Hale High School is an excellent principal. He never forgets that he himself is a teacher who now just happens to be a principal, and sees his job as serving teachers so that they can succeed. When they need a substitute, he gets one. When they need supplies, he finds them. When they need money to do a special project, he tries to find the money in the budget to permit it. He also loves his teachers and finds a hundred little ways to show them how he feels. Every morning, as his teachers come into school, he stands at the front counter and greets them all by name. He remembers their birthdays and puts notes of appreciation in their mailboxes. He celebrates their successes—their achievements with students, their acceptance into graduate programs, their winning of awards for volunteer work outside the classroom—by announcing those successes at staff meetings. And because he knows how hard his teachers work, he rewards them with little presents—bookmarks, plants, a pair of silly little lamps. His gifts have become such a regular part of staff meetings that now teachers bring in gifts for him to give away.

Every spring Eric invites his teachers to a restaurant for a teacher appreciation dinner. There he gives away substantial prizes—gift certificates to restaurants, tickets to theaters, overnight stays at deluxe hotels—that he has solicited as donations from local businesses. But perhaps the most meaningful prizes are the ones where he offers his own services as a substitute for theirs: He'll do the winner's grade sheets at the end of the quarter, or he'll teach her classes on the day before Thanksgiving so she can have the day off.

Eric knows what it means to be a teacher and to work with 150 children every day. He sees his job as meeting his teachers' needs so that they can meet the needs of the children.

But if principals are going to lead their teachers, *they* need the loving support of the superintendent and the school board. The principal's job is hard and complex! She may have as many as 50 teachers, 1,700 students, and a community of parents, all demanding her time, attention, and energy. Many of those people's needs conflict; many ask for what she doesn't have to give. Unless her superintendent supports her, she won't be able to carry the ball. So just as she does for her teachers, the superintendent must look her in the eyes, see her concerns, and work to get her what she needs. When she says, "We can't handle these additional children—we are simply too full," the superintendent must try to place the children elsewhere.

When she has a conflict with parents, the superintendent must support her (unless, of course, she's wrong); he must take the heat of the parents on himself. When she says, "We have fifty children at risk of failing for whom we don't have tutors," the superintendent must help her find community volunteers. And all the while, the superintendent must encourage her, must recognize her successes, must be available to help.

If a principal performs in a way that doesn't advance the district's goals—if she permits an unsafe situation to occur, if she fails to build cohesive teamwork among her teachers, if she lets children in her building fall between the cracks—then the superintendent must be firm with her in a loving way. Love isn't always easy! He must point out her school's needs, must be clear about the goals, must give her the help she needs to achieve them. If with repeated efforts the goals still can't be met, then the superintendent must take the action that is in the best interest of the students. But he must do it in a loving, respectful way. He must not let other people demean her, because when a principal is demeaned, the entire system is tarnished.

At the same time superintendents love and fight for their principals, they must love and fight for their teachers. They must make their entire district a teachers' district, a district that teachers will vie to come to, because victory will occur in the classroom only if teachers feel loved and supported. That means the superintendent must fight for his teachers on two fronts: inside the district and outside in the city.

Inside the district, he must do everything he can to make sure that teachers' needs are met. He must ensure that they have the resources they need—and since resources are strained in public education, he must go outside the district to get them. He must get government grants and corporate donations, he must convince the citizens to vote for education levies, he must get businesses and community organizations to create teaching partnerships, he must recruit volunteers. He must use every channel available to build support for the classrooms, so that teachers feel they have the total capacity to succeed.

He must make sure they have the planning time they need—and since time is at a premium in public education, he must juggle the schedule district-wide to create it. He must help principals and staffs find ways to manage their time and dollars in order to achieve all of their objectives— perhaps by lengthening the school day a few minutes or changing the way specialists are used.

He must get them the training they need—and because training is expensive in public education, he must be creative in order to provide it. He may have to juggle the schedule to give teachers the time off; he may have to raise millions of dollars from the private sector to buy the services they need. But he can't expect them to give and give and give to children with increasingly challenging needs unless he strengthens their skills and provides the training that will rekindle their flame.

He must hold up a vision for his teachers that exceeds their highest vision for themselves, a vision of teachers as professionals who can reach and teach each child. And he must back up that vision with concrete goals so that the path to the vision is clear: We will raise academic achievement by 10 percent each year; we will find tutors for *every* child who is falling behind; we will use a variety of teaching techniques and individual achievement plans to make sure that every child learns.

Outside the district, the superintendent must make sure his teachers get the credit and recognition they deserve. That's why we send articles and photos to the newspapers highlighting the work our teachers and students are doing. That's why I make hundreds of speeches a year describing our teachers' and students' successes. That's why we are creating a special teachers' license plate that will let teachers park in private parking lots for free, a gold credit card that will give them discounts at selected stores, and a program with an airline that will give them discounts on travel. Each of these perks will say to teachers and the community, "Teachers play the most important role in our society; they deserve these special privileges."

> Here in education we don't have a lot of money. We can't give our people more money and gold watches. We *have* to give them love!

But the best way the superintendent can love and lead his teachers, as well as his principals and students, is to get his entire community jazzed about the public schools. I know that if I can get our community fired up about the schools, their excitement will infuse our district. If I can get parents to read to their children at night, if I can get the business community to provide resources to the schools, if I can get taxpayers to recognize the importance of voting for education levies, if I can bring all the city's resources to bear on education, then I will help my teachers, my principals, my families, and my students by creating the best possible public schools. As a superintendent, my value to my school district comes from what I do outside the system as much as from what I do in it. It is my job to put children's education in the media spotlight; to say to the community, "Our children need you;" to stand up in the community and say "This is not right" when a community effort detracts from children. It is my job to launch a children's crusade that makes children's interests *everyone's* interests, because our children are our future.

When the community gets fired up about education, there's no end to what can happen! And when a community loves its children, people from all walks of life become education leaders. In Seattle, Shirley Steuben volunteers once or twice a week at Cooper Elementary School. Her employer, Washington Mutual Bank, gives her an hour off to do so, but often she goes back in the afternoon on her own time to work in the after-school homework center. "If I can help kids learn and give them an understanding of something they didn't understand before we spent that time together, then they'll have that for the rest of their lives," says Shirley. "Seeing them catch on to a math concept or read a new word, seeing their faces light up . . . If I didn't have to work for a living, I'd spend *all* my time tutoring!"

Dorothy Conrad, a retired bookkeeper, sends ten dollars every month to the Alliance for Education because she believes in the public schools.

Grace Wilson, who with her husband had made numerous charitable contributions, wanted to make a gift of her own to something she loved. So she made a $25,000 donation to John Muir Elementary School, the school she had graduated from fifty years before.

Ken Alhadeff believes that the public schools need more black teachers, so he pays African-American high-school students, who have been selected by their principals, to go to college and get a teaching certificate.

A donor (who prefers to remain anonymous) wanted to give inner-city fourth-graders a boost that would get them ready to succeed in middle school, so he launched a program in which thirty children are bused to his daughter's private school for an intensive summer program.

Martina Rodriguez is a single mother of two who realized that the two children next door didn't have anyone to read to them at night. So she began a nightly reading group. Each evening at seven o'clock all four children curl up on Martina's couch while she reads to them for an hour.

Some of these people are fortunate: They've been successful in business and are in a position to contribute money to improve conditions for our children. But it doesn't take money to contribute to the schools. Our schools are filled with thousands of volunteers who are giving small amounts of time. Their impact on the children they touch is every bit as great as the impact of a million dollars because they are making a difference in these children's lives. That's why when people say to me, "I want to help my schools but I don't know how," I say, "Volunteer in a classroom. You don't need training, you don't need special skills. You just need to read to a child, or let a child read to you. You just need to give one child a little extra attention."

If you work all day and can't volunteer, then do something nice for a child. Read to a child at night—your own or someone else's. Check a child's homework. Ask a child about his or her day in school so the child will know that school is important. When you are out on the street in your city, smile at the children you see. Make them feel loved—because self-concept forms early and children who are frowned at learn to feel devalued. If you are standing in line at the supermarket and you are late, impatient, and grouchy, when you catch the eye of a child, don't turn your frown on her. She won't know you're frowning at your own situation; she'll think you're frowning at her. Put your grouchiness aside and smile—because children need smiles and encouragement every single day.

If you're in the mall and you see a child do something helpful, compliment him; go out of your way to tell his parents. But if you see a child who misbehaves, talk to him as well. Tell him warmly but firmly that what he is doing is wrong because that child needs to learn—and it's your responsibility, as well as his parents', to teach him. Why is it your responsibility to teach a child who isn't your own? Because our children belong to all of us; they are our investment in the future.

Sometimes I imagine the year 2050: I imagine a group of historians gathered at a table, discussing the world powers of the past. They mention the Incas, the Romans, the Ottomans, the Soviet Union . . . and to this list they add the United States. Why the United States? When was American supremacy lost? It was lost, in my fantasy, at the turn of the twenty-first century when we failed to educate our children.

As an army general I had intimate knowledge of our nation's most pressing external dangers. Now, as a public-school superintendent, I see that the *internal* threat to our nation's survival is every bit as great. But we need not succumb. With a new kind of army, a citizens' army, we can win the battle for our schools. A community that is mobilized to help its schools is an unbeatable force. That's all it takes to create the public schools we need.

America, our children are waiting and we must not disappoint them. Let's *all* love them and lead them.

QUIZ:
WHAT IS THE KEY TO EFFECTIVE LEADERSHIP?

All of these are—providing clear direction, getting all stakeholders involved in decision-making, holding people accountable, and having a plan—but without love, none of the others is effective.

ACKNOWLEDGMENTS

So many people contributed time, energy, and insight into helping us write this book. First, and most important, John would have wanted to thank all the teachers and principals, administrators and support personnel, and the members of the Seattle School Board who are striving day after day to make the Seattle Public Schools a truly world-class, student-focused learning system. You know, because he told you, that you are the true heroes of this story. He thanked you inexpressibly for all of your efforts on behalf of the children.

As the book was being drafted, John spoke with many people both inside and outside the school district about its contents. He asked many people to read drafts and give him their feedback. I regret that I cannot name everyone he consulted, but please know that he appreciated your advice and support enormously.

Many people in the school district took time from their incredibly busy schedules to talk with me as we were putting the book together. Susan Llewellyn, Aleta Paraghamian, Joseph Olchefske, Susan Byers, Roger Erskine, Mike O'Connell, Hilary Gray, Cathy Profilet, Elaine Woo, Gary Tubbs, Ron Jones, Dr. Jill Hearne, Eddie Reed, Pat Sander, Marta Cano-Hinz, Bruce Hunter, Dorothy Dubia, Dr. Karen Ho'o, Robin Pasquarella, Ruth Walsh, Mike Casserly, Eric Cooper, Collin Tong, Shep Siegel, Lael Williams, Shiela Mae Bender, Pat Kile, Joan Dore, Roger Reiger, Linda Harris, Don Nielsen, John Morefield, David Ackerman, and Paul Patak all gave me more time than they could easily afford and I am eternally grateful.

I also have to thank our agent, Jim Levine of James Levine Communications, for his inordinate patience and wisdom in helping us shape the manuscript, and our editor, Katie Hall, for her support and sensitive suggestions for strengthening the final product.

Finally, I need to thank our families: Bob and Hallie Rosner for forgiving the enormous number of evening and weekend hours I gave this project. Scott and Steve Stanford for sharing their father with me, particularly as we finished the final draft; and most especially Pat Stanford for her enormous support, patience, generosity, and understanding during the long years of Sundays that this book kept John away from home.

To everyone we say thank you.

R. S.

ABOUT THE AUTHORS

JOHN STANFORD became Superintendent of the Seattle Public Schools in September 1995, after four years as Manager of Fulton County, Georgia (the county that encompasses Atlanta), and thirty years as an officer in the United States Army. He had extensive experience in leadership, logistics, procurement, finance, personnel management, and strategic planning. Mr. Stanford served in the Pentagon as military assistant to the Under Secretary of the Army during the Carter administration, and as executive secretary to Secretary of Defense Caspar Weinburger during the Reagan administration. He was also CEO of several billion-dollar logistics operations within the military. Mr. Stanford retired from the military in 1991 with the rank of major general.

A native of Yeadon, Pennsylvania, Mr. Stanford graduated from Pennsylvania State University in 1961 with a bachelor's degree in political science. He earned a master's degree in personnel management and administration from Central Michigan University, and received extensive training in the military at the Infantry School, the Army Aviation School, the Transportation School, the U.S. Army Command, and General Staff College, and the Industrial College of the Armed Forces.

Mr. Stanford served as Superintendent in Seattle for three years, during which the school district began an impressive turnaround. Standardized test scores rose significantly for all student groups, violence reached a ten-year low, and popular support for the schools rose dramatically. These improvements, combined with Mr. Stanford's charismatic personality and frequent media appearances, made him a hero in Seattle and a focus of national attention. Mr. Stanford died from leukemia in 1998 at the age of sixty.

ROBIN SIMONS is the author of seven books, including *The Couple Who Became Each Other: Tales of Healing and Transformation*, co-authored with David Calof (Bantam, 1996), *After The Tears: Parents Talk About Raising a Child with a Disability* (Harcourt Brace, 1987), *Filthy Rich and Other Nonprofit Fantasies: Changing the Way Nonprofits Do Business in the 90's*, co-authored with Dr. Richard Steckel (Ten Speed Press, 1989), and *Recyclopedia: Games, Science Projects, and Crafts from Recycled Materials* (Houghton Mifflin, 1976). She lives with her husband and daughter on Bainbridge Island, Washington.

Before becoming a writer, Robin worked for many years in the museum field, at the Boston and Denver Children's Museums, as a consultant in museum programming and interactive exhibit design, and as a consultant to the National Endowment for the Arts. She has a master's in teaching from Leslie College and a bachelor of arts with a major in art history from Brandeis University.